"FIRE CAST ON THE EARTH - KINDLING":

BEING MERCY
IN THE TWENTY-FIRST CENTURY

Elizabeth Davis, Anne Hannon, Mary Lyons, Sophie McGrath,
Mary Noel Menezes, Mary Sullivan, and Elaine Wainwright,
Editors

INTERNATIONAL MERCY RESEARCH CONFERENCE

9 – 12 NOVEMBER 2007

ISBN: 978-0-557-04759-8

The essays have been previously published on www.mercyworld.org and some of them in the journal *Listen* (Australia) and the *MAST Journal* (United States).

The photograph on the cover is used with the kind permission of Margaret Smith, sgs, a Sister of the Good Samaritan in Victoria, Australia. It captures the fire kindled at a celebration of the Easter Vigil.

The quotation in the title, the theme of the 2007 Conference, is taken from the letters of Catherine McAuley (1778-1841) on June 6, 1840 and July 28, 1840.g

Contents

FOREWORD

"FIRE CAST ON THE EARTH – KINDLING": BEING MERCY IN THE TWENTY-FIRST CENTURY

The fire that touched the hearts of the two disciples on the road to Emmaus and transformed them was the same fire that touched the heart of Catherine McAuley and transformed her into a fearless prophet of her time. It inspired her to write the words that became the theme and clarion call of the International Mercy Research Conference held in Mercy Center, Burlingame, California, from the 9th to the 12th of November 2007.

The Conference arose out of the planning of the Mercy International Research Commission (MIRC) which was established in May 2004 to "encourage research and study of Catherine McAuley and the Mercy charism." It had as its goal the undertaking of an extended theological reflection process over a period of twelve months with a small and necessarily limited group of Mercy researchers (See Appendix 1 for the list of Participants). It was designed not only to engage in theological reflection on mercy for the sake of mission but also to model a process which could be used around the globe to facilitate such reflection.

From the fire burning in the courtyard under the Burlingame night sky on the night of the opening ritual to the candles glowing in the Conference hall to the Spirit-inspired words of sixteen modern-day Mercy prophets to the lively and serious discussions, there was no mistaking the call to Mercy women to summon up some of the deeper resources of the Mercy tradition, and to try to discover in it once more the supports which helped sisters to live and spread the Gospel. The collective prayer was that the fire of Catherine's dream would burn as strongly in us today and into the future as it did in her, and that we, in turn, would be *fire cast on the earth - kindling.*"

Elizabeth Davis's theme question, *"How Can We Dare Wisdom and Mercy in the Mosaic of Our Realities?"* set the tone for the articulation of our story. Among the memorable aspects of her presentation was the image of the Inukshuk, the eternal symbol of leadership in the Canadian Arctic, an apt symbol for Mercy leadership today. Part of the power of Anne Itotia's portrait of the slums of Kibera was that she is a Kenyan with first-hand knowledge of this spirit-sapping devastation. Elizabeth McMillan presented a shocking scenario of the widespread extent of human trafficking in the world, especially in women and children, the most vulnerable. Ana Maria Pineda addressed selected issues affecting the quality of life of Hispanics in the United Sates, among which education, health care, housing and appropriate social services are paramount, while Senolita Vakatā outlined the complex gender structures of Tongan society and the factors that have reduced this once thriving society to scenes of fire, looting, and a general breakdown of values.

Inspired by the papers that articulated contemporary experience, Mary Sullivan reminded participants to listen again to the persistent call of Christ and Catherine McAuley to *"get up again"* and continue to perform in the various situations the actions of mercy to which the Gospel and the Mercy Constitutions have called Sisters of Mercy. Bonnie Brennan invited reflection on the various ways by which participants might *"endeavour to fan the flame of Mercy into a blaze for the future"* in ministries of spirituality. Dolores Liptak recalled the words of Cardinal Leon Joseph Suenens who urged religious to be at the very centre of the drama of human salvation and to break through the restraints of the past to follow Christ's example through active mission, in other words, to *"mobilize our Mercy passion."* Mary Noel Menezes saw the frayed social fabric of Guyana as a microcosm of the global trends highlighted in other papers. Sophie McGrath considered the leadership of women in the political sphere as vital to the common good.

Elaine Wainwright drew the themes and real life situations of the early papers into her dialogue with the Gospel of Matthew as she explored the concept of *embodied mercy/mercy embodied* in Jesus and in other human persons, places, value systems, and cultures. Theresa Lowe Ching spoke from her experience of *"the enkindling of Mercy in a multicultural context."* Janet Ruffing reflected on the spiritual implications of the Conference theme for mercy in the twenty-first century while Doris Gottemoeller highlighted the necessity for a clear and distinctive spirituality, the importance of owning our ecclesial identity, and the centrality of a corporate mission. Margaret Farley's paper, *"Forgiveness: A Work of Mercy Newly Relevant in the Twenty-First Century,"* embraced the *"book of pain"* that constitutes the social analysis papers as she demonstrated the urgency and centrality of forgiveness as a work of mercy with a particular relevance for the Church and the Sisters of Mercy. Drawing from the insights of the previous speakers, Patricia Fox suggested that Sisters of Mercy *"have the capacity to articulate and draw from a rich and deep spirituality of Mercy that is born out of a mature theology of God, of an understanding of the profound importance of knowing women are created in the image of God, and from the accumulated shared wisdom that service of the poor unleashes."*

The theological reflection process in which these papers were situated unfolded over three days from the 9th through the 12th of November. This process will be described in more detail in the following section and in Appendix 2. Suffice it to note here that for the MIRC, the Commission that developed the concept of this Conference, it was an exciting but daunting challenge initially. Constrained as we were by geographical distance, we kept face-to-face meetings to a minimum as we exploited the limits of telecommunications! Watching the Conference develop as papers came online, and finally being present at and participating in the process was a spiritually enriching experience. Putting the finishing touches to the first draft of the *Vision, Theology and Praxis* statements was a rewarding moment, a moment to be grateful for an overwhelming outpouring of Mercy generosity, learning, spirituality, sacrifice, and endeavour. So, it did not end in Burlingame on Wednesday, 14 November 2007. In fact, we can truly say *"nunc coepi" (now* I have begun) – *"Mercy – Kindling"* continues.

Elizabeth Davis RSM
Mary Lyons RSM
Mary Noel Menezes RSM
Elaine Wainwright RSM

Anne Hannon RSM
Sophie McGrath RSM
Mary Sullivan RSM

Mercy International Research Commission

Theological Reflection Cycle

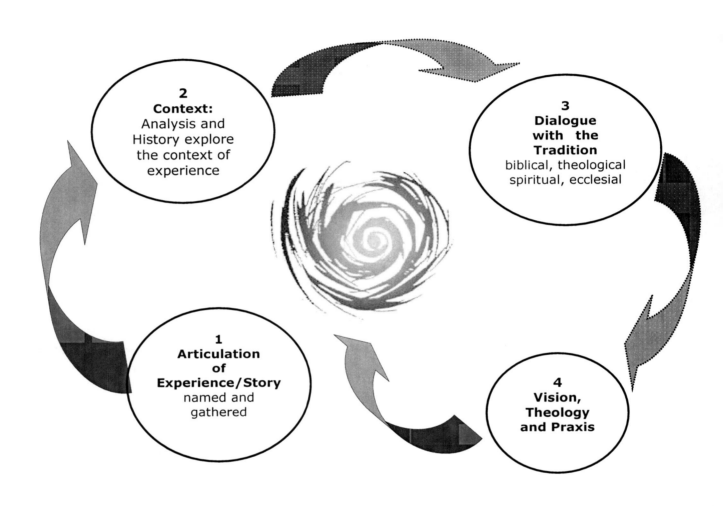

The Theological Reflection Process: An Overview

Stage One of the Theological Reflection Process, **Articulation of Experience/Story: Named and Gathered**, began in November 2006, when those who had been invited to be participants were asked to submit to the Commission a one-paragraph summary in which they identified some of the issues/experiences that were calling forth Mercy in today's world in their contexts. These issues and concerns were summarized and circulated to participants in the following way:

> **Social and Global Trends: Summary Paragraph** (January 2007)
> In the view of those who have been invited to participate in the International Mercy Research Conference scheduled for November 2007, the fundamental social and global trends which Sisters of Mercy need to take account of and dialogue with in order to be Mercy in the twenty-first century center around four widespread phenomena with far-reaching effects:
> - *greed* in all its individual, corporate, and national manifestations, especially among the world's "haves";
> - *lack of respect* for the rights and needs of *all* persons and cultures in the human community, especially when they can be categorized as "different from us" or "expendable by us";
> - resort to *violence* as a legitimate "solution" at all levels;
> - and a fundamental, though often unrecognized, *hunger* for happiness and for genuine spiritual, even religious, understanding and peace.
>
> From these trends flow many specific problems, five of which deserve special attention:
> - the extreme poverty and maldistribution of resources among the world's most vulnerable "have-nots";
> - harsh treatment of migrating peoples, asylum seekers, refugees and persons who in any way appear "different";
> - trafficking in women and children for sexual, military, or other purposes;
> - violation of the earth's natural resources and environment, in apparent disregard of the dire consequences for present and future generations;
> - and debilitating ignorance of basic human, spiritual, and religious understandings, even, as we see it, among Catholics.
>
> Several of these problems disproportionately affect poorer countries and women and children.

This summary of social and global trends informed the choice of focus for those who had been invited to prepare the papers which would be foundational to the ongoing process. The Social Analysis papers were prepared first and circulated to all participants in mid-2007. These, together with the Summary Paragraph, were brought into dialogue with various aspects of Mercy History and with the theological Tradition shaping the group of papers that were circulated by the end of September. All participants had, therefore, read all the papers before coming together for the conference in November. Not only were these papers circulated to participants but they were also uploaded to the mercyworld.org website and hence were available to a much wider audience. They are available in Part II and Part III of this publication.

While Stage Two of the Process, **Context: Analysis and History Explore the Context of Experience**, had already begun in the preparation and circulation of the papers, it, together with the Stage One **Articulation of Experience** informed the beginning of the process as participants gathered on the night of 9 November in an opening ritual. It should be noted here that the process of theological reflection undertaken within the days of the Conference gathering was set in ritual moments and movements co-ordinated by Sheila O'Dea. A group of listeners —M. Francis Añover, Tui Cadigan, Mary Kay Dobrovolny, Elizabeth Dowling, Janette Gray, Anne Hannon, Mary Lyons, Kathleen Murphy, Meta Reid and Penny Roker, divided into three teams—gathered the threads of each stage of the process, presenting them back to the group in a subsequent session so that these threads of theologizing were woven through the three days. The process was very skilfully facilitated by Fran Repka and Veronica Lawson. For an outline of the process as presented to the participants see Appendix 2.

Continuing Stage Two, each participant who had prepared a Social Analysis or History paper provided a 10-minute presentation summarizing or highlighting key aspects of her paper. These were often accompanied by PowerPoint presentations, and contributors had been invited to offer a symbol from their context to the ritual space developed from the previous evening's liturgy. Together with the ritual moments of *Gathering of Threads*, these enabled the theological reflection to be multi-faceted, drawing on a range of analytic and creative skills and modes.

At the end of the first full day of listening and processing of images, symbols, stories, text and tradition, the question was raised: From what we have heard through the process to date, what aspect/s do we take forward into dialogue with our theological tradition that will help us to shape a vision of Mercy into the twenty-first century? Insights from this discussion were carried into Stage Three which began on the second day.

Stage Three, **Dialogue with the Tradition**, brought the questions and insights from Stages One and Two into dialogue with biblical, theological, spiritual and ecclesial traditions. Again 10-minute presentations reminded participants of the focal points of each of the papers in this section. This material was processed by way of conversations between panelists and participants from which images and theological insights began to emerge.

The third day of the conference was given to Stage Four of the process, **Vision, Theology and Praxis**. This emerged from a gathering of the threads of the entire process and was undertaken by way of dialogue among the participants around the key emphases. Below is the articulation of these interrelated aspects of Vision, Theology and Praxis flowing from the process and refined for circulation to the Mercy world.

Vision:

A vision is the reality of the future for which we yearn. Out of the first three stages of our theological reflection process, this vision emerged.

We Sisters of Mercy in the twenty-first century are in radical communion beyond all borders.

We are grounded in the compassion of God.

We are nurtured by the Gospel, and by the story of Catherine McAuley and of Mercy lived and living.

Aware of our own brokenness, we join with others in healing the wounds of Earth and Earth's peoples.

Theology:

Theology emerged from the major themes that both informed and provoked our process of theological reflection. Our theologizing was multifaceted, reflecting the different contexts of Mercy.

Doing theology during these days spiralled into and out of our engagement with experiences of the contextual and historical realities we shared. These then spiralled into dialogue with the biblical, theological, spiritual and ecclesial traditions in which we stand.

> We were touched deeply by the pain of those who are impoverished, especially women and children and the Earth.

> We recognized our own complicity in the brokenness and woundedness and our need for forgiveness.

> We were caught up into the womb-compassion, steadfast love, faithfulness and graciousness of God, of Jesus as embodied mercy and of the Spirit permeating all.

> We were drawn into a theology of communion, of God who is communion.

> We experienced in our theologizing a yearning for God to be imaged female as well as male.

> We were impassioned toward a theology of mercy that is formed and tested by justice as well as compassion.

> We were challenged to break the cycles of violence in our world and in our own realities through radical forgiveness of the other.

Recognizing that what we had begun was but a single moment, we were impelled to continue to develop theologies and spiritualities of Mercy that draw on the rich resources among us as Sisters of Mercy engaged in Mercy across the globe. This will enkindle in us the fire of Mercy in response to the cries and pain of the most wounded, including Earth.

Praxis:

Praxis is reflective and reflected action emerging out of a new vision and theology for liberation and transformation.

We Sisters of Mercy embrace the vision of a radical communion beyond all borders. Therefore, we will:

> Develop theologies and spiritualities for Mercy that flow from ongoing storytelling in our different contexts, in dialogue with our local and global experiences and with our sacred traditions and texts.
>
> Engage in theological reflection processes in ways that deepen and expand our theological understandings and praxis.
>
> Reclaim the motivating force in the call of Catherine McAuley and give new expression to the spiritual and corporal works of mercy.
>
> Use multiple ways to share the passion and pain in the stories of Mercy so that our local experiences resonate with the global.
>
> Deepen and expand images of God in ways that will give women the confidence to know that they have been made in the image of God.
>
> Provide opportunities for cross-cultural, contextual, and global engagement through Mercy International Association, its expanded Mercy International Centre, and other organizations.
>
> Foster increased participation of women in leadership and policy-formation.
>
> Use the new technologies to enable the fire of Mercy to shape anew our local Mercy ministries and to increase our collaboration in global projects.
>
> Share our Mercy human and financial resources to facilitate this praxis.

Mercy — Kindling

These now flow out into the Mercy world inviting you, in all your various locations, to continue the spiral, undertaking your theological reflection processes in dialogue with what has begun here. This ongoing process we name *"Mercy – Kindling"*.

How Can We Dare Wisdom and Mercy in the Mosaic of Our Realities?

INTRODUCTION

Elizabeth M. Davis, RSM

Paul wrote to the Romans (12:15), "Rejoice with others when they rejoice, and be sad with those in sorrow." *Gaudium et Spes* begins, "The joy and hope, the grief and anguish of the people of our time, especially of those who are poor or afflicted in any way, are the joy and hope, the grief and anguish of the followers of Christ as well." Inès Maria dell' Eucaristia wrote to the Daughters of Wisdom in 1994, "In this troubled world, we wish to express God's love for wounded humanity and always we must answer the question: how can we dare Wisdom in the mosaic of our realities?" We cannot know with whom to weep or rejoice or what their joys and anguish are unless we understand the mosaic of our realities. Only then can we dare wisdom and mercy.

In this paper, I seek to describe the mosaic of our realities. I am a woman from a rural community in the poorest province in Canada, a teacher and health administrator by profession, a baby boomer by generation, a Roman Catholic by religious tradition, and a Sister of Mercy by life-choice. Each characteristic influences the way in which I see the world. The choice of elements, sources and structure in this paper will reflect that influence. My analysis will be primarily of society in Canada with significant application to other Western countries and some application to other countries.

The paper is in three parts: (i) my description of realities today, (ii) an analysis of this description through four lenses, and (iii) the naming of questions facing those who minister in the midst of these realities. The paper will not follow a sociological methodology but will be eclectic in its approach.

THE SOCIETY IN WHICH I AND WE LIVE

To put order in the description of today's realities, I envision the image of a spiral with the elements of environment, person, and community swirling in that spiral and connecting with each other in multiple, ever-changing ways. The length of the paper precludes an in-depth discussion of any element.

Environment

A recent report on the state of our environment concludes, "The planet's warming is unequivocal, its impact is clearly noticeable, and *it is beyond doubt that human activities have been contributing considerably to it* [highlighted italics mine]." Adverse effects include: agriculture and food security, oceans and coastal areas, biodiversity and ecosystems, water resources, human health, human settlements, energy, transport and industry, extreme weather events."[1]

---

[1] *Fourth Assessment Report: "Climate Change 2007: Impacts, Adaptation and Vulnerability,"* Report of Intergovernmental Panel on Climate Change, April 2007. Summary for Policymakers.

The report expresses concern about the increased risk of extinction of 20 – 30% of plant and animal species, decreased fresh water availability, loss of biodiversity, significant changes in Arctic and Antarctic ecosystems, ground instability in permafrost regions, and impact on health of humans marked by increases in malnutrition, increased deaths, disease and injury due to heat waves, floods, storms, fires and droughts; increased burden of diarrhoeal disease, and increased frequency of cardio-respiratory diseases.[2]

An internationally-negotiated response to this dire prediction is articulated in the *Earth Charter* (which can be accessed online at www.earthcharter.org). It begins:

> We stand at a critical moment in Earth's history, a time when humanity must choose its future. As the world becomes increasingly interdependent and fragile, the future at once holds great peril and great promise. To move forward we must recognize that in the midst of a magnificent diversity of cultures and life forms we are one human family and one Earth community with a common destiny. We must join together to bring forth a sustainable global society founded on respect for nature, universal human rights, economic justice, and a culture of peace.[3]

Human activities, having led to this threat to our planet, can reduce vulnerability to climate change. Why are we not taking this threat and this opportunity seriously?

Person

Generations

We live in a time and place where, for the first time in the history of humankind, we now have four generations of adults living in large numbers at the same time. Each generation has been formed by different world events and has developed different values and qualities:

CHART ONE: GENERATIONS LIVING TODAY

Qualities	Elders	Boomers	Generation X	Millennials
Time of Birth	Pre-1946	1946 – 1965	1966 – 1979	1980 – today
Formative Elements	Patriotism, families, Great Depression, World Wars I & II, golden age of radio,	Prosperity, focus on children, TV, suburbia, Medicare, Cold War, women's	AIDS, stagflation, latchkey kids, single parents, computers, fall of the Berlin	Internet chat, school violence, TV reality shows, multiculturalism, the Gulf War,

[2] Ibid.
[3] *Earth Charter: A Declaration of Fundamental Principles for Building a Just, Peaceful and Sustainable Global Society for the 21st Century* (New York: United Nations, 2000), preamble.

	growth of labour unions	liberation, space race	Wall, *glasnost*	the Iraq War
Values	Dedication, sacrifice, hard work, conformity, order, patience, respect for authority, duty before pleasure, honour	Optimism, teamwork, personal gratification, health and wellness, personal growth, youth, work, involvement	Diversity, thinking globally, balance, techno-literacy, fun, informality, self-reliance, pragmatism	Confidence, civic duty, achievement, sociability, morality, diversity, street smarts, inclusion
Qualities	Conformists, conservative spenders, past-oriented, belief in logic not magic, loyalty to organization, wisdom, stability, experience	Driven, soul-searchers, willing to "go the extra mile," love-hate relationship with authority, loyalty to profession, strong work ethic, achievement oriented	Risk-takers, sceptical, family-oriented, bosses as colleagues, focus on the job not work hours, innovative, diverse range of skills, entrepreneurial & independent	Optimistic, prefer collective action, techno-savvy, connected 24/7, embrace diversity and change, highly technologically advanced, entrepreneurial and independent, socially responsible

This diversity of underlying values increases the challenges to understanding and respect among the generations.

Three aspects of the generational reality must also be noted:

- ✓ No country has ever before experienced large numbers of people over 65. In Canada, this is paralleled by a declining birth rate and less inter-generational living. There are implications for labour market adjustments, life-long learning, adjustments to pension plans and entitlement, long term care provisions, and policies for "ageing in place" and "active ageing." How we view the elderly, especially elderly women, calls for more intentional consideration especially in an age obsessed with youth.
- ✓ In Canada, the declining birth rate is not consistent across all groups. Aboriginal people and immigrants have higher birth rates resulting in a disproportionate percentage of children living in poverty with poorer health status.
- ✓ Increasing urbanization in Canada (close now to 80%) and most other countries means an increasing rural/urban divide: youth and young families

continue to migrate from rural communities leaving behind an increasingly older population, and they are migrating to cities that are becoming more culturally diverse as migration across the earth intensifies.

These generational and urban/rural complexities challenge governments and communities who strive to build societies that live in harmony while treasuring diversity.

Women

Women in Canada make up 50% of the total population but 69% of the population over 69 years of age. They constitute 47% of the workforce and have an average annual pre-tax income that is 62% that of men. They are more likely than their male counterparts to lose time from work for personal or family responsibilities, and to work part-time.[4] In 2007, the proportion of seats held by women in Canada's Parliament was 20.8% (compare Australia at 24.7%, the United Kingdom at 19.7%, the United States at 16.3%, and the United Nations at 9.4%).[5]

Stereotypical attitudes and practices are working to the disadvantage of women and girls in families, educational institutions, religious institutions, workplaces, political bodies and media. Gaps in efforts to achieve gender equality and empowerment of women include increasing violence against women, under-representation of women in decision-making in all areas, discriminatory laws governing marriage, land, property and inheritance; disproportionate share of household and family responsibilities, lack of equal employment opportunities, lack of attention to mechanisms which support a balance between family and work responsibilities, disproportionate effects of poverty, devastating effects of conflict, impact of AIDS/HIV, and trafficking in women and girls.

Hannan expresses well what is needed: "An enabling environment for enhancing promotion of gender equality and empowerment of women needs to be developed by improving women's capabilities, including through education and health; increasing their access to and control over opportunities and resources such as employment, land and economic assets; enhancing their agency and leadership roles; as well as protecting and promoting their human rights and ensuring their security, including freedom from violence."[6]

Poverty

Growing economic, social and technological gaps exist between the richest and poorest citizens in wealthy countries like Canada and the United States and between the richest and poorest countries. After forty years of stability in the richest countries, income since 1980 has become increasingly concentrated in the hands of the top 0.01% of earners. The

---

[4] Statistics Canada, *Women in Canada: A Gender-based Statistical Report*. Fifth Edition. March 2006, 11 – 16.

[5] *Women in National Parliaments* website. Information accurate for April 2007. Accessed May 15, 2007 at http://www.ipu.org/wmn-e/arc/classif300407.htm.

[6] Carolyn Hannan, *A new world: A vision for gender equality and empowerment of women*, Address to Contemporary Woman Program at Brescia University, Owensboro, Kentucky, April 6, 2006, 14.

ratio of CEO compensation to average production workers' pay, which had averaged 42 to one in 1982, was 10 times higher – 431 to one – in 2004.

> Income in North America is now concentrated in the hands of the very, very wealthy to a degree not seen since before the Second World War. And with greater wealth comes greater political influence; public policy, including health policy, is increasingly driven by the priorities of the wealthy, overriding the concerns of the general population.[7]

In Canada, extreme poverty exists among Aboriginal people, recent immigrants and non-permanent residents, visible minorities, persons with disabilities, lone parent families and unattached individuals. Child poverty rates are disproportionately high among these vulnerable social groups. Approximately half (52%) of low income children in Canada live in female lone parent families. According to the 2001 census, 49% of children in recent immigrant families are poor.[8] The chances of living in poverty decrease as education levels, employment activity and occupational skill levels increase.[9]

For the world's poorest countries, the past decade has continued a disheartening trend: not only have they failed to reduce poverty, but they are falling further behind rich countries. The Human Development Report 2005 describes it this way:

> If the world were a country, it would have had an average purchasing power parity income of $5,533 and a median income of $1,700 in 2000. The gap between median and average income points to a concentration of income at the top end of the distribution: 80% of the world's population had an income less than the average. Meanwhile, the average income of the top 20% of the world's population is about 50 times the average income of the bottom 20%. Global income distribution resembles a champagne glass. At the top, where the glass is widest, the richest 20% of the population hold three-quarters of world income. At the bottom of the stem, where the glass is narrowest, the poorest 40% hold 5% of world income and the poorest 20% hold just 1.5%.[10]

The Millennium Development Goals are a global response intended to reduce extreme poverty by 2015 (see Appendix A). Is the achievement of these goals probable? The 2006 Human Development Report says, "Today, the world has the financial, technological and human resources to make a decisive breakthrough in human development. But if current trends continue, the MDGs will be missed by a wide margin.

---

[7] Robert G. Evans, "From World War to Class War: The Rebound of the Rich," *Healthcare Policy*, Vol. 2, No. 1 (2006), 15.

[8] Campaign 2000, *Oh Canada! Too Many Children in Poverty for Too Long*, 2006 Report Card on Child and Family Poverty in Canada. Accessed on May 12, 2007 at www.campaign2000.ca.

[9] Kevin K. Lee, *Urban Poverty in Canada: A Statistical Profile* (Ottawa: Canadian Council on Social Development, 2000).

[10] United Nations Human Development Report 2005, *International cooperation at a crossroads: Aid, trade and security in an unequal world.* Accessed on May 10, 2007 at http://hdr.undp.org/reports/global/2005/, 36.

Instead of seizing the moment, the world's governments are stumbling towards a heavily sign-posted and easily avoidable human development failure—a failure with profound implications not just for the world's poor but for global peace, prosperity and security."[11]

Health
Today health is usually defined as a complete state of physical, mental, and social well-being, and not merely the absence of disease or infirmity.[12]   An Australian Aboriginal description broadens this definition: "Health does not just mean the physical well-being of the individual but refers to the social, emotional, spiritual and cultural well-being of the whole community. This is a whole of life view and includes the cyclical concept of life-death-life."[13]   Key health issues internationally include food security and nutritional well-being, HIV/AIDS, tobacco, occupational health and safety, mental health, infectious diseases, violence, reproductive health, globalization and water, and globalization and health of indigenous peoples.[14]

Determinants of health such as biology, gender, socioeconomic status, education, ethnicity and age have significant effects on the health of all people. Globally, factors affecting health include widening socio-economic inequalities between the wealthiest and the poorest people, human migration and needs of migrating populations, impact of globalization on health and health systems including increasing mobility of health care professionals, new communication technologies, influence of private companies on provision of health services and insurance, role of international bodies and trade agreements, effects of climate change and environmental destruction, population growth, the overcrowding of urban areas and encroachment of human populations into previously uninhabited ecosystems, war, violence, terrorism, and gender inequalities.

Community

Religion
Eighty-five percent of Canadians indicate affiliation with an established religion yet fewer than 25% attend church regularly.[15]   A Statistics Canada Report concludes that, in Canada, private devotion now plays a more important part in people's lives than

[11] United Nations Human Development Report 2006, *Beyond Scarcity: Power, Poverty and the Global Water Crisis*. Accessed on May 10, 2007 at http://hdr.undp.org/hdr2006/, 17.
[12] *Preamble to the Constitution of the World Health Organization as adopted by the International Health Conference*, New York, June 19 - July 22, 1946; signed on July 22, 1946 by the representatives of 61 States (Official Records of the World Health Organization, no. 2, p. 100) and entered into force on April 7, 1948.
[13] National Health and Medical Research Council, *Promoting the health of Indigenous Australians: A review of infrastructure support for Aboriginal and Torres Strait Islander health advancement* (Canberra: NHMRC, 1996), part 2:4.
[14] *Gender, Globalization and Health,* edited by H. Maclean and S.R. Sicchia (Canadian Institutes for Health Research: Institute of Gender & Health, April 2004).
[15] Interview with Dr. Reginald Bibby, Professor of Sociology and Research Chair for Social Sciences, University of Lethbridge. Accessed online on May 10, 2007 at http://www.innovationalberta.com/article.php?articleid=108.

attendance at religious services.[16] There is increasing attention to activities that reflect spontaneity and community (e.g., meditation, pilgrimage to Iona, Divine Mercy devotions, adoration of the Blessed Sacrament). Sheldrake speaks of "a privatization of spirituality and a concentration of interiority that sometimes separates spiritual experience from a social or public vision of ethics. In contrast to the inherited polarization between sacred and secular, the roots of contemporary spirituality are to be found in an emphasis on human experience in all its variety and pain, as the immediate context of God's self-disclosure."[17]

Today's church members are diverse in their involvement in church. Reese, speaking about younger members, identifies *church in mission* (active in service and volunteer programs), *church in search* (single and divorced young adults over the age of 30), *church youthful* (active in college ministry), *church apologist* (favouring devotional prayer and papal teachings), *church devotional* (Theology on Tap, parish activities), *church busy* (young professionals and young families), *church creative* (open to blending different faith traditions), and *church disconnected* (distant from church).[18]

Marie Chin, reflecting on diversity within religious communities, identifies four prevalent cultures co-existing today: (i) *essentialist* (unquestioning loyalty to church institutions, holding on to tradition and customs), (ii) *existentialist* (emphasis on the individual, democratic say in community, little patience for mutual responsibility, dislike of uniformity), (iii) *liberation* (conviction of preferential option for the poor, priority of justice, critical of unjust structures in church and society), and (iv) *feminist* (empowering self and others, mutuality of relationships, re-visioning and re-imaging, valuing inclusivity).[19]

Technology and Computer
The world has moved from the Industrial Age to the Information Age and now to the Network Age with its distributed, decentralized culture (citizen-centered not institution-centered). Frand characterizes the Network Age in this way: Computers are not technology but part of life, internet is better than TV, reality is no longer real, doing is more important than knowing, multitasking is a way of life, typing is preferred to handwriting, staying connected is essential, there is zero tolerance for delays, and the consumer and creator of information are blurring.[20] Words like iPod, iPhone, Facebook, MySpace, and text messaging define a new way of relating.

Hogue speaks of societal impact when computers are such a part of our way of life:

---

[16] Statistics Canada, *Canadian Social Trends: "Who's religious?"*, May 2, 2006.
[17] Philip F. Sheldrake, "The Crisis of Postmodernity," *Christian Spirituality Bulletin* (Summer 1996), 7.
[18] Mary Anne Reese, "The Broad Spectrum of Young Adult Catholics. Refracting the Light," *America* 189 (September 22, 2003), 8 – 12.
[19] Marie Chin, RSM, *Hunger for Right Relationships*, Presentation to the Congregation of Notre Dame Visitation Province in Halifax, Nova Scotia, July 2003.
[20] Jason Frand, "Thinking About Our Future: Supporting the Academic Mission," *Educause Review* (August 2000).

As consumers, citizens and scholar-educators, most of us live, move and breathe in a technological whirlwind, and this profoundly affects our moral self-understanding, our interactions with others and our cultural and natural habitations. The moral problem of contemporary technology results not from its ubiquity and not from the power of its specific applications but from the dominance of a specific technological pattern, the device paradigm . . . this displacement, in spite of its seductive promises of liberation and enrichment, corrodes creative relationships between and among selves and between selves and their environments.[21]

Conflict, Security and Peace

The last two decades have demonstrated that the main threats to our security now come from terrorism, epidemic disease, organized crime, conflict over natural resources, climate change and environmental degradation. "Security is increasingly interpreted as security of people, not just territory; security of individuals, not just of nations; security through development, not through arms; security of all people everywhere – in their homes, in their jobs, in their streets, in their communities, and in the environment."[22]

Since 1990, more than three million people have died in armed conflict, and many millions more have died as a result of the disease and famine associated with war. Conflict is now strongly associated with poverty. During the period between 1990 and 2003, low income developing countries constituted more than half of all the countries and territories experiencing violent conflict.[23]

At Assisi in 2002, Pope John Paul, together with 200 other religious leaders, articulated the *Ten Commandments of Peace* in response to this reality (see Appendix B). It is worth noting how little visibility this Decalogue has received.

ANALYSIS THROUGH FOUR LENSES

Globalization

We live in a world increasingly ignoring borders. Travel and trade between nations increased fourfold between 1980 and 2000. Four billion dollars in cross-border currency now changes hands every six hours. Eight hundred million persons crossed international borders in 2005. Forty million people migrate a year. The number of migrants working outside their own countries is at least thirty million with billions of dollars yearly going back to their home countries. Scientific projects with international teams; 50,000 global NGOs; drug and private arms trade, arms control, terrorism, money laundering, pollution,

---

[21] Michael S. Hogue, "Theological Ethics and Technological Culture: A Biocultural Approach," *Zygon,* Vol. 42, No. 1 (March 2007), 79.

[22] Dr Mahbub ul Haq (1997), quoted in Oli Brown, "Trade, Aid and Security: an agenda for peace and development," *Commonwealth Ministers Reference Book*, 2007, 1.

[23] Brown, 2 – 3.

refugees, ocean and atmosphere, television, global warming, the Internet, and infectious diseases know no borders and shape a "community of common fate and responsibility."[24]

This trans-border reality is one indicator that never before has change come so rapidly – in so many ways, all at once – on such a global scale, and with such global visibility. The following description captures the inherent imbalance of the resulting globalization:

> Globalization denotes the expanding scale, growing magnitude, speeding up and deepening impact of trans-continental flows and patterns of social interaction. It refers to a shift or transformation in the scale of human organization that links distant communities and expands the reach of power relations across the world's regions and continents. But it should not be read as pre-figuring the emergence of a harmonious world society or as a universal process of global integration in which there is a growing convergence of cultures and civilizations. For not only does the awareness of growing inter- connectedness create new animosities and conflicts, but it can fuel reactionary politics and deep-seated xenophobia. Since a substantial proportion of the world's population is largely excluded from the benefits of globalization, it is a deeply divisive and, consequently, vigorously contested process.[25]

Global governance exists in a limited way today through the United Nations, the World Bank, the International Monetary Fund and the World Trade Organization. Corporations, mostly Western, are pressuring for a more extensive and powerful system of global governance that would allow them to promote global trade policies serving their interests above those of less powerful actors such as smaller companies, indebted nations, or small and vulnerable national enterprises. Such a system will effectively subordinate human rights, social values, ecological concerns and all other dimensions of the common well-being of the planetary community to the economic needs and interests of these corporations.[26]

Others seek a more humane globalization and are working toward a global ethic. The Commission on Global Governance report, *Our Global Neighbourhood*,[27] (which can be accessed online at www.gdrc.org/u-gov/global-neighbourhood) and that of the Commission of the European Catholic Bishops 2001, *Global Governance: Our Responsibility to Make Globalisation an Opportunity for All*,[28] (which can be accessed at

---

[24] John A. Coleman, "Making the Connections: Globalization and Catholic Social Thought," in *Globalization and Catholic Social Thought: Present Crisis, Future Hope*, edited by John A. Coleman and William F. Ryan (Ottawa: Novalis, 2005), 12.

[25] Ibid., 14. Quoting David Held and Andrew McGrew, *Globalization/Anti-Globalization* (Malden, MA: Blackwell, 2002), 1.

[26] James E. Hug, "Economic Justice and Globalization," in *Globalization and Catholic Social Thought*, 60-61.

[27] Commission on Global Governance, *Our Global Neighbourhood* (Oxford: Oxford University Press, Great Britain, 1995).

[28] Commission of the Bishops' Conferences of the European Community, *Global Governance: Our Responsibility to Make Globalisation an Opportunity for All*, 2001.

www.comece.org/comece.taf?_function=euroworld&_sub=_trade&id=4&language=en)
are the most recent expressions of this global ethic.

> Open economies will not be sustainable without the willingness of states to open up politically as well. The political will to achieve and maintain a system of global governance must be nourished by firm convictions and values. In a world where no single power – even the strongest – can or should exert full control, worldwide agreement on a list of basic values and principles is essential. Global governance, as opposed to global government, means a networked approach to global problems that involves governments, business and non-governmental organisations as well as Churches and other religious communities.[29]

Both reports endorse common values for a global world: respect for human dignity, responsibility, solidarity, subsidiarity, coherence, transparency and accountability.[30]

Postmodernity

Postmodernity concentrates on the tensions and similarity erupting from processes of globalization: the accelerating circulation of people, the increasingly dense and frequent cross-cultural interaction and the unavoidable intersections of local and global knowledge.[31] It has been said that postmodernity is both "emancipatory and demonic."[32]

It is difficult to describe all the elements of postmodernity, but the following are key features: (i) *rejection of objective truth* (everything depends on personal perception) leading to many different traditions being equally valued and the seeking of faith without boundaries or definitions; (ii) valuing of *multiple forms of knowledge* leading to an acceptance of symbols, intuition, imagination and experiential learning; (iii) a sense of *all reality being fabricated* leading to a valuing of plurality, multiplicity and diversity; (iv) deep *suspicion of authority* leading to an aversion to meta-narrative because no meta-narrative is open or large enough to include the realities of all people (therefore, they are oppressive or unjust) and leading to rejection of institutions; (v) *search for the transcendent* with craving for reconnection with the spiritual all around us and relationship with all creation; (vi) an understanding of *salvation as intra-worldly* not extra-worldly leading to a separation of religion and spirituality; (vii) sense of *fragmentation* leading to self being constructed in a number of ways to suit the situation and world of isolated individuals and consumerism; (viii) *blurring of morality* leading to multiple standards of morality with expediency priming morality; (ix) *influence of the media* with confusion between truth and fiction; (x) *weakening of government* leading to greater power for multi-national corporations; (xi) *quest for community* with relationship

---

[29] Ibid., forward, #3 and 4, 7.

[30] Ibid. #5, 7.

[31] Shannon Weiss and Karla Wesley, "Postmodernism and Its Critics," *Anthropological Theories: A Guide,* Department of Anthropology, College of Arts and Sciences, University of Alabama. Accessed on May 9, 2007, at http://www.as.ua.edu/ant/Faculty/murphy/436/pomo.htm, 2.

[32] Paul Lakeland, "A Postmodern Apologetics," in *Postmodernity* (Minneapolis, MN: Fortress Press, 1997), 89.

and participation as key to meaning; and (xii) *living in the material world,* wanting the good things in life with time as a commodity.[33]

Holland sets out four contending strategies promoted by societal elites who are attempting to define the new cultural era. He parallels these with alternative cosmological visions to promote a more resourceful creation of the new culture of life.[34]

CHART 2: NON-AUTHENTICALLY ELITE POSTMODERN STRATEGIES

Strategy	Vision	Perspective	Threat
Economic neo-liberalism	Mechanistic colonization of planet	Ultramodern (objective-instrumental)	Ecological-social devastation
Academic reconstructionism	Deconstruction of all meta-narratives	Ultramodern (subjective-expressive)	Ethical relativism and nihilism
Religious restorationism	Reassertion of patriarchal values	Secure defense of ultramodern	Authoritarianism and militarism
Scientific bio-engineering	Scientific conquest of life	Total triumph of autonomous reason	Neo-totalitarianism

CHART 3: AUTHENTICALLY POSTMODERN ALTERNATIVE MOVEMENTS

Strategy	Vision	Perspective	Gift
Bioregional economics	Global network of diverse bioregional communities	Authentically postmodern	Sustainable economic creativity
Neo-realist philosophy	Recovery of practical wisdom rooted in ancient traditions	Authentically postmodern	Re-rooting education in communal needs
Charismatic-prophetic religion	Celebration and defense of culture of life	Authentically postmodern	Celebratory-prophetic spirituality of life
Holistic-evolutionary cosmology	Co-creative participation in evolutionary holism	Authentically postmodern	Ecological-mystical consciousness

---

[33] Ideas drawn from a number of sources including Lakeland, "Postmodern Apologetics," Alan Kirby, "The Death of Postmodernism and Beyond," *Philosophy Now* (58): 34 – 37; Daniel Cadrin, OP, "Postmodernity: Its Implications for Religious Life," Address to the General Conference of the Congrégation de Notre Dame on January 21, 2006; Graham Johnston, "Preaching to a Postmodern World," *A Guide to Reaching Twenty-first Century Listeners* (Grand Rapids, MI: Baker Books, 2001).

[34] Joe Holland, "Toward a Global Culture of Life: Cultural Challenges to Catholic Social Thought in the Postmodern Electronic-Ecological Era," in *Globalization and Catholic Social Thought,* 123.

In a world of fragmentation, ambiguity and the end of meta-narrative, how can we become creators of this new culture of life?

Culture of Technology

Technological innovation and proliferation significantly shape our contemporary existence. The culture of technology is well described by Kirby: "The pseudo-modern cultural phenomenon par excellence is the internet. Its central act is that of the individual clicking on his/her mouse to move through the pages in a way which cannot be duplicated, inventing a pathway through cultural products which has never existed before and never will again."[35] We need to think theologically and ethically about the cultural pattern of technology and a vision for living responsibly within it:

> Technological innovation and proliferation significantly shape contemporary human moral existence. This is because of both the obvious ubiquity of technology and the morally seductive, culturally embedded technological promise to manage the contingency and vulnerability of the good life. In light of this, I contend that one of the primary theological ethical challenges of our time is to think critically through technology's cultural pattern rather than simply its particular applications. . . development of a bio-cultural theological anthropology, then, provides an orientation to human moral life that binds critical appreciation of technological power with vigilant preservation of the cultural and moral ecologies within which the creative goodness of a loving God and others flourishes.[36]

Culture of Consumerism

Consumerism is a way of being in the world expressed in a moral and cultural attitude based on life-orienting beliefs prevalent in contemporary industrial and post-industrial societies. It rests on a flawed anthropology that places a primacy on things by emphasizing *having* rather than *being*. It is a modern (and post-modern) phenomenon that has arisen with the market economy, a distinct cultural distortion of human freedom that occurs in the context of free markets, but it is not a necessary result of free markets.[37]

Wells expresses the tragedy of consumerism in this way:

> Across a broad front we gather materials for the construction of ourselves. We build a public self in what we buy and what we voluntarily choose to do. This front runs from cuisine (Thai, French, or Mexican tonight?), to fashion (Ferragamo shoes or faux furs?), to particular

---

[35] Kirby, "Death of Postmodernism," 35.

[36] Hogue, "Theological Ethics and Technological Culture," 78.

[37] Gregory R. Beabout and Eduardo J. Echeverria, "The Culture of Consumerism: A Catholic and Personalist Critique," *Journal of Markets & Morality*, Vol 5, No 2 (Fall 2002). Accessed online on May 16, 2007.

products (antiques or Swedish contemporaries?), to music (Bach or the Grateful Dead?), to sexual lifestyles (monogamous or casual, gay or heterosexual?), to beliefs (Christian, New Age, or postmodern doubt?). Beneath it all is the same compulsion to be in a state of constant inward evaluation, taking an inventory of needs and wishes, and then reaching out for a "product" to satisfy the felt emptiness and to project who we are. This takes channel surfing to a high art as we slide from product to product, from relationship to relationship, from style to style, seldom lingering long before the shape of our internal inventory tugs us in another direction in search of different fulfillment.[38]

Kavanaugh concludes, "There is no intrinsic human uniqueness or irreplaceable value. The person *is* only insofar as he or she is marketable or productive. Human products, which should be valued only insofar as they enhance and express human worth, become the very standards against which human worth itself is measured."[39] How can we be a counter-cultural witness, negating this lifestyle of consumerism, competition, hoarding, planned obsolescence, and unnecessary waste?

CONCLUSION

As Sisters of Mercy trying to make sense of ministry in this mosaic of realities in contemporary society, we are faced with troubling questions:

- ✓ How can we focus on the centrality of the Word when there is in our time a rejection of objective truth and confusion between truth and fiction?
- ✓ What does theology mean when meta-narrative is no longer trusted or even believed?
- ✓ What will be our expression of Church in a time and place when organizations are no longer credible and culture is person-centered not institution-centered?
- ✓ What does spirituality mean when religion and spirituality are no longer seen as congruent?
- ✓ How can we hold the integrity of multiple traditions while living in harmony?
- ✓ What does solidarity mean in a distributed world, with multiple generations, and increasing gaps between the richest and poorest within and among countries?
- ✓ How can women be leaders in this age when gender equity and empowerment of women are still distant dreams?
- ✓ How do we continue to live viable and credible religious life in a time when freedom and autonomy of individuals are paramount?

---

[38] David F. Wells, *Losing Our Virtue: Why the Church Must Recover Its Moral Vision* (Grand Rapids, Mich.: Eerdmans, 1998), 88.

[39] John Francis Kavanaugh, S.J., *Following Christ in a Consumer Society: The Spirituality of Cultural Resistance* (Maryknoll, N.Y.: Orbis Books, 1986; revised edition, 1991), 22.

- ✓ How can the energy of a woman who lived before the modern age inspire a community that lives in a post-modern age?
- ✓ What can we learn from history in a time when "the maps they gave us were out of date by years?"[40]

And the ultimate question remains, "How can we dare wisdom and mercy in the mosaic of our realities?" Perhaps part of the answer lies hidden in these insightful words from a small Newfoundland outport:

> One boat sails east and one sails west
> With the selfsame wind that blows.
> It's not the gales but the trim of the sails
> That guides where the good ship goes.[41]

Let us have the insight to know that the good ships need to go in multiple directions, seek the wisdom of the winds that blow, and have the courage to trim our sails. Then perhaps we will be better prepared to dare both wisdom and mercy in our church and our society.

---

[40] Phrase from a poem by Adrienne Rich, *Twenty-one Love Poems –The Dream of A Common Language, XIII* (New York: W.W. Norton & Company, 1974-1976).

[41] A verse recited by Newfoundland fishermen, which is a variant of lines by the poet Ella Wheeler Wilcox (1850-1919) in her *Winds of Fate*.

APPENDIX A

UNITED NATIONS MILLENNIUM DEVELOPMENT GOALS (2000)

Goal 1: Eradicate extreme poverty and hunger
> **Target 1**: Halve, between 1990 and 2015, the proportion of people whose income is less than $1 a day
> **Target 2**: Halve, between 1990 and 2015, the proportion of people who suffer from hunger

Goal 2: Achieve universal primary education
> **Target 3**: Ensure that, by 2015, children everywhere, boys and girls alike, will be able to complete a full course of primary schooling

Goal 3: Promote gender equality and empower women
> **Target 4:** Eliminate gender disparity in primary and secondary education, preferably by 2005, and in all levels of education no later than 2015

Goal 4: Reduce child mortality
> **Target 5:** Reduce by two-thirds, between 1990 and 2015, the under-five mortality rate

Goal 5: Improve maternal health
> **Target 6:** Reduce by three-quarters, between 1990 and 2015, the maternal mortality ratio

Goal 6: Combat HIV/AIDS, malaria, and other diseases
> **Target 7:** Have halted by 2015 and begun to reverse the spread of HIV/AIDS
> **Target 8:** Have halted by 2015 and begun to reverse the incidence of malaria and other major diseases

Goal 7: Ensure environmental sustainability
> **Target 9:** Integrate the principles of sustainable development into country policies and programs and reverse the loss of environmental resources
> **Target 10:** Halve, by 2015, the proportion of people without sustainable access to safe drinking water and basic sanitation
> **Target 11:** Have achieved by 2020 a significant improvement in the lives of at least 100 million slum dwellers

Goal 8: Develop a global partnership for development
> **Target 12:** Develop further an open, rule-based, predictable, non-discriminatory trading and financial system (includes a commitment to good governance, development, and poverty reduction both nationally and internationally)
> **Target 13:** Address the special needs of the Least Developed Countries (includes tariff- and quota-free access for Least Developed Countries' exports, enhanced program of debt relief for heavily indebted poor countries [HIPCs] and

cancellation of official bilateral debt, and more generous official development assistance for countries committed to poverty reduction)

Target 14: Address the special needs of landlocked developing countries and small island developing states (through the Program of Action for the Sustainable Development of Small Island Developing States and 22nd General Assembly provisions)

Target 15: Deal comprehensively with the debt problems of developing countries through national and international measures in order to make debt sustainable in the long term

[Some of the indicators listed below are monitored separately for the least developed countries, Africa, landlocked developing countries, and small island developing states.]

Target 16: In cooperation with developing countries, develop and implement strategies for decent and productive work for youth

Target 17: In cooperation with pharmaceutical companies, provide access to affordable essential drugs in developing countries

Target 18: In cooperation with the private sector, make available the benefits of new technologies, especially information and communications technologies.

APPENDIX B

THE DECALOGUE OF ASSISI FOR PEACE

Pope John Paul II
Assisi, Italy –February 24, 2002

1. We commit ourselves to proclaiming our firm conviction that violence and terrorism are incompatible with the authentic spirit of religion, and, as we condemn every recourse to violence and war in the name of God or of religion, we commit ourselves to doing everything possible to eliminate the root causes of terrorism.

2. We commit ourselves to educating people to mutual respect and esteem, in order to help bring about a peaceful and fraternal coexistence between people of different ethnic groups, cultures and religions.

3. We commit ourselves to fostering the culture of dialogue, so that there will be an increase of understanding and mutual trust between individuals and among peoples, for these are the premise of authentic peace.

4. We commit ourselves to defending the right of everyone to live a decent life in accordance with their own cultural identity, and to form freely a family of their own.

5. We commit ourselves to frank and patient dialogue, refusing to consider our differences as an insurmountable barrier, but recognizing instead that to encounter the diversity of others can become an opportunity for greater reciprocal understanding.

6. We commit ourselves to forgiving one another for past and present errors and prejudices, and to supporting one another in a common effort both to overcome selfishness and arrogance, hatred and violence, and to learn from the past that peace without justice is no true peace.

7. We commit ourselves to taking the side of the poor and the helpless, to speaking out for those who have no voice and to working effectively to change these situations, out of the conviction that no one can be happy alone.

8. We commit ourselves to taking up the cry of those who refuse to be resigned to violence and evil, and we desire to make every effort possible to offer the men and women of our time real hope for justice and peace.

9. We commit ourselves to encouraging all efforts to promote friendship between peoples, for we are convinced that, in the absence of solidarity and understanding between peoples, technological progress exposes the world to a growing risk of destruction and death.

10. We commit ourselves to urging leaders of nations to make every effort to create and consolidate, on the national and international levels, a world of solidarity and peace based on justice.

Africa: Urbanisation and Proliferation of Slums
A Case Study of Kibera, Nairobi

Anne Itotia RSM

Abstract

The underlying causes of rights deprivation and marginalization of people create poverty in Africa forcing people to migrate from rural to urban areas. Thus, the rise and high rates of urbanisation and the proliferation of slums are evidence of people's movement in Africa. Many people especially the young dream of a better future. They, therefore, leave the underdeveloped rural areas in search of greener pastures. Many of these migrants end up in very overcrowded urban areas commonly known as informal settlements or slums. Here, they experience very basic needs and crime is rampant. Currently, a staggering one billion people worldwide live in such informal settlements, and "without radical changes the number could double in thirty years."[1] This research, therefore, presents a critical social analysis with a focus on Africa. Within the issues named, some awareness of the socio-economic, political and trade imbalances which create poverty in Africa cannot be ignored.

The focal point for this research is the Kibera slum in Nairobi, Kenya. It is the largest slum in Africa and one of the largest in the world.[2] It is home to one million people, close to that of Swaziland or of Trinidad and Tobago. The problems highlighted in this paper offer a case in point that carries many of the issues named in the summary paragraph offered for this November 2007 Conference.[3] The paper is developed in four sections. Section one gives an overview of the situation, section two characterises the case in point, section three positions the research within the context of Africa and section four offers a conclusion of the research. The pictures below illustrate Kibera's reality that will be unfolding.[4]

Kibera

---

[1] *The Slum Challenge.* United Nations (UN) report.
[2] Christiane Bodewes, *Parish Transformation in Urban Slums: Voices of Kibera, Kenya* (Nairobi: Paulines Publications Africa, 2005), 31.
[3] Issues named include greed, violence, hunger, extreme poverty, and debilitating ignorance.
[4] http://news.bbc.co.uk/1/shared/spl/hi/picture_gallery/07/africa_flying_toilets/html/1.stm

Section One: OVERVIEW

Introduction

Welcome to the story of Africa whose socio-economic and political climate illustrates that forty years after the colonial government, the continent is still underdeveloped. In particular, over the last two decades, the countries of Africa have faced increased poverty, rising levels of unemployment, increased insecurity, bad governance, deterioration of infrastructures and poor social services, just to name a few. As a result, there is a high rise of urbanisation and a proliferation of slums. The UN Human Settlements Programme (UN Habitat)[5] notes that slums exist in all parts of the world. However, they are concentrated in developing countries. As such, Africa has the second largest number of slum dwellers in the world.[6]

Random House College Dictionary defines a slum as "a thickly populated, squalid part of a city, inhabited by the poorest people." According to UN Habitat, a slum is a place of residence lacking one or more of five things: durable housing, sufficient living area, access to improved water, access to sanitation, and secure tenure. Following this definition, in most places of our cities—whether in Lusaka, Zambia's capital, Lilongwe, Malawi's capital or Badia West in Lagos, Nigeria, or wherever—the conditions are complex. In Kenya, for example, slums are informal settlements "hidden away like a dirty secret along railway embankments, rivers, and beside rubbish dumps."[7] Kibera exemplifies this reality.

Kibera presents micro and macro issues of a people living under conditions of extreme poverty. The slum is severely overcrowded and lacks proper infrastructures (e.g. sewage systems, water supply and sanitation, access roads, drainage and electricity, schools, health centres, community centres, recreational facilities, communication services, open spaces and so on). In Kibera, you will find a very high unemployment rate, a huge number of school drop-outs and low income earners. There are also bureaucratic government systems and structures that match the government's lack of social energy, poor local and international policies, trade and debt issues as well as Africa's own problems, i.e., land ownership, traditions and customs, corruption and lack of contingency plans in case of disasters.

Time and space constraints do not permit a detailed conversation on all the issues mentioned above and the questions that they hold for Africa. Nevertheless, Kibera's physical environment is a hotbed of crime, prostitution, rape and other forms of anti-social and immoral behaviours. This slum is featured in the 2005 film by Fernando Meirelles, *The Constant Gardener,*[8] and in the CNN video.[9] As a slum, it is the most

---

[5] *The Challenge of Slums: Global Report on Human Settlements* (2003).
[6] http://www.globalpolicy.org/socecon/develop/2003/1006slums.htm accessed 29 May 2007.
[7] Andrew Harding, *The Third in a Four Part Series: Looking at what life is like for Nairobi residents in Africa's largest slum.* BBC http://news.bbc.co.uk/2/hi/africa/2297265.stm.
[8] *The Constant Gardener* (Film). The story is filmed in Loiyangalan, a small town located on the southwestern coast of Lack Turkana in Kenya, and the slums of Kibera, Kenya.
[9] Christiane Amanpour reports for CNN, *Where Have All the Parents Gone.* The Wind of Hope project in Isiolo, Kenya. http://www.youtube.com/watch?v=33I4rqTx0V0

studied slum in Africa, either because of its historical role in the colonial rule of the 1900s, or its location in Nairobi—a cosmopolitan city with two UN agencies: Habitat (United Nations Agency for Towns and Cities) headquartered in Nairobi, and the United Nations Environmental Programmes (UNEP).

1.1.   The Concept of the Basic Need Basket

In Africa, the concept of the basic need basket asserts that most people are below the poverty line bracket. If we take, for example, any five basic needs: food, shelter, clothing, medicare, and education, you will find that the cost of each item has a shortfall in poor people's expenditure in relation to their income. Moreover, each of these basic needs has much hidden and related cost. For example, food alone takes in fuel (charcoal or firewood, water, vegetables, and other groceries). Hence, to provide a meal for an average family of five to ten (for most families care for other poorer families as well) would cost close to Kenya Shilling (Ksh) 500.00 (US$ 7 to 8). In most cases, a casual labourer earns from Ksh 70.00 (US $1) to Ksh 200.00 (US $3) a day (as of April 2007).

Commodities	Ksh 70.00	US$ 1.00	Malnutrition is very evident and diseases like pneumonia, malaria, TB, typhoid, dysentery, vomiting and diarrhea turn fatal most times. In terms of expenditure, there is nothing left to have a decent life. Herewith, child labour and prostitution are alternative solutions to earning money. Today, the spread of HIV/AIDS is worrying and family resources and welfare are diminishing.
2 kg Maize flour	50.00	00.70	
Vegetables (onions, greens, tomatoes)	100.00	1.42	
Oil, Salt etc	25.00	00.35	
1 kg Sugar	70.00	1.00	
100gm Tea	30.00	00.42	
Water (30 litre)	20.00	00.28	
Charcoal (8kgs)	80.00	1.12	

In summary, given the United Nations' report (2005) on the *Millennium Development Goals* (MDG),[10] I can confirm that Africa is one of those continents where extreme poverty remains a daily reality for people who subsist on less than US $1, i.e. Ksh 70 a day. Therefore, Africa's social capacity in terms of social services is in dire need of attention. This reality weighs heavily on Africa's development which has thirty-four of the world's fifty least developed countries. This geographical handicap has been compounded by war, government failure and mismanagement of power as well as poor international and local policies and bad stewardship. Seemingly, the negative impacts of globalization on Africa have not spared Kenya—robbing away her spirit of goodness and hospitality. Today, communal values are being lost to over-emphases on consumerism, individualism and unethical behaviors. However, if the MDGs were realized, then the basic need basket of every household would be improved in Africa.

---

[10] Goal 1: Eradicate Extreme Poverty and Hunger.
http://www.globalpolicy.org/msummit/millenni/2005/05mdgreport2005.pdf

1.2.   Kibera: A Part of a Whole

From the views of fifty people interviewed from different parts of Africa as well as of those who either lived or worked in Africa, the belief is that Kibera, as a case in point, could well refer to any other slum in the world. For example, in Lilongwe 70 percent of the households are squatters; in Caracas, Venezuela, about 55 percent; in Dar-es-Salaam, Tanzania, about 50 percent; and in Karachi, Pakistan, 45 percent. The World Bank's thinking is that "the world's worst slums can be transformed."[11] This is because "the rapid growth in developing world cities is making living intolerable for the urban poor and threatening the economic, social and environmental progress of these cities."[12]

Although many of Kibera's problems stem from rural to urban poverty, the backbone of the issues is international and national policies. At the same time, the World Bank and the International Monetary Fund's 'Structural Adjustment Programme' (SAP) have worsened conditions in Africa. When we look at Africa today, the burden of foreign debt, over dependency on the dollar/Euro notes, inflation of world markets, reliance on fossil fuel, impact of environmental degradation, low social energy, greed and corruption, poor implementations of national plans and lack of cohesion for development purposes, etc., all add up to the continent's woes and pleas.

Section Two: GROWTH AND DEVELOPMENT OF KIBERA

Introduction

One cannot miss Kibera for "in the grey gloom of first light, it looks like a pile of rubbish, a clutter of cardboard and cloth on a damp pavement."[13] Although one may be tempted to ask, why people should live in such awful places as Kibera, the slum is widely located in cross proximity to employment opportunities. In the cosmopolitan city of Nairobi, Kibera covers only 5 percent of the size of Nairobi which is 684 square kilometres. Kibera is commonly seen as a city within the city of Nairobi. It has its own class of people, its own complete districts, services, churches, shopping areas, medical clinics and bus stations, etc. Nairobi is a city where 60% of the people are accommodated in the slums and half of these residents live in Kibera alone.

The Millennium Goals have highlighted the slums as settlements that need proper attention rather than the preconceived idea that slums are informal settlements and the people in them are squatters. Kibera has been home to many dating back to the 1900s settlements and has been under government control since 1948.

2.1. Geography and Historical Background of Kibera

Nairobi is more than 1,661 metres above sea level. The city has approximately three million people (3,000,000) though unofficially people believe that it has close to four

---

[11] Washington, 3 June 1996.
[12] Ismail Seregeldin, World Bank Vice President for Environmental Sustainable Development, 3 June 1996.
[13] Andrew Harding, The Third in a Four Part Series: *Looking at what life is like for Nairobi residents in Africa's largest slum.* BBC documentary. http://news.bbc.co.uk/2/hi/africa/2297265.stm accessed on 25 May 2007.

million. Kibera is surrounded by affluent suburbs and estates including the famous Karen[14] area, Langata, Upper-hills, and Adams-Arcade. This slum occupies approximately 630 acres of land situated in the "Nairobi South-Western peri-urban zone about seven kilometres from the City Centre."[15] Kibera contains twelve villages and has close to twenty ethnic communities.

Kibera's history goes back to the 'colonial period'[16] when the urban layout was based on government-sanctioned population. This was the era of racial segregation that separated people into the enclaves for Africans, Asians and Europeans.[17] As an informal settlement, Kibera dates back to "the 1920s when the British colonial government decided to let a group of 'Nubian soldiers'[18] settle on a wooded hillside outside Nairobi."[19] The British failed to repatriate the Nubians or to compensate them with title deeds to these lands acquired from the Kenyan people. Consequently, the Nubians built homes, and set up businesses. They were still squatters with no legal rights and they called the place *Kibra*, meaning jungle.[20] This place became a military reserve in order for the soldiers to act as informal military forces should their services be needed again on short notice. In a loose translation of his (2002) writing, Zalot indicates that later, the colonial government needed labour to construct the Kenya to Uganda railway line, to extract natural resources from the land, and to transport these resources to the near port and load them on ship.[21] The Nubians were a means to easily available labour for such British projects.

The legacy of colonisation often shadows the atrocity of the Arabic settlers in Africa. These ruled the land (East Coast of Africa) in the 18th century before the Portuguese gained control on the Indian coast of Kenya for almost two hundred years with Mombasa as their administrative centre. In the early 19th century the British developed commercial ties with the Arab Sultans. We are all familiar with the history of slave trade that relates to systems of domination in Africa where Europe and the Arabs were all part of the trade of the Africans. This simply explains why Africa might be in need of healing and reconciliation with its past. In my opinion, past memories frustrate any plans for development and this escalates greed and corruption. People have not yet renewed their trust of any leadership systems.

---

[14] See Sydney Pollock's film *Out of Africa* (1985).
[15] Kenya Water For Health Organisation http://www.kwako.org/loc-d-kibera.html
[16] In the 1900s when Kenya was a British Protectorate. The capital was transferred from Mombasa to Nairobi in 1905.
[17] Africans were not allowed to enter the city without a permit and because of racial segregation the black people ended up in the black suburbs or in Kibera rather than in the white or the Asian settlement areas.
[18] An ethnic group from Sudan.
[19] The Nubian soldiers had been fighting on the side of their allies in World War One, as part of the King's African Rifles. See Harding, *The Last in a Four Part Series: Looking at what life is like for Nairobi residents in Africa's largest slum.* http://news.bbc.co.uk/2/hi/africa/2297279.stm accessed on 25 May 2007.
[20] BBC Slums Life Series http://news.bbc.co.uk/2/hi/africa/2297279.stm.
[21] Jozef D. Zalot, *The Roman Catholic Church and Economic Development in Sub-Saharan Africa: Voices Yet Unheard in a Listening World* (Lanham: University Press of America, 2002), 3.

The problems that hamper growth and development in Africa are multiple. The present and the past are well connected to the issues of highly inequitable land distribution,[22] the forced *hut tax* [23] introduced by the British systems, "institutionalisation"[24] of money in Africa, collapse of formal institutions, changes in gender roles and in social cohesion more generally, increased population pressure, corrupt systems, subsistence farming and cash-crop production. Today, housing, land ownership, employment, tribalism, crime, and alcoholism are some issues that, if addressed, slums like Kibera could be transformed.

Though Kibera is not attractive from the outside, if invited into a home, feel privileged. Most visitors to the slum never get the chance to see the real living areas there and the routines of daily living. To enter a home, one doesn't knock, but instead calls out "Hodi...Hodi," and the response to enter is "Karibu" (welcome). If you are invited in, you may be invited to enjoy some tea "chai" (boiled water with milk and sugar) and slices of white bread. Inside most of the homes, everything is clean - worn, old, and falling apart - but freshly washed.

2.2. Demographics
With an estimated population of one million (1,000,000) people, Kibera's situation is urgent, just as in many other slums in Africa. In Kenya, the last decade has witnessed heavy influxes of people into the slums since the government instigated ethnic cleansing in 1992-1994 and provoked continued violence in the country. Most slums contain many young people and women's burden in the slums is severe. Thus, the shift in gender roles has intensified and has destabilised families, because now both men and women have to contribute to the welfare of the family. This has a detrimental effect on men-women relationships. In Kibera, women are particularly disadvantaged because half of the population lives in female-headed single-parent households. The education of girls is not encouraged either, and many of them end up marrying young.

2.3. Infrastructures

2.3.1. Housing
The majority of structures are rented on a room-to-room basis. The average home size in Kibera is 3 meters by 3 meters, with an average of five persons per dwelling. Urban

---

[22] This goes back to the colonizers who forbade Kenyans from growing their own coffee crops, lest they compete against settler plantations, and British settlers extracted any material or economic wealth generated within Nairobi. See Mark Kramer, *Dispossessed Life in Our World's Urban Slums* (Maryknoll: Orbis Books, 2006), 59. The post-independence leaders did not make any difference in the realities of the poor who lost their livelihood through colonization.

[23] Communities were put under forced labour to pay for the 'hut tax'. When people lost their lands and homes, they were put into concentration camps and lived in grass-thatched huts. The British enforced payment of a tax per hut. This forced people to start looking for jobs to get money to pay. The jobs were either on the white settlers' farms or in the city. Before this, people did not use money, as the system of trade was barter—exchange of goods for goods. Today, militia groups are using the same methods of harassing slum residents, requiring a "protection fee" per household, capitalising on the sins of the past history.

[24] Before this, people practiced barter trade (exchange of goods for goods), which explains why trade is still an issue in Africa.

services such as water or sanitation are minimal. There is an average of one pit latrine for every 50 to 200 people. People resort to "flying toilets"[25] . Toilets are not easily affordable, for to use one (a filthy private latrine) costs five shillings. Bureaucratic structures disable people to do simple repairs or to build a toilet without dealing with the administrative provincial government through the local chief for permission. Hence, the illustration below can speak for itself.[26]

In terms of housing, it is not simply the problem of affordability that keeps Nairobi's population from access to decent housing. According to a 2002 study, "mortgages range from 15 to 25 percent, with repayment periods averaging about ten years. Borrowers are required to pay up front 20 to 40 percent of the appraised value of the property and all the related legal fees. This can amount to 10 percent of the loan value. To have the land surveyed, marked, and appraised, together with stamp duties and legal fees is likely to cost Ksh 210,000 approx US $ 3,000" (see Consortium of International Urban Organizations: Cities Alliance). Kibera has no electricity service; therefore, at night it is "pure dark with intermittent glimmers of fire."[27]

2.3.2. Health
Kibera's smells are constantly challenging. There is a stink all over that is compounded by lack of toilets, open sewage, and rotten foodstuffs as well as smells from charcoal burners or burning firewood. Cuts and simple injuries are common, and tetanus is dangerous unless one gets a tetanus injection. These injuries are common because the pathways that are narrow alleys are littered with rusty nails, plastic bags, wood, pieces of metal, broken glass, and empty plastic lighters—you name it.

There are several individuals and NGOs who run health clinics within the slum. Mobile health clinics are frequently conducted by the health NGOs and the government. However, HIV/AIDS continues to be a permanent condition in Africa, creating a hundred

---

[25] These are plastic bags which fly over the roof tops at night. Note: AMREF (African Medical and Research Foundation) has constructed a total of 286 pit latrines across the Kibera slum. All the units are in use and are contributing to the reduction of the "flying toilets" menace.
http://news.bbc.co.uk/1/shared/spl/hi/picture_gallery/07/africa_flying_toilets/html/1.stm.

[26] Ksh 5.00 to use a latrine.
[27] Mark Kramer, *Dispossessed Life in Our World's Urban Slums* (Maryknoll: Orbis Books, 2006), 55.

thousand orphaned children in Kibera alone.[28] The disease exacerbates poverty, marginalises people and stigmatises those afflicted and their families.

2.3.3. Schools

There are a few schools within the Kibera slum run by well-wishers. These schools are run by donations from individuals and corporate bodies which occasionally donate items like food, books, desks, pens, building materials and teachers' salaries. The teachers are commonly referred to as volunteer teachers.

2.3.4. Transport System

The Kenya to Uganda railway passes through Kibera. The slum also has a railway station but due to the absence of an effective commuter train system in Nairobi, most Kibera residents use buses and Matatus (Local Taxi) where necessary. Consequently, the already disadvantaged poor are forced to trek long distances on foot to work or just give up seeking work in certain parts of the city. Inside Kibera there are no roads, only pathways. These paths are dirt concrete leading through the homes. The paths are so narrow in places that you can actually touch the buildings on both sides of the path if you stretch out your arms. Many of the pathways are divided right down the middle by a smelly ditch which helps carry the waste water away.

2.3.5. Water

Drinking water is sold to the inhabitants in plastic containers after it has been pumped through metal and plastic pipes alongside sewage trenches. A 30-litre jerry-can costs twenty shillings ($0.28). These trenches carry refuse and human waste to the river at the base of the valley. The river then runs into Nairobi Dam which is used for recreation and other resources. The plastic pipes are brittle and exposed, often breaking, to be repaired without care for sanitation. The 2006 *Human Development Report* argues that "water and sanitation must be put front and centre on the development agenda...."[29]

2.3.6. Security

Turmoil in slums arises when political leaders spur people to vote along tribal lines. Usually, slums are not a major source of urban unrest, but they constitute areas with a higher concentration of crime related activities that range from petty to serious and major crimes. Most of the immoralities arise from congested housing, illiteracy, ignorance of basic constitutional rights and human rights, etc. Idle youth end up as mobs or private vigilantes (militia groups) who patrol the slums sometimes demanding protection fees from the people. These would burn you if you steal one shilling, while at the same time pickpockets mingle with the crowds heading home after their day's work, hiding quickly along narrow alleys, jumping nimbly across open sewers, their paths occasionally lit by the lamps and candles of stall owners selling fruit and fried fish.

---

[28] See CNN video, *Where Have All the Parents Gone.* http://www.youtube.com/watch?v=33I4rqTx0V0.
[29] General Analysis on Poverty and Development (9 November 2006) http://www.globalpolicy.org/socecon/develop/index.htm, accessed 1 June 2007.

2.4. Kibera's Livelihood

Many slum dwellers depend on the 'informal economy,' which involves "some kind of petty retailing," [30] e.g. opening a tiny kiosk named 'Duka', a mini-market. Unbelievably, the size of such a Duka is that of a closet or just a stall, i.e. a place to sell soft drinks, soap, candy, cigarettes, cooking oil, maize flour or fresh vegetables and fruit bought from the main markets. Employment elsewhere is in the service industry, i.e., domestic 'maids,' waiters, bar maids, guards, watchmen and prostitutes, etc. Other people find jobs in small business as charcoal sellers, dressmakers, or in brewing, e.g., the "Nubian gin or *chang'aa*, an illicit alcoholic drink made of maize, sorghum, or sugar cane." [31] In the past, local brews have turned lethal claiming many lives. "Children sell trinkets and newspapers, scavenge through garbage, and shine shoes." [32] Other activities include selling kerosene and serving in small hotels and food stands.

Section Three: THE CONTEXT - AFRICA

Introduction

In etymology, Africa takes the name proposed by a historian Leo Africanus (1488-1554) who suggested the Greek word *phrike* (φρίκη, meaning 'cold and horror' combined with the prefix 'a', indicating a land free of cold and horror. Historically, *afri* was the name of several peoples who dwelt in North Africa near the provincial capital Carthage. The Roman suffix 'ca' denotes country or land. [33]

Africa as the world's second largest continent is "home to 900 million people as per 2005 reports in sixty one territories, accounting for about 14% of the world's human population." [34] Yet, ask someone to tell you quickly what they associate with Africa. The answers in most parts probably range from "cradle of humankind" to "poverty," "corruption," [35] "tribalism," and so on.

3.1. Background

African countries are characterised by an astonishing contradiction: an enormous resource endowment on the one hand, and social and economic deprivation on the other. According to the United Nations Human Development Report in 2003, the bottom 25 ranked nations (151st to 175th) were all African countries. Africa's past colonial history predisposed her to primary products. Today, she is rich in raw materials including natural resources (minerals, precious stones, and fossil oil), unbeatable game reserves and wildlife, and world famous beach resorts like Mombasa. She plays a role in her agricultural exports, e.g., horticultural products, coffee, cocoa, tea, and tobacco, to open markets. She decorates homes, hospitals and hotels with her cut flowers. Her minerals are sold even for high tech computer chips and cell phones. Africa sells her barrels of oil to

---

[30] Mark Kramer, 55.
[31] Ibid.
[32] Ibid.
[33] Consultos.com etymology http://www.consultos.com/pandora/africa.htm.
[34] *World Population Prospects*: *The 2004 Revision*, United Nations Department of Economic and Social Affairs (Population Division). http://en.wikipedia.org/wiki/Africa.
[35] *Africa: Whatever you thought think again. National Geographic*, Special Issue, September 2005.

millions of consumers and she exchanges her wealth for guns and ammunitions as handy resources for war and tribal clashes.

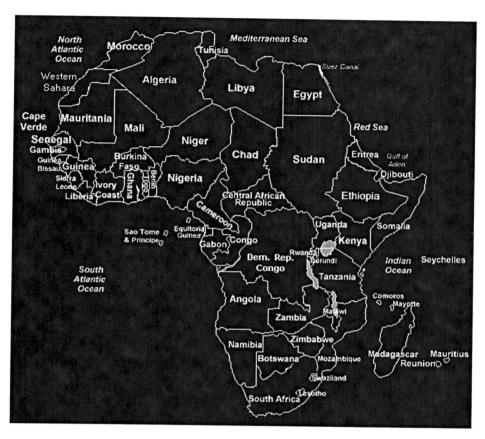

Unfortunately, Africa is still a shadow in the world trade negotiations. However, a look at South Africa will illustrate that the country has access to financial capital, numerous markets, skilled labor, and first-world infrastructure in much of the country. The Johannesburg Stock Exchange[36] is a state of the art resource. Similarly, Nigeria sits on one of the largest proven oil reserves in the world and has the highest population among nations in Africa, becoming one of the fastest-growing economies today. Seemingly, Ghana, Kenya, Cameroon and Egypt are making comparable progress in economic growth. The rivers of central Africa are great generators of hydroelectric power. Africa is mother to the big animals that are a major source of ecotourism revenue in eastern and southern Africa; and her forests in the wetter regions, if managed and logged sustainably, would be renewable as lucrative sources of income. However, the world trade systems, structures, and strategies continue to keep Africa in chains of poverty for the most part. Consequently, Africa is still a weak player in the economic market. Africa completely depends on the dollar or the Euro note to sell her wares and her money is of little value if any.

The problems that beset Africa call for a new paradigm and call people to look beyond Africa's past colonial history which still impinges on her development. As a continent,

---

[36] Economy of Africa. http://en.wikipedia.org/wiki/Africa, accessed 27 May 2007.

tribal divide is becoming a political tool for politicians just as different cultures, languages, and mindsets keep Africa away from her people. This is also exaggerated in the structures of her zones, such as Francophone, Anglophone or the Arab north. Thus, Africa remains her own worst enemy. She has lost her fraternity and sorority that offered her solidarity in the ***ubantu spirit***[37] in the years past. Consequently, she has to constantly challenge some of her own cultural practices, e.g., female genital mutilation (FGM), wife inheritance, and the heart-breaking practice of breast ironing in Cameroon.[38]

Section Four: CONCLUSION

Intervention and Reconstruction

With all the policy-sensitive initiatives undertaken over the last decade, including the *Enabling Strategy* from the Nairobi Informal Settlements Coordination Committee, and the *Nairobi Situation Analysis, the Poverty Reduction Strategy Paper* and the *Local Authority Transfer Fund*, there should be some signs of hope. These have addressed a series of themes, including settlement upgrading of slums, community participation and improved access to services.

Jacinta (not her real name) offers a success story of a woman who knows best that the people in the slums are deprived not only of life-building or coping skills but of opportunities to spot economic gains. Jacinta is today a well-groomed lady whose education, that was supported by an NGO, opened her to a hopeful future. Her word to us is "that we develop a spirit that enables others to challenge socio-economic and political systems through capacity building, training and education, while focusing on those at the bottom of the ladder."[39] This agrees with the arguments of James Mwangi that "Africa needs an environment to help it pull itself out of its system; foreign aid has not changed Africa much in the last 50 years." He continues, "Africa needs support to participate in fair trade where it can export and get an equal share as the rest of the world. Direct investment is the key word." He added, "Access to the markets through the removal of trade barriers and subsidies would place Africa on a fair and realistic scale on the global market."[40]

---

[37] *Ubantu* does not translate into English as it has rich and nuanced meaning. *Ubantu* is the value of human being, it is humanness, it is kindness. *Ubantu* is tolerance, sensitivity, and respect. When you put that together you find *ubantu* as the lifeblood that pumps through your veins and informs the brain to think correctly, to think emotionally correctly. (Anne Itotia, personal notes, Workshop on *African Traditions and Cultures in the Ubantu Spirit,* Pretoria, South Africa, 2000).

[38] The breasts are flattened using heated grinding stones, wooden pestles, heated banana, coconut shell and sometimes herbs and petrol. Breast ironing is a form of body modification in which mothers, aunts or older cousins flatten pubescent girls' breasts to make them less sexually attractive to men. Cameroon women and girls are struggling to fight this cultural practice that is equally devastating and traumatising. *East African Standard*, 27 May 2007.

[39] Jacinta is a university graduate working with an international community in Nairobi. I met Jacinta through Ken Mathews, a Community Aid Worker in San Francisco.

[40] James Mwangi, Equity Bank Chief Executive Officer, was addressing hundreds of economic experts in a technical working group in Berlin ahead of the G8 summit. See "World Bank Challenges G8 on Aid," *East African Standard*, 6 June 2007.

In conclusion, there are many initiatives in Kibera despite people's difficult situations. These include several active community organisations working on issues such as: environment and sanitation, waste management, HIV/AIDS awareness, counselling and testing, domestic violence, education, and unemployment. Seeing the number of people willing to work in harsh environments and the problems that threaten us today in urbanisation, a well coordinated effort is necessary for all who care about people at the bottom of the pyramid – those who live issues of extreme poverty each day. This is because the migration of people arises from many mitigating factors that thwart people's dreams for a greener pasture. Therefore, the conditions forcing people to migrate should be our concern rather than the movement of people worldwide.

Global Human Trafficking: A Mercy Concern

Elizabeth McMillan, RSM

Introduction

At a meeting in November 2006 of the Sisters and Associates who coordinate Mercy Justice ministry in the Americas, Mercy Sister Deirdre Mullan reported that there were "approximately 20 million migrants and refugees worldwide, triple the number estimated by the UN only 17 years ago."[1] Further, she noted, countries such as Ireland, Italy and Spain, which in the 18th and 19th centuries sent millions of citizens abroad, are now countries of destination. Modern communication media reveal to the masses of indigent people worldwide economic opportunities not available to them in their native lands, and trucks, buses, ships, and even airplanes offer them greater mobility than was available in the past.

At the same meeting Mullan reported that "in 2005 the funds migrants sent back to their home countries [were] at least $167 billion, and [that] this revenue now dwarfs all forms of international aid combined." In Honduras, for example, salaries earned abroad constituted the largest or second largest source of the country's GNP in recent years. The percentage of this income sent home by professionals working abroad – mostly in the United States—is insignificant when compared with the percentage earned by those who do manual labor: agricultural workers, maids and janitors, those who work in food service, on factory assembly lines, and in the construction trades. Most of these people who are on the move go willingly, ready to risk and to sacrifice, in hopes of a better future for themselves and their families. The International Labor Organization [ILO] reports that women migrating for work opportunities now constitute about half of all migrant workers.[2]

I.   The Bad News: Exploitation of the Vulnerable

In this socio-economic climate where the extreme poverty of the very poor makes them extremely vulnerable socially and morally, they are ready victims of the form of slavery we call *human trafficking*. Enslaving people for economic gain is an old story. More than 1,000 years before the birth of Jesus Christ, Moses led the captive people of Abraham in flight from their Egyptian masters. In 1619 the first African slaves arrived in Virginia, the first of the English colonies in the land that eventually became the United States. And it wasn't until 1863, almost 250 years later, that President Abraham Lincoln issued the Emancipation Proclamation, declaring that "all persons held as slaves within the Confederate States [of the USA] are, and henceforth shall be free."[3] In the year 1776 indentured servants sailed from Rotterdam in the Netherlands, "packed" into ships carrying "four to six hundred souls; not to mention the farm instruments, tools,

---

[1] Deirdre Mullan, Meeting of Justice Ministers, Sisters of Mercy of the Americas, St. Louis, MO, USA, November 2006. http://www.unodc.en/trafficking_human_beings.html.
[2] Draft ILO Multilateral Framework on Labour Migration, International Labor Organization, Geneva, 2005
[3] www.infoplease.com/timeline/slavery.html.

provisions, water-barrels and other things that likewise occupy much space." After describing in some detail the grotesque conditions of the trip the author of this account goes on to say that "even with the best wind the voyage lasts 7 weeks."[4] The plight of these indentured servants, if they survived the transatlantic voyage, which many did not, prefigured the situation of those who are trafficked today. Not only was the voyage itself a very risky venture, but the indentured were literally the property of those who paid their passage; they belonged to them until it was paid off by their sweat and strain.

The United States Department of State reports on its website that 800,000 to 900,000 persons, principally women and children, are trafficked annually within or across international borders.[5] At the Conference on Human Trafficking sponsored by the McGill International Law Society, Montreal, Canada, March 20, 2006, the estimate reported was 800,000 to four million people. They are kidnapped, forced, or induced into prostitution by deception. Among the children are boys as well as girls. It is reported that "the present rate of trafficking in children is already 10 times higher than the trans-Atlantic slave trade at its peak."[6] Also included in this number are the thousands of infants stolen from their mothers and sold on the international market to families desperate to adopt.[7]

The United States is the destination country for the greatest number of victims of trafficking. Government estimates are that at least 50,000 are trafficked to the US, and that the number could be as high as four million.[8] The US government also estimates that 14,500 to 17,500 are trafficked within the country.[9] The clandestine nature of the activity makes it difficult, even impossible, to know how many people are trafficked into the US, indeed into any country, in a given year.

A classic case of human trafficking was reported by the press in Newark, New Jersey, in the United States in November 2005. A 35-year-old man named Rosales pleaded guilty to keeping young Honduran women in an apartment to work off fees of $10,000 to $20,000 for smuggling them into the United States. Rosales implicated in turn the ringleaders and others involved along with him in a trafficking ring. He told the police that he and several Honduran women had been smuggled into the country by a "coyote." The coyote's sister in Houston made arrangements for them to travel to Newark, New Jersey, where he was asked to "be in charge of" an apartment where a new group of Honduran women were to be housed. He was told by one of the ringleaders of the smuggling ring, "If any of these bitches get out of line, you should beat them." One of the women was pregnant, and after ingesting an abortion-inducing drug, she delivered a baby who died before an ambulance arrived. In his testimony offered as part of his guilty plea, Rosales testified against the leaders of the trafficking ring. Ten people were indicted. They had brought the women to the United States on the promise of decent jobs in restaurants. The young women were forced to drink alcohol and dance with customers. They were forced to work up to seven days a week from 6 p.m. to 2 a.m., and were threatened with deportation or harm to them

---

[4] http://www.let.rug.nl/usa/D/1601-1650/mittelberger /servan.htm.
[5] http://state.gov/p/inl/41444.htm.
[6] http://www.cwin.org.np/press_room/factsheet/fact_trafficking.htm.
[7] R.T. Naylor, *The Wages of Crime*, Cornell University Press, 2002.
[8] U.S. Department of State. Trafficking in Persons Report, June, 2002. http://www.state.gov/g/inl/rls/tiprpt
[9] Ibid.

or their families in Honduras if they did not comply. The newspaper article invites readers to report other cases of human trafficking or slavery to a 1-888 phone number, and offers a web address to readers who want to find out more about trafficking and exploitation.

According to statistics collected by the US State Department in the late 1990's, of those 700,000 to four million trafficked worldwide, at least 50,000 are trafficked to the United States annually. US officials also estimate, on the basis of available data, that the majority of victims around the globe come from Southeast Asia (225,000) and South Asia (150,000). An additional estimated 100,000 are from the countries which are former members of the Soviet Union. Over 100,000 come from Latin America and the Caribbean, and over 50,000 come from Africa. These (mostly) women are trafficked to Asia, the Middle East, Western Europe and North America.[10] The United Nations Office on Drugs and Crime reports, "Economic and Sexual slavery is a highly lucrative global industry controlled by powerful criminal organizations, such as the Yakuza, the Triads and the Mafia."[11]

A related issue is the question of the legalization of prostitution. Those who advocate legalization allege that making it illegal deprives women of the right to decide for themselves whether they want to earn a living by offering sexual companionship for a price. Women's groups who oppose the legalization argue that there is no such thing as a "right" to the exploitation of one's body. In 2006 the Joint Project Coordinated by the Coalition Against Trafficking in Women (CATW) and the European Women's Lobby (EWL) on Promoting Preventive Measures to Combat Trafficking in Human Beings for Sexual Exploitation published the report, *The Links Between Prostitution and Sex Trafficking: A Briefing Handbook*. The report concludes:

> Legalization removes every legal impediment to pimping, procuring and brothels. Traffickers can use work permits to bring foreign women into the prostitution industry, masking the fact that women have been trafficked, by coaching them to describe themselves as independent "migrant sex workers."[12]

The authors cite the testimony of prostitutes who have been subject to degrading and dangerous, even life-threatening abuse, such as "slashing with razor blades; tying women to bedposts and lashing them until they bleed; biting women's breasts; burning the women with cigarettes, cutting [their] arms, legs and genital areas; and urinating and defecating on women."[13] The Report also cites a Canadian report on pornography and prostitution that found that "the death rate of women in prostitution was 40 times higher than the general population."[14]

---

[10] www.usdoj.gov/crt/crim/traffickingsummary.html
[11] "Trafficking in Persons: The New Protocol," United Nations Office on Drugs and Crime. www.usdoj.gov/crt/crim/traffickingsummary.html.
[12] Raymond, Janice et al, *A Comparative Study of Women Trafficked in the Migration Process: Patterns, Profiles and Health Consequences of Sexual Exploitation in Five Countries*. N. Amherst, MA, 2002.
[13] Ibid., p. 14.
[14] Loc.cit., p.16.

II.   Attempts to Monitor and Control International Trafficking

In 2002 the United Nations issued what became known as the Palermo Protocol, a Protocol to Prevent, Suppress and Punish Trafficking in Persons, Especially Women and Children. Its stated purposes are

(a) to prevent and combat trafficking in persons, particularly women and children;

(b) to protect and assist the victims of such trafficking, with full respect for their human rights; and

(c) to promote cooperation among State Parties in order to meet those objectives.

The protocol aims to supplement the United Nations Convention against Transnational Organized Crime. Some of the international criminal organizations that traffic in weapons and drugs also traffic in people.

The International Labor Organization

In 2005 the International Labor Organization negotiated a Multilateral Framework on Labor Migration which offers "principles and guidelines for a rights-based approach to labor migration."[15] Section VI of the Framework calls for the "Prevention of and protection against abusive migration practices," stating that "Governments should formulate and implement, in consultation with the social partners, measures to prevent abusive practices, migrant smuggling and trafficking in persons; they should also work towards preventing irregular labour migration."[16] The document further calls for "addressing the specific risks faced by women and, where applicable, promoting opportunities in the workplace".[17]

In 2004 the UN Global Programme Against Trafficking in Human Beings (GPAT) housed in the United Nations office on Drugs and Crime produced a report on human trafficking that was based on data collected from 1996 and 2003.[18] Their working definition of human trafficking reads:

> The recruitment, transportation, transfer, harbouring or receipt of persons, by means of the threat or use of force or other forms of coercion, of abduction, of fraud, of deception, of the abuse of power or of a position of vulnerability or of the giving or receiving of payments or benefits to achieve the consent of a person, having control over another person for the purpose of exploitation. Exploitation shall include, at a minimum, the exploitation or the prostitution of others or other forms of sexual exploitation, forced labor or services, slavery or practices similar to slavery, servitude or the removal of organs.[19]

---

[15] ILO Multilateral Framework on Labor Migration, Geneva, November 2005.
[16] *Draft ILO Mutilateral Framework on Labour Migration: Non-binding principles and guidelines for a rights-based approach to labour migration*, Geneva, 31 October – 2 November 2005, International Labour Office, Geneva.
[17] Ibid., #V.9.12.
[18] *Programme Against Trafficking in Human Beings*.
[19] http://www.unodc/en/trafficking_human_beings.html

The UN definition includes a specific reference to the *act,* the *means*, and the *purpose*. Thus the "recruitment, transportation, transfer, harbouring or receipt of persons" would be criminal, as would threat or the use of "force, abduction, fraud, deception, abuse of power or vulnerability, or giving payments or benefits to a person in control of the victim."[20] The definition is comprehensive. However, one of the difficulties in its application is that a person may have consented to – and even *paid* for—the services of a person to transport her illegally across the border, and then *subsequently* found herself without passport or funds in the hands of her "coyote."[21]

The United States is the global destination for the greatest number of trafficked persons, an estimated 50,000 persons annually, although the number could be much higher. In 2000 the United States Congress passed the Victims of Trafficking and Violence Protection Act, strengthening the Criminal Section of the Civil Rights Division, enabling it to "reach the more insidious forms of coercion" and to "come to the aid of more victims and to bring more cases than allowed under prior laws." The report characterized trafficking as "one of the fastest growing areas of international criminal activity" and noted that the overwhelming majority of those trafficked are women and children.[22]

The Act defines human trafficking as "the recruitment, harboring, transportation, provision or obtaining of a person for commercial sex, labor services through the use of force, fraud, or coercion, for the purpose of subjecting that person to involuntary servitude, peonage, debt bondage, or slavery."[23] In 2002 the US State Department issued the first of annual reports in which countries are ranked according to the efforts they are making to combat trafficking. The report employs Tier Placement categories, Tier 1 being the group of countries which have in place the legal structure and law enforcement apparatus to monitor and control human trafficking. In Appendix B can be found excerpts from the 2007 report on the countries in which the Sisters of Mercy are ministering.

The Tier 2 class of nations are those that are not doing enough, and the countries on the Tier 2 Watch List are those who are not able to show that they are making sufficient effort to address the problem. Specifically, the statute challenges each country to:

- Create new laws that criminalize trafficking with respect to slavery, involuntary servitude, peonage or forced labor
- Permit prosecution where nonviolent coercion is used to force victims to work in the belief they could be subject to serious harm
- Permit prosecution where the victim's service was compelled by confiscation of documents such as passports or birth certificates
- Increase prison terms for all slavery violations from 10 years to 20 years and add life imprisonment where the violation involves the death, kidnapping, or sexual abuse of the victim
- Require courts to order restitution and forfeiture of assets upon conviction

---

[20] Ibid., p. 51.

[21] The term used for those who lead illegal migrants across the border between Mexico and the United States.

[22] Ibid.

[23] Ibid.

• Enable victims to seek witness protection and other types of assistance
• Give prosecutors and agents new tools to get legal immigration status for victims of trafficking during investigation and prosecution

Initiatives to combat human trafficking have come as well from Canada and countries in the European Union, the Group of Eight, and the Organization for Security and Cooperation in Europe (OSCE). Regional conferences such as the Joint Bali/Budapest Processes meeting in Vienna in October of 2005 have also been convened. At this conference the Chair, Turkey, underlined the connection to international organized crime and the "key role of awareness raising campaigns directed at the general public, judicial and law enforcement agencies."[24] Reference was also made at the meeting to "the development of an European Union plan on best practices, standards and mechanisms to prevent and combat trafficking in human beings," and to the group's recent communication, "Fighting trafficking in human beings –an integrated approach and proposals for an action plan." The plan calls for yet stronger cooperation at the regional and global level and continued promotion of regional initiatives like the "Nordic Baltic Task Force against Human Trafficking and the Budapest Process."[25]

A UN Report on Human Trafficking Trends, published in April, 2006, documents the trafficking of people from 127 countries to be exploited in 137 other countries. A global map of human trafficking [see Appendix A] reveals the global patterns.

Countries of origin are countries from which people are trafficked.[26] Among those where there is a *high* or *very high* number of reported incidents are:
• In Africa: Nigeria, Ghana and Morocco.
• In Asia: China, Thailand, Bangladesh, Cambodia, India, Laos, Myanmar, Nepal, Pakistan, the Philippines, and Vietnam.
• In Central and South Eastern Europe: Albania, Bulgaria, Lithuania, Romania, the Czech Republic, Estonia, Hungary, Latvia, Poland and Slovakia.

The main destination countries:

• The United States is a country where there is a very high incidence of cases of people being trafficked into the country.
• Australia, Canada and the United Kingdom are also on the list of destination countries with a high incidence of persons brought in.

The countries which are both origin and destination countries are Poland, the Czech Republic, China, India, Thailand, Cambodia.

---

[24] www.icmpd.org/fileadmin/ICMPD-Website/Budapest/_Process/Working-Groups/Bali.BP_Meeting_Conclusions_Vienna_2005.pdf
[25] Ibid.
[26] See Appendix A for global maps from the UN report.

Victims of trafficking are abducted or recruited in one country, transported through transit regions, and then taken to destinations in other countries where they are exploited.[27]

Global Patterns of Trafficking

This analysis by regions of the world reveals a global pattern of dominant destinations as well as a pattern of regions in the world where the majority of victims of trafficking originate. The principal countries of *destination* are found in North America, Western Europe, Western Asia and Turkey, and Oceania. The principal countries of *origin* are those in the Commonwealth of Independent States (former members of the Soviet Union), Africa, Asia, Central and South Eastern Europe, and Latin America and the Caribbean. Some of these counties are significant regions in terms of both origin and destination. Central and South Eastern Europe, Asia, Africa and Western Europe are mainly *transit* areas. Among the countries of Western Europe that are cited as *destination* countries, Belgium, Germany, Greece, Italy and the Netherlands rank very high in the numbers of persons trafficked, and Nigeria ranks very high as a "source country" from which many are trafficked. The destination of these Nigerians is predominantly Western Europe.[28]

Within the Americas, the countries of Latin America (Central and South America) and the Caribbean are primarily countries of *origin*. The United States and Canada are the destinations of most of the victims of trafficking, although persons are also trafficked to Europe and to destinations within the region. Central America is cited most frequently as the sub-region from which most victims are trafficked, followed by the Caribbean and South America. Brazil, Columbia, Dominican Republic, Guatemala and Mexico are rated as countries with considerable traffic northward. Within Oceania, Australia is high on the list of destinations for those trafficked primarily from Thailand and the Philippines.

The U.N. researchers employed three fundamental categories in their analysis of the data: (1) criminal acts, (2) the means used to commit these acts, and (3) goals, the purpose for which the traffickers were engaged in the activity. The available figures range from the reported number of those rescued or repatriated to the reported number of trafficked persons in existence. The difficulties involved in collecting current and reliable data reflect the challenges of trying to monitor and control an enterprise that is by its very nature clandestine. Much of the activity goes undetected. Some of the other shortcomings of effective data management that hindered the researchers are:

- a definition of *trafficking* in terms of only one kind of exploitation, e.g., sexual
- the definition does not cover adult males, who are also trafficked

---

[27] *Trafficking in Persons: Global Patterns*, United Nations Office on Drugs and Crime (UNODC), April, 2006.
[28] Ibid.

- the affected population is not identified as "victims of crime", but as "smuggled migrants" (with the underlying assumption that these people have engaged the smuggler)
- the victims are afraid to supply information for fear of retaliation or harm to their family members
- many countries lack a centralized system of data collection; also, some produce annual figures, while the data produced by others covers a period of several years
- countries mix categories of data: e.g., trafficked persons with migrant smuggling and other forms of irregular migration
- countries collect data solely on trafficking across borders, whereas *smuggling across borders is a transnational activity that terminates with the arrangement once having crossed over the border; trafficking involves non-governmental organized exploitation.*

Finally, researchers note, data collection is complicated by the difficulties in verifying *consent*. A child under the age of 18 cannot legally have given his or her consent, and those adults responsible for children do not have the legal right to consent to the child's commercial exploitation.

A critical issue for those charged with enforcement of laws governing trafficking is the important distinction between *trafficking* and *smuggling*. The law enforcement community in the United States in its guide for those charged with patrolling its borders uses the following conditions to distinguish smuggling from trafficking.

In the case of smuggling:

• The person being smuggled is usually cooperating
• There is no coercion
• Those being smuggled are knowingly violating the law
• Once over the border, the person is free to leave the smuggler
• It always involves the crossing of an international border
• It has to do only with entering a country, i.e., crossing a border illegally

Whereas, trafficking:

• Involves force, fraud or coercion, or the involvement of minors in commercial sex
• Is forced labor or exploitation
• Enslaves, isolates, leaves the person without passport or visa
• Can occur without crossing an international border
• Involves working in commercial sex acts or other forced labor

Fraud, force and *coercion* are the key components that distinguish trafficking. Under United States law, whenever any *minor* is induced to perform a commercial sex act, it is considered trafficking regardless of whether fraud, force or coercion is involved.[29]

---

[29] Human Smuggling and Trafficking Center. HSTC@State.gov.

Mercy in the Context of Global Trafficking

Since the year 2000 the US Department of State has been collecting data and publishing reports from their files on human trafficking around the world. The countries profiled in Appendix B give some idea of the current situation in the countries where the Sisters of Mercy are present. Excerpts from these reports can be found in this Appendix. Most of what appears in the profiles is cited textually from the State Department's 2007 report. The report identifies the countries as *source, transit* or *destination* countries.[30] The *source* countries are those from which the victims are trafficked by force or deception, and the *destination* countries are those where they are put to work, in some cases having passed through a *transit* country.

Conclusion: Organizations Committed to the Effort

The only good news in this distressing overview of one of the most serious challenges to our generation is that there are a number of organizations that are either exclusively dedicated to an anti-trafficking agenda, or are participating in the effort to inform, protect, protest or prosecute. The list of these organizations can be found in Appendix C.

Faced with this shocking scenario, what might we be called to do with the special charism given to Catherine McAuley to rescue and care for endangered women and children?

---

[30] http://www.state.gov/g/tip/rls/tiprpt/2007/82806.htm The excerpts cited from the report are largely quoted *verbatim*, though not in their entirety.

APPENDIX A

Global maps from the April 2006 report, *Trafficking in Persons: Global Patterns*, United Nations Office on Drugs and Crime (UNODC)

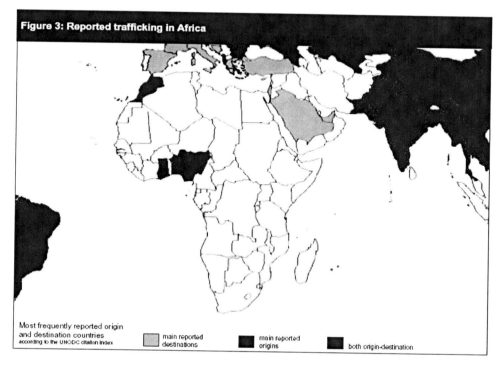

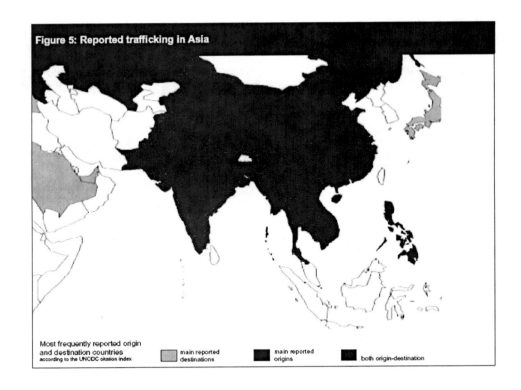

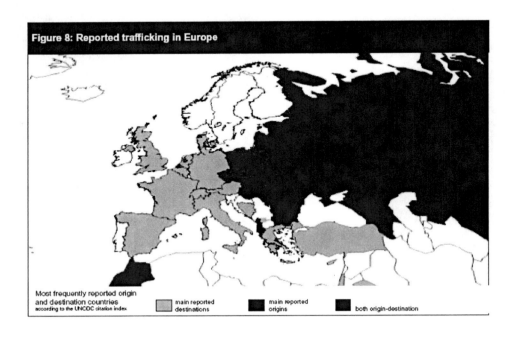

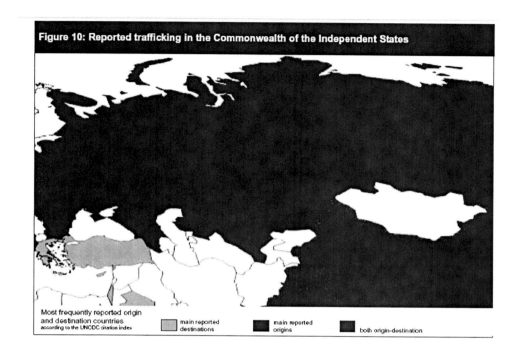

Figure 10: Reported trafficking in the Commonwealth of the Independent States

Most frequently reported origin and destination countries according to the UNCDC citation index — main reported destinations — main reported origins — both origin-destination

Figure 13   Reported Trafficking in the Americas

Most frequently reported origin and destination countries according to the UNCDC citation index — main reported destinations — main reported origins — both origin-destination

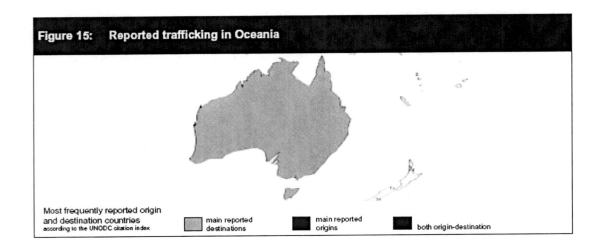

Figure 15:   Reported trafficking in Oceania

Most frequently reported origin and destination countries according to the UNODC citation index

main reported destinations | main reported origins | both origin-destination

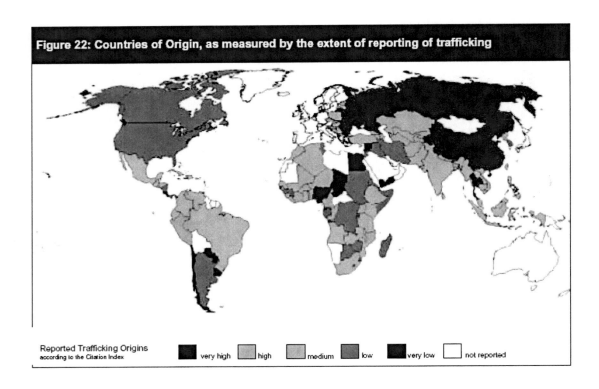

Figure 22: Countries of Origin, as measured by the extent of reporting of trafficking

Reported Trafficking Origins according to the Citation Index

very high | high | medium | low | very low | not reported

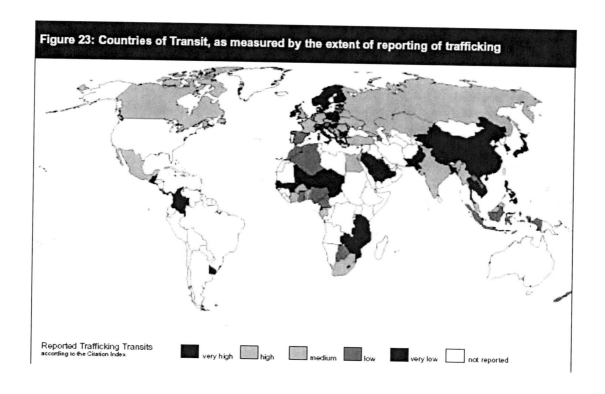

Figure 23: Countries of Transit, as measured by the extent of reporting of trafficking

Reported Trafficking Transits according to the Citation Index — very high, high, medium, low, very low, not reported

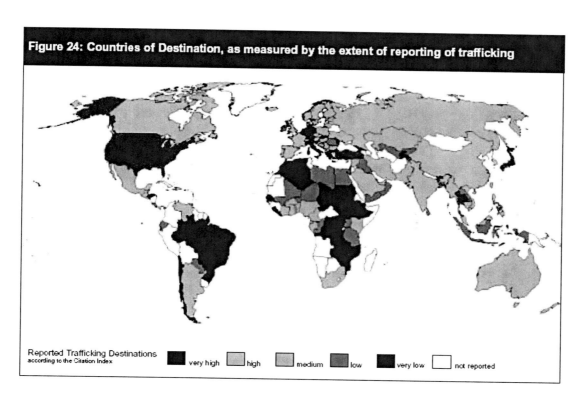

Figure 24: Countries of Destination, as measured by the extent of reporting of trafficking

Reported Trafficking Destinations according to the Citation Index — very high, high, medium, low, very low, not reported

APPENDIX B

In **Europe** the Sisters of Mercy are in Ireland, the United Kingdom, and Italy.

Italy is a *transit* and *destination* country for men, women, and children trafficked for the purposes of commercial sex exploitation and forced labor. Most victims are trafficked from Nigeria, Romania, Moldova, Albania, and the Ukraine. Ireland and the United Kingdom do not appear on the US State Department report.

In the **Near East** they are in Pakistan.

Pakistan is a *source, transit* and *destination* country of severe forms of trafficking. Women and girls from Middle Eastern and Eastern European countries are trafficked for commercial sexual exploitation and bonded labor. Men, women and children are trafficked for bonded labor to the Middle East and East Asian countries. Pakistan faces a significant internal trafficking problem reportedly involving thousands of women and children trafficked to settle debts and disputes or forced into sexual exploitation or domestic servitude. Unconfirmed estimates of Pakistani victims of bonded labor are in the millions. Women and children from Bangladesh, India, Burma, Afghanistan, Sri Lanka, Nepal, Azerbaijan, Iran, Kazakhstan, Kyrgz Republic, Turkmenistan, Uzbekistan, and Tajikistan are also trafficked to Pakistan for sexual exploitation and internal servitude.

In **Africa** the Sisters of Mercy are present in Kenya, Nigeria, South Africa, Zambia, and Zimbabwe.

Kenya is a *source, transit* and *destination* (SDT) country for purposes of forced labor and commercial sex exploitation, including the coastal sex tourism industry. Children are trafficked within the country for domestic servitude, street vending, agricultural, and commercial sexual exploitation, including sex tourism. Kenyan men, women, and girls are trafficked to the Middle East, other African nations, Europe, and North America for domestic servitude, enslavement in massage parlors and brothels, and forced manual labor. Foreign employment agencies facilitate and profit from the trafficking of Kenyan nationals to Middle Eastern nations, notably Saudi Arabia, the United Arab Emirates, and Lebanon, as well as Germany. Chinese, Indian, and Pakistani women reportedly transit Nairobi en route to exploitation in Europe's commercial sex trade. Brothels and massage parlors in Nairobi employ foreign women, some of whom are likely trafficked.

Nigeria is a SDT country. Within the country and internationally women and children are trafficked for forced labor and street begging (mostly boys) and for sex and domestic servitude (mostly girls). Nigerian women and girls are trafficked to North Africa, Saudi Arabia and Europe, notably Italy, France, Spain, the Netherlands, Belgium, Austria, and Norway. Small numbers are also trafficked to the United States. Nigeria prohibits all forms of trafficking through its 2003 Trafficking in Persons Law. The government demonstrated steady efforts to protect trafficking victims during 2007.

South Africa, Zambia, Zimbabwe made some progress in addressing anti-trafficking concerns since the release of the 2006 Report. In June 2006, President Mbeki signed the Children's Act, which specifically criminalizes child trafficking. In August 2006, the National Prosecuting Authority (NPA) sponsored a two-day seminar on prosecuting human trafficking cases in the South African context for provincial prosecutors and chief prosecutors from other African countries. The South African Police Service's Organized Crime Unit received training from International Organization for Migration (IOM) on the role of organized criminal groups in the trafficking of women and children. In October, police officers from South Africa, Mozambique, and Swaziland met to discuss cross-border trafficking, including trafficking in persons. In August, the Women's Parliament conducted a two-day meeting focusing on human trafficking. The Department of Labor funded a national radio campaign on child labor that ran during the annual "16 days of activism against violence to women and children" campaign.

In **Asia Pacific** the Sisters of Mercy are in Australia, Aotearoa NZ, Papua New Guinea, the Philippines, Samoa, and Tonga.

Australia is a *destination* country for some women from East Asia and Eastern Europe trafficked for the purpose of commercial sexual exploitation. The majority of trafficking victims were women from India, the People's Republic of China, and South Korea migrating to Australia temporarily for work whose labor conditions amounted to slavery, debt bondage, and involuntary servitude. The Government of Australia has strengthened its domestic trafficking laws to cover offenses involving deception, exploitative employment, conditions and contracts, or debt bondage. The government has also increased penalties for trafficking in children and for employers who exploit workers in conditions of forced labor, sexual servitude, or slavery. It provides significant resources to support anti-trafficking efforts throughout Southeast Asia.

Transnational Sexual Exploitation and Trafficking Teams (TSETT) within the Australian Federal Police investigated 14 possible trafficking cases in 2006. Australia, as co-chair and co-founder of the Bali Process on People Smuggling, Trafficking in Persons, and Related Transnational Crime, continues to play a prominent leadership role in several regional projects aimed at building awareness of trafficking, increasing law enforcement capacity, and enhancing victim support. The government supported a public awareness campaign with advertisements in daily and suburban newspapers encouraging victims and concerned members of the community to call the police hotline.

Aotearoa New Zealand is a *destination* country for a significant number of foreign women from Malaysia, Hong Kong, People's Republic of China, and other countries in Asia, who are illegally in the commercial sex trade. The law prohibits both sex and labor trafficking. In 2003 the Prostitution Reform Act legalized prostitution for those over 18 and decriminalized solicitation. Other laws prohibit child sex trafficking and tourism. Penalties for trafficking for commercial exploitation are commensurate with those for rape – up to 20 years imprisonment. While there have been no prosecutions under the new anti-trafficking law, which requires movement across an international border, instances of internal trafficking can be prosecuted under laws on forced labor, slavery, other forms of abuse and the Prostitution Reform Act.

Papua New Guinea is a *destination* country for women and girls trafficked for the purpose of commercial sexual exploitation. Papua New Guinea does not prohibit all forms of trafficking in persons, though its criminal code prohibits the trafficking of children for sexual exploitation. Internal trafficking of women and children for sexual exploitation and domestic servitude occurs. Children are held in indentured servitude as domestic workers. Women are trafficked from Malaysia, the Philippines, Thailand, Indonesia, and the People's Republic of China for sexual exploitation in brothels in the capital and at isolated logging and mining camps. Children are held in indentured servitude either as a means of paying a family debt or because the natural parents cannot afford to support the child. Papua New Guinea has a significantly increasing problem of trafficking in persons.

The Philippines are a *source*, *transit* and *destination* country for men, women and children trafficked for sexual exploitation and forced labor. They are often lured with false promises of legitimate employment, and are trafficked to destinations throughout Asia, the Middle East, Africa, Europe and North America. To a lesser extent, the Philippines are a transit point and destination for women from the People's Republic of China. Within the Philippines there is internal trafficking from rural to urban areas. Children are also exploited. The government passed an anti-trafficking law in 2003, and provides a range of social services to victims. However, corruption and a weak judiciary remain serious impediments to the effective prosecution of traffickers. Despite widespread allegations of law enforcement officials' complicity in trafficking, the government reported no prosecutions of trafficking-related corruption.

In **North America** Sisters of Mercy are present in Canada and the United States. Canada is principally a *transit* and *destination* country for women and children trafficked for the purpose of commercial sexual exploitation. Women and children are trafficked mostly from Asia and Eastern Europe for sexual exploitation, but victims from Latin America, the Caribbean, Africa, and the Middle East also have been identified in Canada. Many trafficking victims are from Asian countries such as South Korea, Thailand, Cambodia, Malaysia, and Vietnam, but some victims are trafficked from Romania, Hungary, and Russia. A significant number of victims, particularly South Korean females, transit Canada before being trafficked into the United States. Canada prohibits all forms of human trafficking through Law C-49, which was enacted in late 2005, and which prescribes a maximum penalty of 14 years imprisonment. Transnational human trafficking is specifically prohibited by Section 118 of Canada's Immigration and Refugee Protection Act (IRPA), which carries a maximum penalty of life imprisonment and a $1 million fine. Withholding or destroying a victim's identification or travel documents to facilitate human trafficking is punishable by up to five years in prison. Canada also prohibits child sex tourism through a law with extraterritorial application. In November 2006, the Royal Canadian Mounted Police (RCMP) organized anti-trafficking training in Eastern Canada for law enforcement, victim service providers, and non-governmental organizations (NGOs). The RCMP also has developed anti-trafficking videos, pamphlets, and posters, which are distributed widely. Canada works closely with foreign governments, particularly the United States and Mexico, on international trafficking cases.

Canadian law provides for formal victim assistance in court and other services. Canada coordinates anti-trafficking policies through its Interdepartmental Working Group and the Human Trafficking National Coordination Center, which received increased staffing and resources in 2006. The government continued awareness-raising campaigns, such as supporting an anti-trafficking Web site and distributing posters and materials, including anti-trafficking pamphlets printed in 14 languages. Canada annually funds anti-trafficking programs domestically and around the world, and contributes funds to international organizations such as UNODC.

The United States is the *destination* country for the greatest number of victims of trafficking worldwide, an estimated 50,000 annually. On March 11, 1998, President Clinton issued a directive establishing a US government-wide anti-trafficking strategy of (1) prevention, (2) protection and support for victims, and (3) prosecution of traffickers. Within the United States the Civil Rights Division of the federal government employs what they term a "victim centered approach" to the investigation and prosecution of cases. In addition to the prosecution of cases, they work to secure the victims' safety and housing as well as medical and psychiatric services.

The Intelligence Reform and Terrorism Prevention Act of 2004 of the US State Department established the Human Smuggling and Trafficking Center to "work with other governments to address the separate but related issues of human smuggling, trafficking in persons and criminal support of clandestine terrorist travel." The US Attorney General's Trafficking Prosecution Unit works with Human Trafficking Task Forces throughout the United States, training officers and collaborating with them in the prosecution of cases. At the time of filing the 2007 report, there were 725 cases under investigation. "Working with US Attorneys' offices, the Civil Rights Division has prosecuted 360 human trafficking defendants, secured almost 240 convictions and guilty pleas, and opened nearly 650 new investigations since 2001. That represents a six-fold increase in the number of defendants convicted in comparison to 1995-2000."[31] The US Attorney General also approved in 2007 the formation of a Human Trafficking Prosecution Unit to focus specifically on human trafficking. This unit is also charged with providing training, technical assistance, and coordination with 42 Anti-Trafficking Task Forces throughout the United States. The Division is also providing training and technical assistance to other countries at their request.

In the **Caribbean** the Sisters of Mercy are in Belize, Guyana, and Jamaica.

Belize is a *source, transit,* and *destination* country for women and children trafficked for the purposes of forced labor and commercial sexual exploitation. Central American women and children are trafficked to Belize for exploitation in prostitution. Girls are

---

[31] Ibid.

trafficked within the country for sexual exploitation, sometimes with the consent of close relatives. In February 2007, the government took a critical step to confront official trafficking-related corruption by arresting two police officers for human smuggling; a third police officer was arrested for allegedly exploiting a trafficking victim.

The Government of Belize prohibits all forms of trafficking through its Trafficking in Persons Prohibition Act, which prescribes punishment of up to five years imprisonment and a $5,000 fine. An interagency trafficking-in-persons committee leads government efforts to prosecute traffickers, protect victims, and raise community awareness about human trafficking. The government also cooperates with foreign governments on international trafficking cases, and joined the Latin American Network for Missing Persons in 2006. Complicity in trafficking by law enforcement officials appears to be a significant impediment to prosecution efforts. Since June 2006, the government has sponsored anti-trafficking campaigns and messages on television, radio, and in newspapers. The government also worked with Belize's tourism industry to draft a code of conduct to prevent child sex tourism.

Guyana is principally a *source* country for men, women, and children trafficked within the country for the purposes of commercial sexual exploitation and forced labor. Most trafficking takes place in remote mining camps in the country's interior. Amerindian girls from the interior also are trafficked to coastal areas for sexual exploitation, and young Amerindian men are exploited under forced labor conditions in timber camps. Guyanese women and girls are also trafficked to Suriname, Barbados, Trinidad and Tobago, Venezuela, Brazil and the United States. Guyana prohibits all forms of trafficking through its comprehensive Combating of Trafficking in Persons Act of 2005. The government made limited law enforcement progress against traffickers over the last year.

Jamaica is a *source* country for women and children trafficked within the country for purposes of commercial sexual exploitation and forced labor. The majority are women and girls and, increasingly, boys who are trafficked from rural areas to urban and tourist areas for sexual exploitation. In November 2006 the government launched a compre-hensive study of human trafficking, focusing on vulnerable persons and communities to gain a better understanding of the problem and to set up a system for collection of trafficking data. No reports of public officials' complicity in human trafficking were received in 2006. The government recently enacted the Trafficking in Persons Act of 2007 and has made intensive law enforcement and prevention efforts. The new law prescribes penalties of up to ten years imprisonment. A police Airport Interdiction Task Force, created through a memorandum of understanding between Jamaica and the United States, actively investigates cases of drug trafficking and human trafficking at ports of entry.

In **Latin America** there are Sisters of Mercy in Argentina, Brazil, Chile, Guatemala, Honduras, Panama, and Peru.

Argentina is a *source*, *transit*, and *destination* country for men, women, and children trafficked for the purposes of commercial sexual exploitation and forced labor. Most victims are trafficked within the country, from rural to urban areas, for exploitation in prostitution. Argentine women and girls also are trafficked to neighboring countries and Western Europe for sexual exploitation. Foreign women and children, primarily from Paraguay and Brazil, are trafficked to Argentina and Western Europe for commercial sexual exploitation. Bolivians and Peruvians are trafficked into the country for forced labor in sweatshops and agriculture. Reported cases of human trafficking have increased in Argentina, which may be due to growing public awareness of the issue, as well as a higher number of migrants in the country, some of whom are vulnerable to being trafficked.

Argentina does not prohibit all forms of trafficking in persons. Widespread corruption and collusion with traffickers at provincial and local levels has been reported and is considered to be a serious impediment to prosecuting cases. The government increased anti-trafficking training for judicial and law enforcement officials, including in the critical tri-border area with Brazil and Paraguay. Additional training for judges and police is sorely needed.

The government lent strong political support to anti-trafficking campaigns and has taken the lead within Mercosur for a regional anti-trafficking campaign. In October 2006, the government conducted a nationwide campaign against child labor.

Brazil is *source* country primarily for women and children trafficked within the country for the purpose of commercial sexual exploitation, and for men trafficked internally for the purpose of forced labor. NGOs (non-governmental organizations) estimate that 500,000 children are in prostitution in Brazil. Brazilian women are also trafficked for sexual exploitation to destinations in South America, the Caribbean, Western Europe, Japan, the United States, and the Middle East. In October 2006, President Lula directed the creation of a national plan of action against trafficking for all forms of exploitation. Prosecutions and convictions of trafficking offenders appeared to increase, and the Supreme Court strengthened the hand of the federal government in punishing slave labor through a November 2006 ruling. In 2006, Brazil issued a new regulation that requires state financial institutions to bar financial services to entities on the Ministry of Labor's "dirty list," a public listing of persons and companies that have been documented by the government as exploiters of forced labor.

Chile does not prohibit all forms of trafficking, though it criminalizes transnational trafficking for sexual exploitation through an article of its penal code. Penalties under this statute range from three to 20 years imprisonment. An anti-trafficking law is pending [2007] before the Chamber of Deputies. Chilean police engaged in covert anti-trafficking operations and stings and incorporated trafficking into training programs in 2006. The government made solid efforts to assist trafficking victims and funds victim-assistance programs. Trafficking victims may remain in Chile during legal proceedings against their traffickers, and may apply for legal residency. The government works with foreign governments to facilitate the safe return of Chilean victims trafficked abroad. The government conducted regular education and outreach campaigns, which were geared to prevent the sexual exploitation of minors. The government also continued to conduct joint public awareness-raising projects with NGOs (nongovernmental organizations) and international organizations, and it funded anti-trafficking training programs and projects.

Guatemala is a *source, transit* and *destination* country for Guatemalans and Central Americans trafficked for purposes of labor and commercial sexual exploitation. Human trafficking is a significant and growing problem in the country. Guatemalans and women and children trafficked through Guatemala from El Salvador, Honduras, and Nicaragua are subject to commercial sexual exploitation in Mexico, Belize, and the United States. Border areas with Mexico and Belize remain a top concern due to the heavy flow of undocumented migrants, may of whom fall victim to traffickers. The government sponsored nationwide public awareness campaigns targeting potential victims of trafficking to warn them of the dangers. However, the government failed to convict and punish traffickers or to provide special training for judges, prosecutors and police. Credible reports indicate that some local officials have facilitated acts of human trafficking by compromising police investigations and raids of brothels, accepting bribes, and falsifying identity documents. Last year [2006] 564 people, mostly from Central America, were rescued from brothels but then were deported; many were potential trafficking victims. The government also rescued 300 children, who were transferred to NGOs. Due to resource constraints and the volume of migrants in the country, many aliens are simply left at the border; some are potential trafficking victims who fall back into the hands of their traffickers. No meaningful government mechanism for screening potential trafficking victims exists.

Honduras is a *source* and *transit* country for women and children trafficked for sexual exploitation. Honduran women and children are trafficked to Guatemala, Mexico and the United States. Most foreign victims trafficked into Honduras for commercial sexual exploitation come from neighboring countries; some of them are economic migrants en route to the United States. According to the government and NGOs, an estimated 10,000 victims have been trafficked in Honduras, mostly internally. Many victims are children trafficked from rural areas to urban and tourist centers such as San Pedro Sula, the North Caribbean coast, and the Bay Islands. Child sex tourism is growing in the country. Tourism is likely to grow with a concomitant growth in the local sex trade, particularly child sex tourism. In light of this situation, and because Honduras' new anti-trafficking law is not yet fully enforced, the country's lack of a stronger law enforcement response to trafficking crimes is of concern. The government should intensify efforts to initiate prosecutions under its new anti-trafficking law to achieve more convictions and increased sentences against suspected traffickers. It should also make greater efforts to increase shelter and victim services.

Panama is a *source, transit* and *destination* country for men, women and children trafficked for the purposes of labor and sexual exploitation. Women and children are trafficked internally for sexual exploitation. Also, there are credible reports of women and children trafficked from Columbia and the Dominican Republic to Panama for sexual exploitation, as well as through Panama to Costa Rica and the United States (through Central America) and Europe. Child domestic laborers, who may be trafficking victims, are trafficked from the western provinces to Panama City. Panama's anti-trafficking legislation [2004] is ambitious, and the authorities are in the process of implementing provisions to improve victim protection; however there were no convictions using the new law in 2006. The government funds NGOs that shelter or assist trafficking victims and operates a foster family program.

Peru is primarily a *source* country for women and children trafficked internally for sexual exploitation and forced domestic labor. Most are girls and young women trafficked from rural to urban areas. Although the country does not have a comprehensive law against trafficking, the penal code covers trafficking-related crimes such as slavery, pimping, sexual exploitation of children, and forced labor. In the Lima region alone, police removed 81 underage victims from raided premises. Peruvians are also trafficked to Japan and Africa. The government produced a draft of a legal framework for future anti-trafficking actions in coordination with the Office of Migration. The Public Ministry provided support and substantial in-kind support including travel expenses and staff time for a US government-sponsored program on trafficking in persons for 1,389 prosecutors, police, health workers, educators, and local government officials in thirteen cities. An interagency group monitors the enforcement of trafficking laws and the progress of cases through the judicial system. They have created a nationwide hotline for reporting trafficking in persons; however, the government lacks the resources to provide adequate protection for victims.

APPENDIX C

Organizations and Networks Involved in Anti-Trafficking Efforts

Campaign to Rescue and Restore Victims of Human Trafficking
US Dept of Health and Human Services
http://www.acf.hhs.gov/trafficking/
Main menu:
About Human Trafficking
About Rescue and Restore
Coalition Information
Campaign Tool Kits
Resources

Center for Women Policy Studies.
Founded in 1972 for feminist policy analysis, research and advocacy.
http://www.centerwomenpolicy.org/
Women's health
Women and poverty
US Foreign Policy and Its Impact on Women
Women Engaging Globally
Global POWER
"No More Business as Usual"
The Barbara Waxman Fiduccia Papers on Women and Girls with Disabilities

GABRIELA Network
gabnet@gabnet.org
A Philippine-US Women's Solidarity Mass Organization that educates women, and organizes them around issues, such as trafficking, that are of urgent concern to women.

Anti-Slavery International
Thomas Clarkson House
The Stableyard
Broomgrove Road
London SW9 9TL
info@anti-slavery.org
An organization dedicated to raising awareness about the evils of the 18th century slave trade, and lobbying the government of the United Kingdom to provide "guaranteed protection and assistance to all trafficked people."

Make Way Partners
www.makewaypartners.org/human-trafficking.html
A Christian agency working to combat and prevent human trafficking as well as to end all forms of modern-day slavery through education and humanitarian assistance to the victims of trafficking.

Network of Victim Assistance [NOVA]
www.novabucks.org/index.htm
A network in Bucks County, Pennsylvania, USA, which offers services to victims of sexual assault.

Stop Trafficking Newsletter
stoptraffick@aol.com
A monthly newsletter on human trafficking sponsored by the Sisters of the Divine Savior (Salvatorian Sisters). A number of religious communities, including the Sisters of Mercy of the Americas, co-sponsor the publication. The website also offers education materials, e.g., a parish packet of educational materials.

The History and Experience of Latinos/Hispanics in the United States

Ana Maria Pineda, R.S.M.

In the United Status, a nation built by immigrants over the bones of the indigenous people, there have been waves of immigrants. In the current waves, there are immigrants from every continent, culture, every ethnicity, every religion, and sub-groups within these groups. Latino immigrants are one of the largest, if not the largest immigrant group challenging the reality of the United States.

In writing about the reality of Latinos/Hispanics in the United States, it is important to provide an ample historical context to understand where we have come from and where the journey is taking us.[1] Another dimension of this history is to become acquainted with U.S. Hispanic Ministry, its demographics, and significant facts and figures.[2] Lastly, I will suggest areas that as Sisters of Mercy, we need to take into account as we search out the meaning of Mercy in the Twenty-first Century.

A History of Conquest

Long before the Pilgrims landed on Plymouth Rock, Hispanics were a presence in these lands. It began immediately with Christopher Columbus's first voyage of discovery in 1492, and the first Christian evangelization began in 1493 with the Spanish settlements on Hispaniola.[3] The "discovery" of the Americas by Spain was marked by violence. The missionary efforts of Spain were unfortunately linked with the conquerors' greedy pursuit of wealth. In a very short time, the culture and history of the indigenous peoples of the Americas were substantially altered. The encounter of Spain with the indigenous peoples of the Americas produced a people, the Hispanic/Latino people. This mestizo (mixed blood) people today live in Mexico, Central American, South America and the United States. The history of Latinos has geographically unfolded in unique ways. This paper focuses on the reality of Hispanics/Latinos in the United States.

Hispanic Diversity

The term Hispanic, although useful in referring to a cultural group, is nevertheless limited. Using it leads to homogenizing the rich diversity of the peoples it attempts to represent. Other terms such as Spanish-American, Mexican-American, Chicano and Latino have been used over several decades. None has found singular approval over the years, but the term Hispanic, used broadly by U.S. Hispanic Catholics since 1977, has become a popular one. The heterogeneous reality of the Hispanic/Latino population defies ready identification.[4] People of Mexican heritage (66.9%) are the largest among the Hispanic constituency of this country. Puerto-Ricans (8.6%) and Cubans (3.7%) comprise the second and third largest groups within

---

[1] For this paper, I am drawing significantly from work that I have already written, and from studies, surveys and Census Bureau information.

[2] I rely substantially on a report provided by the United States Conference of Catholic Bishops, Inc., Washington, D.C., 2002.

[3] National Conference of Catholic Bishops 1988:4.

[4] I will use the terms Latino and Hispanic interchangeably to acknowledge their importance, and the unsettled situation of defining the identity of Latinos/Hispanics in the United States.

the Hispanic population. The fourth group of Hispanics is made-up of those coming from the countries of Central and South America (14.3%), e.g., Salvadorans, Nicaraguans, Costa Ricans, Panamanians, Hondurans and other Hispanics (6.5%).[5] Hispanics from the Caribbean include those from the Dominican Republic as well as those already mentioned from Puerto Rico and Cuba. While these national groups share similar cultural values, the Spanish they speak is flavored differently, and a distinct appropriation of customs, values and attitudes mark their particular way of being Hispanic. Other social, economic and educational factors shape these diverse groups differently.

The issue of what term to use poses the question of appropriation. How does the group or do the individuals relate to the ancestral origins that are part of their history? The birth of the Hispanic people occurs with the encounter of Spain with the indigenous inhabitants of the "New World" in 1492. A "mestizaje" was produced or, as Virgilio Elizondo describes it, "the process through which two totally different peoples mix biologically and culturally so that a new people begins to emerge, e.g., Europeans and Asians gave birth to Eurasians: Iberians and Indians gave birth to the Mexican and Latin American people."[6] The historical process of becoming this "new race" is only five hundred years old. It is a process which has been marked by a variety of colonial experiences, such as that of the French, the English and others. Each political power has established and eliminated geographical boundaries in following its political agendas and goals. And although Hispanics did not cross the borders of the territories that they had occupied for five centuries, the border crossed them.

In this ongoing political process, an appropriation of cultural identity is a challenge for United States Hispanics. Born out of a violent historical moment of the *Conquista*, they face a range of possibilities as they attempt to accept the consequences of that history. This is not an easy choice, especially for U.S. Hispanics who are faced with the degrees of shame or pride that they personally attribute to the reading of their particular history. It is a choice which is influenced by the attitudes of the dominant cultural society in which they were raised.

The challenge of identity is extended along generational lines. The question that faces the youth of any ethnic group is shared by young Hispanics as well. As the immediacy with one's parental cultural roots is more a reality of the past, the young experience a tension between their parents' values and that of the dominant society in which they function. The choices they will ultimately make span a continuum from the decision to maintain only the Hispanic culture as passed on to them by their parents to opting for total assimilation into the social, cultural, and religious norms of the dominant society.

Hispanic Religiosity

The question of identity will significantly impact the particular Hispanic experience and expression of "religiosity" of this diverse population. For Latin Americans who migrate to the United States from primarily rural areas, their experience of religiosity may often be highly devotional and rely more on the piety of the individual and/or that of the community. The infrequent attention given to rural communities due to the scarcity of ministers nourishes

---

[5] The percents indicated here are taken from the U.S.Census Bureau report on the Hispanic Population in the United States, March 2002.
[6] Virgilio P. Elizondo, *La Morenita: Evangelizer of the Americas* (San Antonio: Mexican-American Cultural Center, 1980) 17.

a reliance on popular expressions of faith which are intimately connected to the rhythm of rural life. A strong adherence to traditional religious practices and beliefs may be the foundational pool from which they will draw.

However, all Latin Americans will not necessarily fall into this religious category. Latinos who have lived in political contexts of oppression, in which their human rights have been violated as in El Salvador or Guatemala, may have discovered in that struggle a new model of church. This was part of the liberating process for Archbishop Oscar Romero who urged change in the Salvadoran church in order to be faithful to its mission:

> Therefore, in the different circumstances of history, the criterion that guides the church is not the satisfaction of human beings or its fear of them, no matter how powerful or feared they may be, but [it is] its duty to lend to Christ through history its voice so that Jesus can speak, its feet so that he can walk the world of today, its hands to work in the building of the kingdom in today's world, and all its members to "fill up what is lacking in his suffering" (Col. 1:24).[7]

For these Latinos, religiosity is shaped in an ongoing way by human events that occur at all levels of life. The political arena is not separate from that of one's faith, and the presence of Christ is sacramentally embodied in the community of believers. Other Hispanics/Latinos choose to retrieve the religiosity of their ancestors and seek ways of appropriating it either in the context of modern-day realities or in re-enacting ancient religious traditions and rituals. Pilgrimages to sacred sites, such as that of Chimayo or the basilica of Our Lady of Guadalupe, nourish the collective religious memory of their ancestors as well as their own. A mestizo ritualization of ancient Mesoamerican traditions intertwined with the Catholicism of Spain will be sought by others in an attempt to claim a religiosity that is proper for those born in the United States.

The Catholic Church in the United States has not always understood how to respond to the religious expressions that are an integral part of Hispanic/Latino Catholicism. In particular, the area of popular religion has been looked upon suspiciously. Neglect of Hispanic Catholics by the Catholic Church has a long history.

U.S. Hispanic Catholicism
As a group of people in the United States, Hispanics were often neglected in the life of the Church. Moises Sandoval writes that Hispanics were silent participants in Church pews. The difficult truth of the matter is that the first significant movement toward establishing Church structures for the Hispanics occurred in the 1920's. In 1923, an immigration office was established by the U.S. Catholic Bishops in El Paso. But the most significant developments came in the waning days of World War II. In 1944, Archbishop Robert E. Lucey of San Antonio sponsored a seminar for the Spanish-speaking.[8] The seminar convened fifty delegates from the western and southwestern regions of the United States to discuss the pastoral attention given by the Church to Hispanics. Archbishop Lucey's initiative motivated other dioceses to follow suit. In 1945, Archbishop Lucey established the first office for Hispanic concerns on a regional level. The leadership for the position of director resided in

---

[7] James R. Brockman, *Romero: A Life* (Maryknoll, N.Y.: Orbis Books, 1989) 82.
[8] Moises Sandoval, *On the Move: A History of the Hispanic Church in the United States* (New York: Orbis, 1989) 47.

the hands of non-Hispanics until 1967, when a layman, Antonio Tinajero, was hired. In 1968, the office would assume national dimensions when it was moved to Washington, D.C., as part of the National Conference of Catholic Bishops. The office was primarily directed toward the social and material needs of the Hispanic community, and not on their pastoral needs.

In 1971, Pablo Sedillo, Jr., was appointed director, and under his leadership the office finally assumed a more pastoral role with the responsibility of urging the Church to respond concretely to the pastoral needs of Hispanics. Other significant movements began to occur, marked by the consecration of the **first** Hispanic U.S. bishop, Patricio Flores, in 1969. In 1972 the first National Hispanic Pastoral Encounter (Encuentro Nacional Hispano de Pastoral) was celebrated, initiating a grass-roots process by which the Hispanic community, for the first time in its history, began a search to identify its pastoral needs and its relationship to the U.S. Catholic Church. A succession of Encuentros would follow, in 1977 and 1985. This process resulted in the formulation of the National Pastoral Plan for Hispanic Ministry, approved by the National Conference of Catholic Bishops (NCCB) in 1987.[9] The net result was a growing consciousness on the part of the Hispanic people of their identity as Church and their role within it. For many Hispanics it brought about a greater cultural awareness and with it self-confidence. Hispanics would no longer conform to being a passive presence in the U.S. Church, nor would they readily accept a position of non-leadership.

The Significance of the *Encuentros*

The overall significance of the Encuentros process (1972-1985) cannot be sufficiently emphasized. Prior to this movement, U.S. Hispanics had virtually no say within the Church structures of either Spanish or American Catholicism. The Encuentros represented a first step across the border of pastoral indifference and neglect. For the first time, Hispanics found themselves exploring the question of Church and their place in it. The Encuentros offered a major opportunity for communal reflection and decision making for Hispanics on matters of faith and religious values.

I Encuentro Nacional Hispano de Pastoral (1972)

During the I Encuentro keynote addresses were given by Bishop Zambrano of Colombia and Reverend Virgilio Elizondo of San Antonio, Texas. Both touched upon several aspects of ministry that would later be recognized as important elements for the entire Church: 1) the identity of Church; 2) the place of the Church in the modern world: 3) the incarnational reality in which the Church is rooted; 4) pastoral activity as the proper exercise of the salvific mission of the Church; and 5) the implicit understanding that the response of love expressed through pastoral activity inherently belongs to all baptized women and men.

Specific mention was made of the critical need to establish centers and programs for leadership training of bishops, priests, religious, and laity (Hispanic and non-Hispanics). Recommendations were made for non-Hispanic clergy and religious preparing to work in Hispanic ministry:

---

[9] Despite its approval by the United States Conference of Catholic Bishops, the plan was not supported. It was not implemented and consequently the growth of Hispanic Ministry was compromised.

The style of ministry of foreign (non-Hispanic) clergy and religious who work in Spanish-speaking communities in the U.S. must be, in the best sense of the world, missionary. That is to say that there must exist, on their part, familiarity, adaptation, and acceptance of the language, culture, and style of Catholicism of the Spanish speaking people. They must have, as their principal goal, the development of native Christian and ecclesiastical leadership, such as, bishops, priests, deacons, religious, and lay leaders.[10]

Recommendations were made for the preparation of Hispanic priests that stressed the importance of cultural identity, bilingual and bicultural formation, strong identification with the Hispanic community, and team-work as the preferred style of ministry.

II Encuentro Nacional Hispano de Pastoral (1977)

Five years later the Hispanic community gathered again to consider six major themes that had emerged since the 1972 Encuentro. The umbrella theme of Evangelization was the principal focus aligned with the topics of Ministries, Human Rights, Integral Education, Political Responsibility and Unity in Pluralism. During the process of the II Encuentro the significance of ministry emerged as one belonging to all Christians through their baptism. The articulation of the emerging concept of ministry was based on the fact that the Hispanic people identified themselves as Somos Pueblo (We are a People) and Somos Iglesia (We are Church). Ministry is understood as the mission of all the members of the Church without distinction or exception. The gifts and talents of the community are given by the Holy Spirit for the good of the whole. Finally, service is seen as a concrete expression of faith and a way of living the two great commandments.[11]

But in order to accomplish this type of transformative service, it was necessary to know the culture, historical reality, and the actual needs of the community. It was clear as all the themes were explored that it was impossible to evangelize without having knowledge of the realities that Hispanic people lived.

III Encuentro Nacional Hispano de Pastoral (1985)

The III Encuentro was not an isolated event in the history of the pastoral ministry of the Hispanic people in the United States. It was rather one more step in a process of ecclesial participation that began with the establishment of Church offices for the care of Hispanics in the first half of this century, for example, in Philadelphia in 1915 and in San Antonio in 1945.[12]

Now what clearly emerged was that for those of the Hispanic community who had been involved in the process of the Encuentros, the earlier question that plagued Hispanics regarding who could participate in ministry was no longer an issue. The issue now was the fact that goodwill alone was not sufficient. Time had proven that given the complexity of

---

[10] Office of Hispanic Affairs, *Proceedings of the I Encuentro Nacional Hispano de Pastoral*, 1972. Printed in binder form for the participants of the I Encuentro.

[11] United States Catholic Conference, *Proceedings of the II Encuentro Nacional Hispano de Pastoral* (Washington: United States Catholic Conference Creative Service Office, 1978) 31.

[12] United States Catholic Conference, *Prophetic Voices: The Document on the Process of the III Encuentro Nacional Hispano de Pastoral* (Washington: United States Catholic Conference, 1986) 31.

U.S. society and of the existing structures of the institutionalized Church, Hispanics needed adequate educational formation not only for ministry within the Church but for all dimensions of life.

Several decades have passed since the process of the Encuentros. Despite the enthusiasm of those years, it has become painfully clear that even with educational formation, Hispanics continue to be minor players in the life of the Catholic Church. While Hispanic Pastoral Centers flourished during the decades of the 80's and 90's, poor financial support resulted in the closing of some of those offices. In other cases, some of the offices had to limit their services. In 2006 the United States Catholic Conference of Bishops restructured its main office in Washington, D.C. and eliminated the Secretariat for Hispanic Affairs (1968-2006). This decision was made despite the statistics that indicate the importance of the general Hispanic population in the U.S., and their adherence to the Catholic Church.

Demographics
Population: The 2000 census lists the Hispanic population in the U.S. at 35.3 million.[13] This represents 12.5% of U.S. population.[14] The Hispanic population is young, with 37.5% under age 18. Another 59% of the population is between 18-64 years. And 5.3% of the Hispanic population is 65 years or older.[15]

In 1980, 80% of the Hispanic population was native born. In 1990, 64% of the Hispanic population was native born. According to the 2000 census, 60.9 % of all Hispanics are native U.S. citizens, while only 39.1% are foreign born.

Seven states had more than one million Hispanic residents in 2000: Arizona, California, Florida, Illinois, New Jersey, New York, and Texas. Fifty percent of the Hispanic population in 2000 lived in California, the highest of any state.[16]

Hispanics can be found in almost every state in the United States. They can be found in unexpected places such as Hawaii and Alaska. Hispanics migrate to places where they can work.

U.S. Catholics
The 2002 Official Catholic Directory lists the U.S. Catholic population at 65,270,444. Catholics represent 22.9 percent of the total population of the United States. According to a recent survey, 72.6% of Hispanics living in the United States (26 million) are Catholic. Sixty-four percent of all Hispanics attend church services regularly.[17] The ten dioceses of Los Angeles, Miami, New York, Galveston-Houston, San Bernardino, Chicago, Brooklyn, Fresno, San Antonio and Orange have the largest Hispanic populations.[18]

---

[13] Total population of U.S. Hispanics: U.S. Census Bureau, *Census Brief*, May 2001.
[14] Ibid.
[15] U.S. Census Bureau. *The Hispanic Population in the United States: Population Characteristics*, March 2001.
[16] U.S. Census Bureau Demographic Profiles, 2002.
[17] Survey commissioned by The Latino Coalition and conducted by McLaughlin & Associates, *Opinones Latinas*, August 2002.
[18] Ruth N. Doyle, Ph.D., Dioceses Ranked by Total Hispanic (All Races) Population, 2002.

Of the nation's 46,000 priests, 6.3% or 2900 are Hispanic.[19] Of these 2900 Hispanic priests, approximately 500 were born in the U.S.[20] Fifteen percent of the priests ordained in 2002 were Hispanic. There are approximately 9925 Hispanic Catholics per Hispanic priest, while there are 1230 Catholics per priest in the general Catholic population.[21] Approximately 500 or thirteen percent of current seminarians are Hispanic.[22] Nine percent, or twenty-five of the nation's 281 active bishops, are Hispanic. There is a ratio of one bishop to every 231,000 Catholics in the United States and a ratio of one Hispanic bishop to every one million Hispanic Catholics in the United States.

Despite the significant population of Hispanic Catholics there are only a small percent of Hispanic clergy and Hispanic Bishops that can attend to their pastoral needs or who are in a position to effectively advocate for Hispanic Catholics. Some dioceses have the practice of "importing" priests from Latin America, but their lack of familiarity with the realities of the U.S. context makes it problematic. Oftentimes they bring with them cultural attitudes that disregard the values of lay participation, and the roles of Latinas as agents of change in the Church and in society. Clergy from Latin America are sometimes used to a "privileged" status and treat their Hispanic parishioners with arrogance and disrespect.

The Catholic Church in the U.S. has encouraged appropriate priestly formation that will make it possible for the ordained to serve Hispanic Catholics, but this has not proven successful. An increasing numbers of Hispanic Catholics are joining other religious denominations, and are turning away from the Catholic Church. Others are searching for a spirituality that will nourish their faith and relationship with God, and decide that the Catholic Church has nothing to offer. While this affects Hispanic adults, it has more serious consequences for Latino/a youth.

Latino/Hispanic Religious Affiliation
While all this is true, it has been noticeable for several decades that changes in Latino/Hispanic religious affiliations are taking place. Recent studies on issues of faith and public life published in *Latino Religions and Civic Activism in the United States* [23] report that almost one quarter of all Latinos in the United States are Protestant. Seventy percent of Latinos are Catholic, translating into 29 million Catholic Latinos in the United States. This is compared to 22 million white mainline Protestants. Twenty-three percent of Latinos are Protestant or identify as "other" Christian that includes Jehovah's Witnesses and Mormons. This translates to 9.5 million people. Eighty-five percent of all U.S. Latino Protestants identify themselves as Pentecostals or evangelicals (6.2 million people). Thirty-seven percent of the U.S. Latino population (14.2 million) self-identifies as "born-again" or evangelical.

[19] A survey on Hispanic priests ministering in the United States, conducted by the National Association of Hispanic Priests, 1999, reports 2900 Hispanic priests, and the 2002 Official Catholic Directly reports that there are approximately 46,000 priests.
[20] Survey on Hispanic priests ministering in the U.S., conducted by the National Association of Hispanic Priests, 1999.
[21] USCCB Committee on Hispanic Affairs. *Hispanic Ministry at the Turn of the New Millennium*, 1999, 5. Study by Stewart Lawrence of Puentes, Inc.
[22] USCCB Committee on Priestly Life and Ministry. The Study of the Impact of Fewer Priests on the Pastoral Ministry was done by the Center for Applied Research in the Apostolate (CARA) at Georgetown University, June 2000.
[23] Statistics compiled in the volume, *Latino Religions and Civic Activism in the United States*, Oxford University Press, 2005.

This figure includes Catholic charismatics, who constitute 22 percent of U.S. Latino Catholics. Twenty-six percent, or 7.6 million, of all Latino Catholics self-identify as being born-again. One percent of Latinos identify with a world religion, such as Buddhism, Islam or Judaism.[24] And .37 percent of all Latinos are atheist or agnostic.[25]

For both Latino Catholic and Latino Protestant, the relationship with the churches is a complex one. There is an experience of cultural marginalization. The religious sensibilities of both groups are historically shaped by Spanish Catholicism. This has not escaped the attention of Justo Gonzalez, a noted Latino Protestant Church historian who claims that all Latinos are "culturally Catholic." Gonzales calls for a "New Reformation" where both the richness of Catholic Latino popular religion and the Protestant emphasis on Scripture are integrated. While the call to ministry is more accessible for Latinos in the Protestant churches, few of them occupy roles of authority and decision-making. Overall the treatment of women continues to be a challenge for Latinas in both denominations. And the religious expression of faith lacks the fervor typical of the Latino culture.

The tension between Latino Catholics and Latino Protestants is divisive to the unity of a community that already faces innumerable obstacles in the United States. More Latino Catholics are feeling emotionally alienated from the life of the parish communities where little is done to welcome them. Latino Protestants find themselves deprived of the rich experience of ritual that is part of the culture, and their experience of leadership is minimal.

Education

According to the 2002 U.S. Census Report, the educational achievements of Latinos are significantly lower than non-Hispanic whites. Less than 27.0 percent Hispanics have less than a ninth grade education compared to 4.0% non-Hispanic whites. Only 16.0 percent Hispanics attain an education in the 9th to 12th grade but do not obtain a high school diploma compared to 7.3 percent non-Hispanic whites. Hispanics who graduate from high school or who have some college study experience represent 45.9 percent compared to 59.3 percent of their non-Hispanic counterparts. Only 11.1 percent Hispanics obtain a bachelor degree compared to 29.4 percent non-Hispanic whites.

Given these percents, over 50 percent of Hispanics will not be eligible to attend college or obtain a higher educational degree.

The lack of access to quality education seriously impacts the ability of Hispanic youth to enter the workforce. Hispanics (8.1%) are much more likely than non-Hispanic whites (5.1%) to be unemployed. They are more likely than non-Hispanic whites to work in service occupations. Hispanics (20.8%) are twice as likely to be employed as operators and laborers than non-Hispanic Whites (10.9%). This has serious consequences on the ability of Hispanics (14.2%) to occupy managerial or professional occupations compared to non-Hispanic whites

---

[24] Some Latinos are discovering that they are Sephardic Jews. The re-conquest of Spain from the Moors led to the exile of the Jews in 1492, and forced Catholicism on Jews wishing to remain in Spain. Often times, this conversion was only publicly assumed. In recent years, a number of Latinos are re-discovering their Jewish roots.

[25] This information is the results of the national survey *Hispanic Churches in American Public Life*. I am drawing substantially from the data provided by Bruce Murray, in "Latino Religion in the U.S.: Demographic Shifts and Trends," FACSNET. See: www.facsnet.org/issues/faith/espinosa.php

(35.1%). This reality impacts the earning ability of Hispanics which is significantly lower than that of non-Hispanics whites.

Income/Poverty
The median income of white households in the United States is $45,904; for Hispanics it is 27 percent less at $33,455. In 1999, 7.7 percent of non-Hispanic whites were living in poverty. In the Hispanic community, the poverty rate was 21.2 percent, or approximately 7.2 million people. The poverty level of Hispanics in the U.S. has serious consequences for the overall health of the Hispanic communities. The consequences are felt in every area of life.

Latino Youth and Gangs
The level of poverty forces adults in the household to spend extended times away from home. An increasing number of households are headed by single-mothers. Children are often left on their own while the parents are working. In the absence of adult supervision, youth seek out ways of belonging. For many, gangs provide "community" for children who have nowhere else to occupy their energies. Latino youth have fallen prey to a gang culture which promotes violence and destroys the hope of a better future for Hispanic families and communities. The city of Salinas in California is a sad example of an escalating gang culture which endangers the young of the community. The number of deaths due to gang violence has become one of the leading causes of death for the young in Salinas. The crimes committed by gang members have threatened the security of the local community, and civic leaders are at a loss about what to do. Gang members are also migrating to Latin America. Gang culture is being exported outside of the United States and threatens the health of the communities on both sides of the border.

Immigration
The poverty in other parts of Latin America forces people to look elsewhere for jobs. The proximity to the United States makes it easier for the poor of Latin America to migrate legally or "illegally" to the United States. It is difficult to estimate the exact number of undocumented from Latin America. It is estimated that it numbers over 10 million.

The September 11, 2001 attack on the World Trade Center has made this an even more explosive reality for Latinos in the United States. The political rhetoric post September 11th has unjustly targeted Hispanic immigrants as potentially dangerous to the security of this country. The punitive treatment of Hispanic "undocumented" has forced many to forgo services for their children and themselves. In some cases, the fear of deportation has led Hispanic immigrants to endanger their lives. A recent example of risking one's life occurred a few weeks ago during the raging fires in Southern California. While searching through the rubble of one of the fire sites, the charred bodies of four migrant workers were discovered in an area that had been evacuated. In another situation, the migrant workers fearing that they would lose their jobs refused to leave the fields. The owner of the fields insisted that they continue working despite the proximity of the fire. Law enforcement officers intervened demanding that they evacuate. After several hours of negotiating with the owner, the officers finally succeeded in convincing the migrant workers to evacuate. Despite the denial of immigration services, it is a fact that "undocumented" who sought out help during the fire were taken into custody and deported. It is still unclear how many "undocumented" died in the fire. The hotly debated issue of immigration has serious implications for Latinos/Hispanics on both sides of the border.

Women and Children

Poor Mexican women who are desperate to find ways to provide for their children become the ideal labor force for transnational industry. Little attention is given to just wages or to the safety of the work environment. The health and safety of women are often in jeopardy. Women often occupy these low paying jobs and are exposed to toxic working conditions. The careless use of pesticides over fields endangers the health of those working in the field. Pesticides have caused sterility for some women. The involuntary immigration of the "poor" in pursuit of jobs is another example of exploitive labor practices. Since 1993 more than 320 young women have been abducted, raped and murdered in the Mexican border city of Juarez. These are mostly young women who are employed in "maquiladoras," enormous assembly plants where they often work in U.S. owned factories for 12 hours shifts for $4-8 dollars a day. Their desperate search for work places them in harm's way.

Another situation along the border is the migration of men who come to the U.S. in pursuit of jobs. They leave their families behind. The women and children are left dependent on the monies sent by the husband. In the meanwhile, the mother is burdened with the full responsibility of fending for the needs of her family. The separation of spouses and families often leads to establishing a two family situation: a wife across the border and a partner or second wife in the U.S. Unjust labor practices affect the entire family, but since women are represented disproportionately among the world's poor and marginalized, it is especially harmful for women. This cycle of suffering is experienced by Latinas on both sides of the border.

The quality of food has become an issue as the environment is degraded. Due to lack of funds, poor women can only purchase poorer quality food. This affects the health of the family members especially the children. Approximately 20 percent of children live in poverty in the U.S. The feminization of poverty has become a global phenomenon with women comprising 70 percent of the world's 1.3 billion poor. And the feminization of poverty is experienced within the Hispanic/Latino communities on both sides of the border.

According to the American Community Survey Reports published in 2007, Hispanics have a lower median income level and a larger proportion of their households are maintained by women (19%).[26] Women from Puerto Rico and the Dominican Republic as well as the elderly (those 65 and older) have a poverty rate of about 20 percent compared with about 7 percent for non-Hispanic whites. Hondurans often migrate to the U. S. by themselves. Their numbers increase the percent of households maintained by women (Puerto Rico-26.6%; Dominican Republic 32.3%, Honduras 26.1%). In contrast, about 9 percent of non-Hispanic white households have no husband present. In addition, about 33 percent of Hispanic mothers who have given birth are unmarried compared with about 20 percent of non-Hispanic white mothers. The poverty rate was generally higher for Hispanic children (under age 18).[27] About 29 percent of Hispanic children and 11 percent of non-Hispanic white children live in poverty.[28] Among some of the Hispanic national groups, the poverty rate for children is about

---

[26] *The American Community-Hispanics: 2004*, drafted by U.S. Census Bureau's Ethnicity and Ancestry Branch, Pew Hispanic Center, Washington, D.C.(2007) 3.
[27] Ibid. 20.
[28] Ibid. 20.

30 percent higher. This is true for children of Mexican, Puerto Rican, Dominican and Honduran backgrounds.[29]

Conclusion

In the interest of time, I have limited myself to addressing select issues that are affecting the quality of life of Hispanics in the U.S. The needs in health care, housing, quality education, and appropriate social services are important issues that should be explored. What may be evident is that the realities lived by many Hispanics in the United States call for our consideration as Sisters of Mercy. The charism of Mercy has always responded to needs that are known. As a young woman, I was drawn to Mercy by the life of Catherine McAuley and her love for the poor and vulnerable. In particular, the women and children of her times called for her attention.

The colonization of the Americas by Spain has negatively marked the history of Latinos/Hispanics in the United States. We continue to live out the consequences of a history of conquest and colonization. Five hundred years later, the lives of those in the Hispanic community have not greatly improved. This is true of the Latino reality on both sides of the border. What is experienced in Latin America is shared in similar ways by the Hispanic/Latino community in the United States. The constant migration of Latinos from south and north of the U.S. border makes this a local and global reality for Sisters of our foundresses were called to bring Mercy to a world in need. Mary Baptist Russell, California's first Sister of Mercy, answered the call to serve the wide diversity of languages, customs and religious traditions in San Francisco[30] during the Gold Rush. It is important to note that Mother Francis Bridgeman corresponded at length with Father Gallagher of San Francisco. She only accepted the invitation to come to San Francisco when she was reassured that accepting the mission would not compromise the commitment of the Sisters.[31] The same was true of Mary Baptist Russell who before accepting a mission would make it clear that the primary duties were the instruction of poor Girls, the protection of unemployed Women of good character, and the visitation of the sick,[32] and any work of Mercy in accordance with the Spirit of the Mercy rule.[33]

We share in the history and heritage of Catherine McAuley whose dedication to the poor and especially women and children was the motivating force in her religious vocation. Can that same motivating force inspire us to accept a new call and challenge? Together we search for ways of being Mercy in the Twenty-first Century. The Catholic Church has not given this migrant group the pastoral attention it needs.

---

[29] Ibid. 20.
[30] Mary Katherine Doyle, RSM, *Like a Tree by Running Water*, Blue Dolphin Publishing, Inc., Nevada City, 2004) 62.
[31] Ibid. 47.
[32] Ibid. 215.
[33] Ibid. 215.

Gender Development in Oceania Region

Senolita T. Vakatā RSM

Background

The Pacific Ocean, also known as *the liquid continent,* covers about a third of the earth's total surface area. It covers about 176 million square kilometres, of which only 10 million square kilometres are land. Of this 10 million, 9.2 million square kilometres are Australia and New Zealand. The rest is made up of tiny island nations called the Pacific Islands. The Pacific Ocean's area is so great that if you put all the earth's landmass in it, there would still be water around![1] There are three major cultural, ethnic sub-regions in the Pacific: Melanesia, Micronesia and Polynesia. Each sub-region boasts a diverse and rich cultural history.

Melanesia comes from the Greek word meaning "dark islands." On these islands live the oldest of the Pacific people who arrived in the Pacific at about forty to fifty thousand years BC.[2] Fiji, Kanaky (New Caledonia), Solomon Islands, Vanuatu, Papua New Guinea and Torres Strait Islands are traditionally considered part of Melanesia because of their shared colonial history and common regional situation rather than because of a racial classification. Melanesian countries are the more populated island countries in the Pacific. In fact, the largest island country in the Pacific is Papua New Guinea, where five million out of seven million Pacific Islanders live.[3]

Micronesia comes from the Greek word meaning "small islands." It consists of hundreds of small atolls or low lying islands spread over a large area of the western Pacific. It is divided into seven territories: the Federated States of Micronesia, the Marshall Islands, Palau, the Northern Mariana Islands, Nauru, Kiribati, and Guam.[4]

Polynesia means the "many islands." Polynesians are well known for their sea-faring skills. The Polynesian triangle has its three corners at Hawaii, Aotearoa New Zealand and Rapa ui (Easter Islands). American Samoa, Cook Islands, French Polynesia, Niue, Rotuma, Samoa, Tokelau, Tonga, Tuvalu, and Wallis and Futuna are all located within this triangle.

Here are a few interesting facts about the Pacific:[5]

- The smallest eco-zone in the world, Oceania, is in the Pacific Ocean, including Micronesia, Polynesia and Fiji.
- There are an estimated 2500 languages and dialects in the Pacific region.
- There are about 25,000 islands in the Pacific (more than the total number of islands in the rest of the world's oceans combined) with only 20% of these islands inhabited.

---

[1] Norman and Ngaire Douglas, eds., *Pacific Islands Year Book*, 16th ed. (Australia, 2002).
[2] Ibid., 30-40.
[3] Ibid., 51-55.
[4] Ibid., 56.
[5] Ibid., 58.

- Ninety percent of Pacific Islanders are Christians as a result of the arrival of the foreign missionaries in the late 19th and early 20th centuries.

Pacific peoples are diverse and different in our cultures, languages, environments and histories, but we are united in our struggles to address the concerns and needs of our people.[6]

I am grateful to be able to participate in this conference and to share our struggle to address the needs and issues that affect the lives of the people in the region. I am a Tongan and a Sister of Mercy, and I work as the co-ordinator for the Catholic Commission for Justice and Development (CCJD) of the Episcopal Conference of Catholic Bishops of the Pacific (CEPAC) – Central Region and as the Caritas Oceania representative on the Caritas Internationalis Gender working group.

In this presentation, I will share with you some important factors that we are facing in the region today. It will mainly focus on *Gender Development in the Oceania Region*. Information for this paper was collected from written texts and oral sources and has been shared at various national, regional and international meetings.

Introduction
The term *gender* refers to the characteristics and roles that societies define for women and men. Customs, traditions, religion and education determine these roles. Gender is related to how we are conditioned to perceive women's and men's attributes and roles in the family and in society. The process of socialization, from birth to adulthood, shapes our perception of gender. Gender, along with factors such as age and class, determines how we are perceived and expected to think and act as women and men because of the way society is organized and not solely because of our biological differences.[7]

Gender includes roles (what we think women and men should do), stereotypes (what we think women and men should be like), and values (what we think is good for a woman or a man).

Roles ascribed on the basis of gender are socially constructed. We are not born with a specific disposition for any particular role; therefore, it can be argued that the roles are changeable, learned, and vary among cultures. Gender is a key organizing principle in the distribution of labour, property and other valuable resources in society.[8]

Gender Roles
The cultural beliefs and values practised in the Pacific have survived a long time. They are closely identified with the people and are used to maintain law and order, instil respect and enhance the role of traditional leaders. These cultural norms and traditions influence *gender roles* – what women and men do. For example, in many societies men are traditionally assumed to be the breadwinners while the women are expected to take

---

[6] Ibid., 60.
[7] Forum Secretariat, *Gender through Pacific Eyes* (Forum Secretariat Suva, 1998).
[8] Ibid., 60.

care of the children and household.[9] Today, some values have been questioned and challenged, and some have changed. Now, in some of the Pacific countries, gender and development mainstreaming are seen as threats to traditional values and cultures.

Understanding the issue of gender means appreciating that it will actually enhance and strengthen the culture and values as it strengthens the relationship between men and women, the relationship between women and children, and family living as a whole. Giving women equal opportunities in education and employment allows them to strengthen their ability to provide upkeep for the family, thus improving their status.[10]

To empower women does not mean removing or lessening the powers traditionally held by men; it means women working alongside men without discrimination and/or victimization. Empowerment can be facilitated by accepting gender issues as a part of development, by putting it in its right perspective and by introducing it at a pace acceptable to the people.[11]

Essential to the discussion of gender roles is the **gender division of labour** – the difference between the tasks done by women and by men. The division of labour differs among cultures and within cultures and may also vary between a culture's rural and urban communities. In some cases within Pacific cultures, it may be appropriate for a woman to do her own housekeeping or for a man to work as a labourer.[12] There are also certain tasks that are always referred to as men's tasks and women's tasks. Men were expected to attend meetings, build structures of homes, sell women's produce, drink kava and do some fishing (boats and diving). Women were expected to do housework, take care of children, collect herbal medicines, plant, plait thatching mats and do some fishing (collecting seafood from shore).[13]

Understanding past and present influences on gender relationships can give insight into future constraints and opportunities for affecting social change in general, and gender relations in particular. For example, the rise of religious fundamentalism can impose new restrictions on women, limiting their ability to participate in other responsibilities and non-traditional work, or it can help them gain greater independence. Crises such as war or drought can significantly alter gender relations and lead women into new roles as leaders, organizers and skilled workers. Sometimes these new roles are temporary, but often they lead to changes in the community that improve the status of women.[14]

Realities to Consider

In order to understand gender development, it is important to understand what is meant by the following terms:

---

[9] Ibid., 66.
[10] Ibid., 79.
[11] Ibid., 88.
[12] *Building Capacity for Change: A training manual on the Convention on the Elimination of all Forms of Discrimination against Women* (IWRAW/Asia Pacific, 2001).
[13] Ibid., 67.
[14] Ibid., 80.

Socio-cultural:	Socialization through education and family upbringing, tradition, belief systems, cultural practices that teach gender roles; changes in culture and lifestyles
Economic:	Access to and control of land, employment, other economic resources (e.g., agricultural produce, forest resources), economic policies (e.g., structural adjustment programmes)
Political:	Commitment of the government and church to the advancement of women, including the provision of resources to promote affirmative action and provide mechanisms to facilitate active and full participation of women in the development process
Religion:	Religious beliefs/teachings about women and men; religious practices
Media:	The images of men and women that the media project either reinforcing or weakening gender biases and gender stereotyping
Environmental:	Status of natural resources (e.g., forests, water resources) that have some bearing on the activities of women and men; natural disasters (e.g., cyclone, hurricane, earthquake)
Legal:	Ratification of the Convention on the Elimination of All Forms of Discrimination against Women (CEDAW); constitutional provisions that have a bearing on women's rights (e.g., land rights, reproductive rights); all laws that affect men and women differently
Education:	The level and quality of education for boys and girls; gender stereotypes in the curriculum; exposure to Western lifestyle and values.[15]

Gender Issues

Gender issues are matters related to the conditions and position of men and women in society. Where there are differences in opportunities, roles and situations between women and men, particularly differences in access to power and control, gender issues arise.

Class, poverty, ethnicity and physical location may also create inequalities but gender tends to make them more severe. Gender-intensified constraints refer to the rules, norms and values that are part of the social construction of gender and are found in such things as workloads, return on labour efforts, health and education, and access to productive assets. They reflect the uneven distribution of resources and opportunities between women and men in the household. Where resources are scarce, women find themselves at greater disadvantage than male members of the family. Some inequalities may be the result of community norms, such as customary laws governing inheritance. Others arise from decisions in the household, often because females are seen as having less value than males.[16]

---

[15] RRRT: Regional Rights Resource Team Pacific, *Human Rights Training Manual* (August 2002).
[16] Ibid., 25.

The following are examples of gender issues:

- In some countries women cannot own land. Tonga is among the countries in the Pacific where women cannot own land, but they are allowed to lease land.
- In many cases women are paid less than men are to do the same tasks, or are paid less to work just as hard as men. In Tonga women are given the same wages as men. Men are known to do the hard physical work.
- For many years, women were not represented in government. They are still not represented equally with men in decision-making bodies. This is true in Tonga where men outnumber women in the government. It is a slow process. Women are climbing rapidly in education, and this might cause changes to come about.
- Domestic violence, rape, sexual harassment and other forms of violence against women are often accepted. Gender is the core reason for discrimination against women within the home, and for women not being consulted and involved in decision making in the home or community. Women are expected to constantly cook and clean and look after the welfare of the children in spite of having a job. There is a lack of support in activities which are considered unconventional, e.g., study and sports. Another reason is the cultural attitude based on the idea of the inferiority or the superiority of men or women or on stereotyped roles of men and women.
- If a family does not have enough money to send all their children to school, boys are sent first. This is not practised in Tonga where parents believe in the education of their children. The statistics report of the Ministry of Education shows that Tonga has 100% literacy and a higher percentage of the population with university degrees.
- A lack of female management executives and a lack of male nurses are the result of gender roles ascribed to these positions. This does not apply to Tonga. Female management executives in Tonga are progressing; women are climbing high in the academic field, and it is now recognised that they can do the same work as men or even better.[17]

Gender and Poverty

This is one example of how women are badly affected by the issues because of gender inequality. While nearly two thirds of the world's poor are in Asia and Pacific region, two thirds of the region's poor are women, and poverty is particularly acute for women living in rural areas.[18]

In poor families, the gender division of labour and of responsibilities for household welfare means that the burden of poverty falls most heavily on women. Given gender disparities in education, health care, economic participation and incomes, women are in the most vulnerable category.[19]

---

[17] Kingdom of Tonga, *National Policy on Gender and Development: Towards Gender Equity, Harmonious Society and a Better Future for All* (August 2001).
[18] Ibid., 20.
[19] Ibid., 45.

Youth unemployment has increased in Tonga. Youths tend to depend a lot on their parents for their financial support so more and more families live in poverty. Mothers become more and more the breadwinners in the families. Because of shortage of land, some families have to find some ways to plant mulberry trees for making tapa and pandanus for weaving mats. Tapa and mats play a very important role in the culture of Tonga. They are used for traditional attire in wedding celebrations and decorations of the dead; they are used in traditional presentations and for decorations and indicate an identity of the wealth of a mother in collecting them. It is a disgrace and often regarded as foreign when a Tongan woman has no collection of mats and tapas.

The number of women living in poverty has increased disproportionately over the past decade compared to the number of men. Male migration as men search for work and consequent changes in household structure have placed additional burdens on women, especially those with several dependents. In the Pacific region, the proportion of households headed by females ranges from 20 to 40 percent.

The disproportionate numbers of women among the poor poses serious constraints on human and social development because their children are more likely to repeat cycles of poverty and disadvantage.

***Improving the political, legal, cultural, economic and social status of women is thus pivotal to escaping the poverty trap.*[20]**

Manufacturing Sector
Increased industrialization and manufacturing sectors in a country result in replacement of a lot of labour with machines and new technology in order to increase productivity and efficiency.[21] As a result, the level of unemployment increases, and the majority of unemployed are women. Most of these women are in female-headed households and are the sole breadwinners for the family. This is not a reality in Tonga, but it is more present in our neighbouring countries, for example, Pago Pago Samoa. Tonga does not have much manufacturing business because of the lack of natural resources.

Access to Land
The land tenure system in Pacific countries is a major obstacle for women's full participation in and contribution to trade. In Tonga, women are not allowed by law to own land; this is a cultural issue. There are social roles separating women and men; the women are to concentrate on household duties and childcare, and the men are to farm on the plantation.[22]

Access to Quality Education
In most of the Pacific countries, men have priority in accessing education in a family so whatever resources a family has are dedicated to educating the son. Girls will have to

---

[20] *A Research Project Publication in Collaboration between UNV/APC Noumea/UNIFEM Pacific and CWL Tonga* (November 2005).
[21] Ibid., 25.
[22] Ibid., 30.

work hard to gain a scholarship or will enrol as far as high school, then stay home and assist their mothers in household duties. In Tonga, education at all levels gives equal opportunities to both girls and boys.

Conditions of Work

The recent change in women's employment in export-oriented industries mostly involves poor quality jobs. Women are mainly employed in the garment manufacturing sector which means long hours of standing and sitting in the factory. This has created an adverse impact on the health of women. Another example is the Tuna cannery in Fiji and Solomon Islands where canning is mainly done by women who stand for long hours inside the factory and endure poor conditions such as poor ventilation while men drive trucks, and load and unload produce.[23]

Differences in Salary

Women's and men's educational levels are usually the same, but their social roles create the female pay differential. This form of inequality and discrimination affects the working morale, motivation and contribution of women. This inequality is caused by the social and cultural ideologies used to decide which jobs are for men and which ones are for women. Even though some women have been able to break into better jobs, previously male dominated, the majority of women are still in low paying jobs with little training or opportunity and no prospects for promotion.[24]

There is a marked difference between the work of chiefly women and those of the lower rank. Women of chiefly rank are in a privileged position indeed. They do not have to labour to produce commodities. They can supervise the work of other women, make garlands for personal decorations, and even design kupesi for tapa making. The heavy planting, hoeing and harvesting of crops, fishing, cooking and heavy craft work such as canoe making and house construction are all the domains of men. Light agricultural duties such as weeding of home gardens, growing plants with scented flowers, leaves, roots or barks for scented oil-making, mat weaving, tapa cloth and craft work relating to these are considered appropriate for women. The raising of children, although largely the responsibility of women, is shared among members of the extended family including the males.[25]

Women in the Churches

It is unfortunate that some churches in this region are still very much influenced by our social setting of responsibility. Regardless of how many women succeed in their theological education like their male colleagues, they are still not considered for higher positions in the churches. They are either expected to teach or work in the school libraries or just stay at home and assist their husbands who are already in ministry.[26]

---

[23] Ibid., 78.
[24] Ibid.
[25] Ibid.
[26] Ibid.

Many of the churches in the region still do not recognize the capacity of their female members to do theological studies. Therefore, the question arises as to how the churches think they are responding to their prophetic call of promoting justice in Oceania. How can they speak to the full participation of all in church ministry?

Gender Differences

Differences are influenced by the following factors:

1. Unequal access to resources and control over these resources such as land, forest, marine resources, education and training, decision-making, and finance. The impact in Tonga is that the rich become richer and the poor become poorer. This also creates more unemployment and forced migration from rural to urban areas. The King and government own all the resources and make final decisions in Tonga. This has a great impact on the people.[27]

2. Unequal access to and control over benefits that are generated from resources or development interventions. The King's household have the ownership of all the resources in the kingdom of Tonga. Princess Pilolevu, the king's sister, owns Tonga Satellite space.[28]

3. Gender division of labour within the families and communities. Churches influence the health and social and economic conditions of women and men. The division of labour between the sexes in Tonga is a direct manifestation of the societal and religious concepts of the essences of female and male. Work which requires hard physical labour and implies sweat and dirt is allocated to men.[29]

4. External factors that influence gender relations and access to control over resources and benefits. The economic and political structures in Tonga have undergone big changes. The introduction of a market or money economy from the 'Westernised' countries has been the controlling factor in changing the roles of women and men.[30]

Gender Equality

Women and men have identical rights and status. There is a need for women and men to be treated equally under the law and in society.[31]

Gender Equity

Women and men are treated fairly. In theory, women and men are equal; therefore they have equal human rights. These rights include the right of choice and security in marriage, the right to land, property and inheritance; reproductive rights, the right to education and employment, the right to their individual identities, and the right to freedom from violence.[32]

In practice, however, gender equality and gender equity are often different. The social and economic structures and conditions disqualify women from getting just treatment,

---

[27] A United Nations Volunteer, "Bringing CEDAW Home to Tonga," *CEDAW Information Research Report 2005.*

[28] Ibid.

[29] Ibid.

[30] Ibid.

[31] Ibid.

[32] South Pacific Commission, *Pacific Platform of Action*, 1995.

and support advantages and privileges for men; and even though both are entitled equally, the issue of equity remains. In international human rights law, for example in interpreting CEDAW, this distinction is seen as the difference between "formal equality" and "substantive equality."

CEDAW stands for the Convention on the Elimination of all Forms of Discrimination against Women. It was adopted by the UN General Assembly in 1979, and in September 1981 the convention entered into force when twenty states ratified the convention. As of May 2000, 165 countries had acceded to or ratified CEDAW. CEDAW is also known as the Women's Convention or the Women's Bill of Rights. Tonga has not yet signed CEDAW.[33]

Tongan traditional society was and is still highly stratified. Both the social and political structures are based on units linked loosely together through elaborate kinship networks. It is a very complex system made more difficult by the fact that the social and political units are sometimes synonymous or overlapping and at other times contradictory.[34]

However, it should be noted that the social and political units more or less operate under similar principles. Tongan society continues to be organised in a form of a pyramid. At the top are the ruling monarchs, the Tu'iTonga, Tu'iHa'atakalaua, and Tu'iKanokupolu, in descending order. Below these groups are the chiefly families or 'Eiki who are members of the aristocracy by virtue of impeccable blood lines and hereditary titles. In the next level are those known as Matapule who are functionaries of title as hereditary chiefs. Below these are ranked the vast majority of Tongans who are known as Tu'a or commoners. There are different languages used in these rank categories.[35]

The concept of rank is pivotal to an understanding of the Tongan socio-political structure. "Rank" is the quality commanding respect and deference, and is inherited from one's parents. It cannot be altered either by one's own achievements or by one's failures. The kinship links or blood ties in Tonga determine to a large extent the political and social rank of any individual in the society. But, although blood ties are all important, it is not the only element in the equation. Sex and age are also important considerations, and all these are mediated through the further principles of "power" and "authority."[36] These principles operate at the "famili" (limited extended family) level as well as in the larger political society.

Priests and religious in Tonga are in the second unit of the pyramid, that is, the aristocracy and nobles. Different languages are used for the King, chiefs and commoners. Society has put priests and religious in the second category. This is very challenging to the priests and religious because most of them are commoners. Yet, as soon as they

---

[33] A United Nations Volunteer, "Bringing CEDAW Home to Tonga," *CEDAW Information Research Report 2005.*
[34] S. Latukefu, *Church and State in Tonga* (Canberra: Australian National University Press, 1974).
[35] Ibid.
[36] Ibid.

become a priest or religious, they are already in the chiefly rank, and the society expects them to act likewise.

In the social structure, women outrank their male relatives. The father's eldest sister has the highest rank within the family and is accorded 'fahu' status. The fahu has been defined as the person (usually woman) with unlimited authority over others within her blood kin. This means, in social terms, that the woman and her children have the right to ask and expect goods and services from her brothers and mother's brothers and kin over whom she is fahu.[37] Both societal and social ranks are predominantly determined by the rank of the mother.

In Tonga the family unit is the basis of society and the Church. Therefore, since Tonga is a patriarchal society, the father is the head of the family. The father is invested with some privileges within the family circle where he is respected and often treated specially. Traditionally, it is disrespectful for the children to touch father's head, because the head is regarded as sacred. Children do not use father's clothing in any way, or eat his leftover meals, or sleep in his bed. All his belongings are not to be touched; this is a symbol of power and sacredness. Moreover, whatever the father says ought to be obeyed for he is the most powerful figure in the family unit. To disobey the father is to violate the Tongan tradition.[38]

There is also a matriarchal element in Tongan society, though it is quite a complicated one. To touch just the surface of it, women have socio-cultural power. In this sense, within a family unit, the girls have higher status than the boys. For this reason, for example, in a social occasion such as a 21st birthday or wedding of one of the boys, the eldest sister has the privilege of receiving the 'top cake' with the best fine mat and tapa cloth (Tongan treasures).[39] This is a symbol of love and respect from the brother to his sister. This "sort of privilege" held by women is known as the "Fahu System." It is well practised in the island even today. Therefore, women hold some kind of socio-cultural power. Unfortunately, with the penetration of the money economy into traditional culture, the elements of materialism and consumerism complicate the medium of gifts and interchange of gifts; hence the relationship in this case tends to be based on materialistic values rather than genuine love and respect for one another.

In the early 1960s, the Bishop of Tonga at the time, Bishop Rodgers, appealed to the Christchurch Mercy Sisters to meet a felt-need in the diocese of Tonga in the area of education. In response to this appeal, four pioneer sisters were sent to Tonga in 1964. They worked in the area of education, village development, and visiting the sick, the aged and the prisoners.

As women and Sisters of Mercy, we play a big part in society. Sisters of Mercy are empowering women and encouraging girls in Tonga through their ministry in education.

---

[37] Ibid.

[38] S. Latukefu, *Church and State in Tonga* (Canberra: Australian National University Press, 1974), 4-5, 8-9, 30-1.

[39] Ibid., 32.

Sisters provide counselling at the Women and Children Centre. Women who experience any form of discrimination and children who are deprived of their rights call in at this house of refuge. There a Sister of Mercy gives them counselling. This is a big step forward for the Tongan government. It is also the first time for the government to employ religious as civil servants.

Mercy Sisters working with women at the community development groups train and encourage them to find ways in which they can earn money to help their families. Through the community development groups, most families are able to pay school fees for their children and to build family houses and water cement tanks.

The sisters are involved in the Commission for Justice and Development which empowers women to speak up on injustices in church and society. They work to inform and form people, to open their eyes and to find ways to free people from their oppression, especially when they are marginalized and at risk.

The most important needs that we encounter today are the need to empower women to obtain professional teaching skills and the need for adult education where the impact of western education and economy is great. There is a need among the people for technical skills to earn a living alongside subsistence farming. There is also the important need of adult education in the spiritual aspect of Tongan life where people today are influenced by the media and overseas contact.

The Mercy Sisters in Tonga today continue to follow the Spirit of Catherine McAuley. She would move along with the people in periods of social change:

> As Catherine McAuley's contribution to the history of social service is our precious heritage, we should act with courage and initiative like hers in serving others in our pastoral and parish work. We seek out the aged, the poor, the lonely, the immigrant, children deprived of parental care, to show them the spirit of Mercy, a genuine love and compassion. Taking into account social needs of our times, and our own resources, we provide residential care for such people.[40]

The Spirit of Catherine McAuley is still alive today seeking out new ways and lifestyles in order to meet the needs of the new century in Tonga.

A Tongan Sister of Mercy already has the power within a family, church and society. She is challenged in how she uses her power.

Gender Issues to be Considered
- Identify the division of labour between women and men at the level of household and community, and identify intra-household transfers between men and women.
- Analyse the patterns of access to and control over resources/benefits at the household and community levels.

---

[40] *Constitutions of the Federation the Sisters of Mercy of New Zealand*, "'Sent by God': Apostolate," 19 no. 77, 22 no. 90, 20 no. 84.

- Determine the factors that influence the above two points.
- Define practical gender needs and strategic gender interests of women and men as inputs to project planning and policy recommendations.
- Do not assume that men and women do the same things, have the same access to or control of resources, or have the same needs.

Conclusion

Undoubtedly, some progress has been achieved in the region in reducing gender disparities and advancing the status of women. However, in spite of these achievements, much remains to be done to reduce the gender gap and achieve greater improvements in women's social, economic and political status.

Gender equality is needed to move us forward, not only to advance the status of women in society and church but hopefully to provide a just and sustainable future for all.

These are my hopes and dreams for the future of Sisters of Mercy in Tonga:

To contextualize God's mercy in Tonga, we start with a very rich heritage. Tongan hospitality and Mercy hospitality are both rich expressions of God's mercy. My dream is that this hospitality can be experienced and shared by the whole family of Mercy throughout the world, but first of all by our Oceania family.

To contextualize mercy in relation to each cultural dimension gives an openness to contemporary emphases like the development of people, enculturation, justice and peace. In practise, enculturation means that we be open and look with the eyes of respect at the differences in cultures and values of other countries.

My hope is that Mercy in Tonga is always a voice for the voiceless in society, that it respects the dignity of every person, and that it lives Gospel values. We need not be afraid to be different in our mission in order to respond to the most vulnerable people. We need more sisters working in Tonga, doing more adult education in all areas, more theological education, and more training of clergy so that they are aware of gender issues and cultural clashes. One of my dreams is that there will never be a time when only Tongan sisters work in Tonga; or that Tongan Sisters of Mercy work only in Tonga. Finally, my dream is that ongoing knowledge and understanding of the story of Catherine McAuley and of the culture of Tonga will be crucial for future planning of mission work. I hope that the Mercy Charism will be alive in all decision making in Tonga. In this way, Mercy Mission will be re-visited and evaluated to empower Sisters in Tonga and in the Pacific to hear the call to plant the seed of faith as the early missionaries did with great enthusiasm and for the love of Jesus Christ.

Catherine McAuley in the Nineteenth and Twenty-First Centuries

Mary C. Sullivan, RSM

One might say that Catherine McAuley (1778-1841) lived in a very different world from that of the twenty-first century. She lived intermittently on two islands, on one of which was the seat of the British colonial empire. On the other were the colonized Irish Catholics controlled politically, socially, and economically by the British Parliament and by Anglo-Irish politicians more or less resident in Ireland, but directed by London.

From another perspective, Catherine's smaller world was not all that different from the present world – at least not in deliberately inflicted misery. The rapacious penal laws against Irish Catholics in the years after the Battle of the Boyne in 1690 to roughly 1720 were by 1778, the year of Catherine's birth, in part repealed or somewhat generally unenforced. Other penal laws were repealed in subsequent years, climaxing in the Act of Catholic Emancipation in 1829. But the worst of the dire social, economic, and religious effects of these laws remained for decades: widespread destitution throughout the country with consequent slums in the cities; disease, epidemics, and famines among the poorer classes; widespread begging; widespread lack of education for poor Irish Catholics who would not succumb to Protestant proselytizers; virtually nonexistent health care for poor Catholics (i.e., 75% to 80% of the population); foundling hospitals with abysmal mortality rates; and workhouses such as those Charles Dickens portrays in *Oliver Twist*.

Edmund Burke said of the penal code: "It was a complete system, full of coherence and consistency, well digested and composed in all its parts. It was a machine of wise and elaborate contrivance, as well fitted for the oppression, impoverishment, and degradation of a people as ever proceeded from the perverted ingenuity of man."[1] William Lecky, a British historian writing in the nineteenth century, says:

> Almost all the great persecutions of history, those of the early Christians, of Catholics and Protestants on the Continent, and, after the Revolution, of Catholics in England, were directed against minorities. It was the distinguishing characteristic of the Irish penal code that its victims constituted at least three-fourths of the nation, and that it was intended to demoralize as well as degrade….

> …The penal code, as it was actually carried out, was inspired much less by fanaticism than by rapacity, and was directed less against the Catholic religion than against the property and industry of its professors. It was intended to make them poor and to keep them poor, to crush in them every germ of enterprise, to degrade them into a servile caste who could never hope to rise to the level of their oppressors.[2]

---

[1] Quoted in W. E. H. Lecky, *History of Ireland in the 18th Century*. 1:144.
[2] Lecky, *History of Ireland*, 1:145, 152.

Catherine McAuley's World:

Catherine McAuley founded the Sisters of Mercy in 1831, amid the after effects of this savage conquest. Because her Catholic father took advantage of the oath of allegiance to the King of England in 1778, which Catholics who wished to own property were then allowed to sign, and because she lived for over twenty years with Protestants (from at least 1800 or 1801 until the death of William Callaghan in 1822), she was in those early years, personally spared the economic plight of the majority of Irish Catholics. However, when she became independently wealthy in 1823, as a result of the Callaghan legacy, she began the process of ever deeper solidarity with the poor of Ireland and England, and of gradually more thorough identification with and ministry to their needs and deprivations, their ignorance and sufferings. She did not become like "The Ladies from the Ladies' Betterment League" who "Walk in a gingerly manner up the hall" of the "worthy poor," allowing "their lovely skirts to graze no wall" in the Chicago slums, as in Gwendolyn Brooks' satiric "Lovers of the Poor." Rather, she became in her lifestyle, and for the rest of her life, as far as she could, *one with* their sufferings and "dejected faces," seeing in them "the person of our Divine Master, who has said, 'Amen, I say to you, as long as you did it to one of these my least brethren, you did it to Me'" (Rule 3.1, in Sullivan, *Catherine McAuley,* 297).

Contemplating Catherine's life and work in the early nineteenth century, and then reflecting on what might be—perhaps ought to be—the life and work of Sisters of Mercy in the early twenty-first century, one could be easily overwhelmed with the magnitude of vocational responsibility, and then resort to silence, inertia or escape. Therefore, one has to try to espouse Catherine's two-fold commitment to trust and urgency: "While we place all our confidence in God – we must act as if all depended on our exertion" (*Correspondence,* 323).

In November 2006, Mercy scholars, reflecting on their experience of the present world, identified many serious global trends and problems. Among the trends noted were "greed in all its individual, corporate and national manifestations, especially among the world's 'haves'; and "a fundamental, though often unrecognized, hunger for happiness and for genuine spiritual, even religious, understanding and peace." These Mercy researchers saw the following two problems as flowing from these and other trends: "extreme poverty and maldistribution of resources among the world's most vulnerable 'have-nots'"; and "debilitating ignorance of basic human, spiritual, and religious understandings, even …among Catholics."[3]

While many other phenomena characterized the world Catherine McAuley experienced, the realities noted above were central to them. When she had the freedom and means to do so, Catherine's response was to create a House of Mercy to shelter homeless girls and women; and a poor school in which to educate poor girls. She did this not only at Baggot Street in Dublin, but in every town or city in Ireland and England where she made a foundation. In these places she also visited sick and dying poor adults, instructing them in

---

[3] "Summary Paragraph" (26 December 2006). Participants in Mercy International Research Conference, November 9-12, 2007. See page 9 of this volume.

Christian faith, in neighborly love, and in the love and consolation of God. These were her clear priorities. In the first paragraph of the Rule she composed, she declared: "The Sisters admitted into this religious congregation besides the principal and general end of all religious orders," such as attending to their own personal and communal growth in fidelity to the Gospel, "must also have in view what is peculiarly characteristic of the Sisters of Mercy, that is, a most serious application to the Instruction of poor Girls, Visitation of the Sick, and protection of distressed women of good character" (Rule 1.1, in Sullivan, *Catherine McAuley*, 295).

It was in view of the congregation's commitment to these endeavors that Catherine so strongly admired the self-sacrifice of the six English women who came to Baggot Street in early 1840 to serve a novitiate and prepare for a new foundation in Birmingham, England. She wrote of them to Frances Warde:

> They renew my spirit greatly – fine creatures fit to adorn society, coming forward joyfully to consecrate themselves to the service of the poor for Christ's sake. This is some of the fire He cast on the earth – kindling. (*Correspondence*, 282)

She had earlier written in the same way to Elizabeth Moore in Limerick about the first five to arrive:

> It is very animating to see five persons most happily circumstanced, leave their friends and country, to enter on a mission so contrary to our natural inclinations, but the fire Christ cast upon the earth is kindling very fast. (*Correspondence*, 270)

As to the "happy circumstances" of these young English women and their fitness "to adorn society," Catherine remarked of Marianne Beckett:

> Sister Beckett…is quite equal to Sister [Clare Augustine] Moore in all arts and sciences – languages – painting, etc., etc. She brought her finery to Ireland, her under dresses trimmed with lace. (*Correspondence*, 270)

By now, Catherine's own "under clothing," as Clare Moore informs us, "was always of the meanest description" (Bermondsey Annals, in Sullivan, *Catherine McAuley*, 114), and it is doubtful that Marianne Beckett herself had lace underwear in Birr where she eventually became the assistant superior, then the superior, of that very poor community.

Voluntary Poverty:
The voluntary material poverty of Catherine McAuley and the earliest Sisters of Mercy was directly related to their works of mercy, to their "being Mercy in the 1830s." Their vow of poverty was not primarily regarded as a separate requirement of religious life, disconnected theoretically and practically from their mission. For Catherine and for them, it was a *necessity*, and not because the available money from Catherine's inheritance was almost completely depleted in the early years of the decade – which it was. Voluntary

poverty was for them a theological and practical necessity because it was the only means of funding more and more needed works of mercy; it was a necessity if they wished to live in credible solidarity with the impoverished people among whom they served, the "have nots" of their world; it was a necessity if they wished, as Catherine certainly did, to "bear some resemblance" to the earthly example of Jesus Christ; and it was a necessity if they truly believed that all women, men, and children were their sisters and brothers with whom Jesus Christ was identified, the children of a common God.

Twice in the early chapters of her Rule, Catherine cites Matthew 25.40: "Truly I tell you, just as you did it to one of the least of these who are members of my family, you did it to me." This scriptural verse was the guiding text of Catherine's life and work. Although she never spoke about the "prophetic" quality of religious life or about its "countercultural" character – such vocabulary and analysis were unavailable to her—her life and that of the first sisters *was* fully and voluntarily prophetic, not the least in their mode of relating to material goods. As Sandra Schneiders notes: "the greed and self-centeredness of an approach to material goods as to be acquired for oneself to the greatest extent possible regardless of the need of the neighbor is challenged by the commitment to evangelical poverty."[4]

For the sake of their mission the first Sisters of Mercy intended to be and were in fact voluntarily poor in their lifestyle. They held Charity Sermons, lotteries, and bazaars to raise money for the works of mercy, not to improve their own living conditions; they begged for the needs of the poor from door-to-door (Catherine euphemistically called this "collections"); using a legacy they had just received, they built a commercial laundry to support and train the 60 homeless, unemployed women then in the House of Mercy, and Catherine rejoiced in this prospect: "What a comfort if I am permitted to see some secure means of supporting our poor women & children established, not to be entirely depending on daily collections which are so difficult to keep up" (*Correspondence*, 132).

When Catherine moved permanently into Baggot Street in 1829, at age fifty, she slept in a dormitory with seven others; later their cheap mattresses were stuffed not with horse hair, but "cow's or dog's or something so dreadful that," according to Clare Moore, "the smell for several months was most sickening"; and for the first reception ceremony on January 23, 1832, the "postulants dresses [of the seven novices] were altered and patched up into habits," and they got the "white veils, only one new one, old guimpes" that had been worn by Mary Ann Doyle, Elizabeth Harley, and Catherine at George's Hill (13 September 1844, in Sullivan, *Catherine McAuley*, 94-95). Moreover, the meals at Baggot Street were "wretched," according to the artistically refined and blunt Clare Augustine Moore:

> Even when I entered [in 1837] the diet was most unfit for persons doing
> our duties. Leg of Beef with onion sauce, beef stakes [*sic*] that seemed as
> if they had lain in a tanpit, hash of coarse beef, and for a dainty, fried liver
> and bacon, though boiled and roast mutton came in sometimes.

---

[4] Sandra M. Schneiders, *Selling All*, 109-110.

The breakfast table was a trial to one's nerves; sugar of the very blackest and coarsest kind with no sugar spoon, and for that matter the juniors seldom had a little lead spoon apiece, weak tea, very little milk, plates of very stale thick bread with a very thin scraping of butter. ("Memoir," in Sullivan, *Catherine McAuley*, 207)

(The purpose of citing Clare Augustine Moore's account is not to endorse malnutrition as a positive value, but to illustrate the poverty of the community, as she experienced it.)

Catherine McAuley and the respective founding parties traveled to make new foundations by "the poorest and cheapest mode of traveling, often to her own great inconvenience, and her bed [in these foundations] was usually on the floor," according to Clare Moore who often accompanied her: "she never waited for a new Convent to be comfortably arranged, being satisfied to have any kind of opening to extend the good effected by the Institute" (Bermondsey Annals, in Sullivan, *Catherine McAuley*, 114-115).

Catherine's letters repeatedly allude to the community's poverty for the sake of mission. She speaks of what one might call "common life" in ways that extend its meaning far beyond those living within Mercy convents to the people they sought to serve. The description in Acts 4 was broadened in Catherine's behavior to solidarity and sharing with those off the streets, in slum hovels, in cholera depots, and on rural roads.

During the cholera epidemic of 1832, after the death of a woman who had just given birth, she brought the infant home in her shawl and put it to sleep in a little bed, probably a small cabinet drawer, in her own room. In 1835, in order to create "a school for the poor girls whom we every day saw loitering about the roads [in Kingstown] in a most neglected state," Catherine gave "the coach house, stable, and part of our garden, with some gates, doors, and other materials for the purpose," as well as the total proceeds of that year's bazaar (£50), even though they were "six pounds in debt for things got at Nowlan's on the Bachelor's Walk" (*Correspondence*, 86). In December of that year the community had to borrow £20 from Charles Cavanagh, their volunteer solicitor, because "We have so often cautioned all those who supply us – not to give any credit on our account – I doubt would they now, if we were to ask them" (*Correspondence*, 70). In 1836 when she discovered on arrival how extremely damp the Charleville house was, with little chance of postulants joining them, she considered abandoning the foundation, but "yielded to…her own compassion for the suffering members of Christ (being greatly touched by hearing a poor woman exclaim, 'Ah! it was the Lord drove you in amongst us!')" (Bermondsey Annals, in Sullivan, *Catherine McAuley*, 120). In 1838, when she could not pay the court's judgment (£375) in the unjust lawsuit brought against her by the builder of the poor school in Kingstown (the lawsuit apparently brought with the parish priest's acquiescence), and the sisters in Kingstown had to leave suddenly, before an eviction notice was levied, Catherine said, not just of this circumstance: "God knows I would rather be cold and hungry than the poor in Kingstown or elsewhere should be deprived of any consolation in our power to afford" (*Correspondence*, 164).

In 1868 Clare Moore, who had lived with Catherine in Dublin for eight years, and after that for brief periods in Cork and Bermondsey, compiled and published the *Practical Sayings* of Catherine McAuley, the first and most authentic source of her sayings. Clare's draft was, she says, reviewed and verified by other eyewitness Sisters of Mercy, including those still living at Baggot Street and elsewhere. Ursula Frayne then in Melbourne wrote to Clare: "How exactly dear Reverend Mother's words are noted down, I could almost fancy myself listening to her once more" (Bermondsey Annals (1868) 2:[125]). The *Practical Sayings* notes that on the topic of voluntary poverty Catherine frequently said:

> In the use of temporal things a Religious should always remember that she has not come to a house of plenty, but to a state of strict poverty.
>
> The truest poverty consists in seeing that our wants are scantily supplied and rejoicing in the scarcity....
>
> The fruits of poverty are: 1st. Great peace of mind under all circumstances....2nd. Great joy in the Holy Ghost which the want [lack] of temporal comforts will never lessen....
>
> We find those who can enumerate very particularly all that Jesus Christ said and did, but what does He care for that? He said and did so, not that we should recount it in words, but show Him in our lives, in our daily practice. (*Practical Sayings*, 6-8, 25)

Catherine's most formal description of the voluntary poverty she advocated is presented in Chapter 17 of the Rule she composed in the mid 1830s. Here she focuses on the example of Jesus Christ and on self-restraint in the use and accumulation of material goods. Her placement of this chapter (and those on Chastity and Obedience) at the *end* of Part I of the Rule and Constitutions (i.e., at the end of the Rule proper), whereas she places the chapters on the works of mercy (chapters 1-4) at the very *beginning* of this Part (contrary to the arrangement in the Presentation Rule) reinforces the belief that for her the vows were at the service of the works of mercy and ordered toward them. They were not ends in themselves but a necessary means of following Jesus Christ and furthering the mission of the Sisters of Mercy in the world. In the Rule Catherine writes:

> As the Sisters in order to become more conformable to...Christ Jesus have...renounced all property in earthly things, they should frequently revolve in mind how tenderly He cherished Holy Poverty. Born in a stable, laid in a manger, suffering hunger, cold and thirst in the course of this mortal life, not having a place to lay His head, naked on a cross, He consecrated this virtue in His sacred Person and bequeathed it as a most valuable patrimony to His followers. (Rule 17.1, in Sullivan, *Catherine McAuley*, 312)

Catherine's language is, understandably, dated, but beneath her vocabulary she is conceptually very close to the thinking of, for example, Sandra Schneiders: "The vow of poverty is a global declaration of embracing the kind of detachment, insecurity, vulnerability, dependence – in short, the homelessness – that Jesus [embraced and] asked of his itinerant disciples."[5] Where Jesus asked his disciples to "carry no purse, no bag, no sandals" (Luke 10.4), Catherine McAuley says simply:

> The Sisters shall therefore keep their hearts perfectly disengaged from all affection to the things of this world, content with the food and raiment allowed them and willing at all times to give up whatever has been allotted to them. (Rule 17.2)

> Nothing shall appear in their dress, but what is modest and grave, nor can they keep in their cells anything superfluous, costly or rich, in furniture or decorations…. (Rule 17.3)

The woman who wrote those words voluntarily laid aside Coolock House, its land and carriages, its comfortable way of life, her inheritance, her future security. Her life became a powerful witness against greed and the wanton consumption of resources it entails and fosters, as well as a credible witness of genuine solidarity with those who had nothing and whom others considered "the least," and so, expendable and castaway. For her the economic plight of the poor became her plight. What she chose to forgo was for their sakes, so as to share with them. In this she chose to resemble Christ who "though he was rich, yet for your sakes he became poor, so that by his poverty you might become rich" (2. Cor. 8.9).

The Spiritual Works of Mercy:
Today Mercy scholars throughout the world see in those among whom they work, and discern in those about whom they read, a "hunger for happiness and for genuine spiritual, even religious, understanding and peace" which is often related to their "ignorance of basic human, spiritual, and religious understandings, even…among Catholics."[6] This present-day hunger and ignorance – whether in the rich or the poor – is not unlike the lack of religious understanding Catherine McAuley perceived in women, men, and children of her world, nor unlike the poverty of religious awareness to which she ministered through the spiritual works of mercy which were always her stated goal, in and through the corporal works.

In creating schools for poor girls in every foundation except Carlow (where the Presentation Sisters already had such a school); in urging the opening of a House of Mercy in each foundation, with a program of religious education and employment training in each House; in visiting the sick and dying poor; in going out to and welcoming adults for religious instructions, especially in Tullamore, Cork, Bermondsey, Birr, and Birmingham – the ministry of Catherine McAuley was always directed to enhancing people's knowledge of and faith in God, with its obligations and consolations. The central

---

[5] Schneiders, *Selling All*, 260.
[6] "Summary Paragraph."

message of her teaching was the Mercy of God, the mercifulness with which God regards and relates to all human beings.

Using the theological language of her day, she wished to "inspire" children "with a sincere Devotion," to teach them how "to implore [God's] grace to know and love Him and to fulfil His Commandments" (Rule 2. 2-3). In visiting the sick and dying she believed that "The Sisters shall always have spiritual good most in view" – for example, awareness of God's pardon and mercy, the need for repentance, the peace and joy of resignation to God's will, the principal mysteries of faith, God's divine care (Rule 3. 9-10). Where death was "not immediately expected," she believed it was "well to relieve the distress first and to endeavor by every practicable means to promote the cleanliness, ease and comfort of the Patient, since we are ever most disposed to receive advice and instruction from those who evince compassion for us" (Rule 3. 8).

She felt that the distressed women admitted to the House of Mercy ought "if necessary be instructed in the principal mysteries of Religion" and "their religious obligations." They should also be instructed in the habits necessary for "suitable employment" so as to develop the grounds for a positive recommendation from the House and the skills "on which they can depend for their future support." Catherine sadly realized that "Many leave their situations not so much for want of merit as incapacity to fulfil the duties they unwisely engaged in" (Rule 4. 1, 2). In general, she was convinced that

> no work of charity can be more productive of good to society or more conducive to the happiness of the poor than the careful instruction of women, since whatever be the station they are destined to fill, their example and advice will always possess influence, and where ever a religious woman presides, peace and good order are generally to be found. (Rule 2. 5)

This is why – at such enormous future financial trouble to herself – Catherine asked to have a poor school built in Kingstown for the poor girls she saw "loitering about the roads in a most neglected state" (*Correspondence*, 86). This is why she defended the sacramental needs of the 60 women in the Baggot Street House of Mercy against the parish priest who refused to appoint a regular chaplain and at a salary she could manage. This is why she trudged through mud and melted snow to visit poor deluded families in Birr who were deeply wounded by the longstanding parish schism. This is why she resisted Protestant proselytizing in Dublin, Kingstown, Birr and London. This is why she founded a convent in "poor Limerick," a barracks town where women were exploited, and why she visited there "a respectable person who is in a desponding state of mind" (*Correspondence*, 156-157). This is why she urged that poor children and adults be well instructed in the meaning of the sacrament of Confirmation and "the gifts and graces it imparts" (*Correspondence*, 92-93).

Even as early as her years at Coolock she was, "indefatigable in her exertions to relieve the wants and sufferings of the poor." Her charity "did not confine itself to relief of their temporal wants only; she took pity on their spiritual ignorance and destitution....She collected the poor children of the neighbourhood in the lodge, which was placed at her disposal, and devoted a great portion of her time to their instruction." Apparently the religious instruction Catherine offered to poor children soon called forth another audience, for Mary Vincent Harnett continues:

> Her solicitude for the interests of the poor soon drew around her many who hoped to derive from her advice, relief and consolation. Everyone who had distress to be relieved, or affliction to be mitigated, or troubles to be encountered came to seek consolation at her hands, and she gave it to the utmost of her ability; her zeal made her a kind of missionary in the small district around her. (Limerick Manuscript, in Sullivan, *Catherine McAuley,* 144)

Concern is often raised today about use of the word "ignorant" in the Act of Profession of Sisters of Mercy, on the assumption that the word is intended to indicate materially poor people, and so demeans them. This is a limiting assumption. Though Catherine's primary efforts were focused on those who were poor in material ways, for her "ignorance," even debilitating ignorance, was not equivalent to "uneducated" or "undereducated." Highly educated people were often, in Catherine's day as they may be today, spiritually ignorant of a mature theology of God, of the full meaning of the Gospel, of the obligations of universal charity, of the common humanity and dignity of all people before God, and of the ungodly greed, violence and selfishness on the part of some that often lie at the root of the extreme poverty of others. Wherever there was spiritual ignorance Catherine sought to relieve it because she believed in the universal mercy and consolation God initiates and bestows, and hence in the dignity of all human beings.

Conclusion:
If Catherine McAuley lived in the flesh today, she would exert herself and her sisters to do three very specific works of mercy, works that would seem to her to be the greatest present obligations of Sisters of Mercy, make the strongest use of their talents and expertise, and have the most potential to enable them to be effectively "Mercy in the Twenty-First Century":

1. She would renew her own, and ask others to renew their, vowed commitment to *voluntary material poverty* – not primarily as a canonical requirement, but as an act of solidarity with the world's poorest people, as a witness against the widespread greed in all its manifestations that leaves them in extreme poverty, and as a necessary means to mount new works of mercy among them.

2. She would use her own and the sisters' long accumulated educational expertise, in fidelity to one of the primary reasons why they were founded, to create for women and children new *Mercy schools* of all types in destitute areas of the world where they are most needed.

3. She would dedicate herself and the sisters more extensively and explicitly to the specific work of *spiritual/religious instruction* of children and adults, in all its formal and

informal modes – the spiritual works of mercy which have always underlain the mission of Sisters of Mercy as she envisioned it – so that all in the human community may know and experience the merciful consolation of God and their common humanity before God.

When Catherine quoted Luke 12.49 – without any biblical training on her part, though she had read widely – she was amazingly close to present-day interpretations of this difficult text. In applying Jesus' words, on the eve of his journey to Jerusalem—"I came to bring fire to the earth, and how I wish it were already kindled!" (NRSV)—to the self-sacrificing readiness of the Birmingham postulants for the mission to be entrusted to them, Catherine was interpreting these words much as Daniel J. Harrington has recently interpreted them:

> The fire that Jesus came to light was the Kingdom of God. Jesus was convinced that in his own person and mission a new phase in God's plan for the world was beginning. Through his teachings and miracles, and especially in his passion, death and resurrection, Jesus was igniting a fire that will culminate in the fullness of God's Kingdom.[7]

When Catherine McAuley founded the Sisters of Mercy on December 12, 1831, there were only thirteen sisters; two of these died, two left, and two more entered within the next year. From the life, example, and effort of these eleven have come, through the providence of God, the 9710 Sisters of Mercy in the world today. Surely these 9710 are enough to be powerfully "Mercy in the Twenty-First Century." If they generously welcome into their lives the Spirit's kindling of the "fire Christ cast on the earth," they could be this even if they were only eleven.

---

[7] "Fire, Baptism and Division," *America*, 13-20 August 2007, 38.

Works Cited

Bermondsey Annals (1868). Archives of the Institute of Our Lady of Mercy. London.

Harrington, Daniel J. "Fire, Baptism and Division." *America*, 13-20 August 2007, 38.

Lecky, William E. H. *History of Ireland in the Eighteenth Century*. Vol. 1. London: 1892.

[Moore, Mary Clare, comp.] *A Little Book of Practical Sayings of...Mary Catharine* [*sic*] *McAuley...*. London: Burns, Oates & Co., 1868.

Schneiders, Sandra M. *Selling All*. Vol. 2, of Religious Life in a New Millennium. New York: Paulist Press, 2001.

Sullivan, Mary C. *Catherine McAuley and the Tradition of Mercy*. Notre Dame, Indiana: University of Notre Dame Press, 1995. This volume includes the following biographical manuscripts about Catherine McAuley: Mary Clare Moore, Bermondsey Annals (1841); Mary Clare Moore, Letters, 1844-1845; Mary Clare Augustine Moore, "Memoir of the Foundress"; and Mary Vincent Harnett, Limerick Manuscript; as well as the "Rule and Constitutions of the Religious Sisters of Mercy" composed by Catherine McAuley.

Sullivan, Mary C., ed. *The Correspondence of Catherine McAuley, 1818-1841*. Washington: Catholic University of America Press, 2004.

History of the Sisters of Mercy of Ireland in Terms of the Ministry of Spirituality

Bonnie Brennan, RSM

Introductory Clarification:

In dealing with the development of the Ministry of Spirituality of the Sisters of Mercy of Ireland there is a point of clarification that needs to be addressed at the outset, that is, the distinction between the 'Spirituality of Ministry' and the 'Ministry of Spirituality.'

The basic, predominant spirituality which each of us brings to ministry, that which motivates us at the very core of our being, enriches the diverse expressions of Mercy ministries in which we are engaged, and in this way all of them may be said to be 'spiritual.' On the other hand, there is the specific ministry of spirituality which, in an intentional way, puts the focus on learning about God; fostering a relationship with God; and finding meaning in our lived experiences in accordance with this relationship. It is the latter that will be dealt with in this paper.

The paper hopes to look briefly at the Ministry of Spirituality, offered by the Sisters of Mercy of Ireland through the years, under four headings:

1. The lifetime of Catherine McAuley and her early associates;
2. The long period of mainly institutionalised ministry;
3. Post Vatican II diversification;
4. The present-day, more collaborative style of the ministry.

1. Catherine and her Early Associates

On being asked by Fr. Gerald Doyle what the requisites were for acceptance of candidates into her new Institute Catherine replied, 'Besides an ardent desire to be united to God and to serve the poor she must have ....'[1] Whatever other gifts or talents these young women possessed they were deemed secondary to these two fundamental desires. Catherine, herself, undertook the formation of new members, and while they had a well-balanced life between prayer, work and recreation, she put a lot of energy into the spiritual formation of the young Sisters. She read to them from spiritual books on a daily basis;[2] tediously transcribed from the few spiritual books available;[3] and encouraged those who were able to translate religious works from other languages, especially French.[4] She guided them through their retreats prior to reception and profession,[5] and prepared them in every way to transmit these spiritual values in their future ministries.

---

[1] Sullivan, Mary C., RSM, *The Correspondence of Catherine McAuley – 1818 - 1841*, Four Courts Press; The Catholic University of America Press, 2004, p. 77 (Letter to Rev. Gerald Doyle, Sept. 5th. 1836).

[2] Degnan, M. Bertrand, RSM, *Mercy Unto Thousands,* Browne and Nolan Ltd., Dublin, 1958, pp.137,138.

[3] Letter of Mary Clare Moore, Bermondsey, August 23, 1844.

[4] Muldrey, Mary Hermenia, RSM, *Abounding in Mercy – Mother Austin Carroll,* Habersham, New Orleans, 1988, pp. 123 and 371.

[5] *Retreat Instructions.*

One has only to take up Catherine's original Rule[6] to see the importance she placed on the Ministry of Spirituality. It is threaded through the three chapters on ministry: *Of the schools; On Visitation of the Sick; Of the Admission of Poor Women;* and gives her followers explicit instruction on how they are to implement this aspect of their care of 'the poor, sick and ignorant.' It is summed up in her words, *'the good of souls is what the sisters shall have principally in mind.'*[7]

Catherine's early life experiences were the springboard for her future ministry. Among these was the inadequacy she felt of her knowledge of Catholic Doctrine when confronted by the taunts of visitors to the Armstrong and Callaghan households. Obviously she was determined to ensure that such ignorance of faith would not continue in the new age of *Catholic Emancipation,* won for the Irish people by Daniel O'Connell in 1829. It is interesting to note that in the chapter, *Of the Schools,* there is not one mention of the secular curriculum, not even *'the Three R's',* but Catherine goes into great detail about religious instruction, preparation for the sacraments, and devotional practices to be encouraged.[8]

It was in order to bring spiritual solace to the patients of Sir Patrick Dunn's Hospital that Anna Maria Doyle urged Catherine to approach Archbishop Murray for permission to undertake visitation of Catholic patients in the hospital.[9] It was the same desire, that people would be comforted in their last days and prepared for a happy death, which encouraged the early Sisters of Mercy to respond to the request to work in the Townsend Street Depot during the cholera epidemic of 1832.[10] Of course the sisters also ministered to the physical needs of those afflicted with the disease, but it was the spiritual dimension of the sisters' care that distinguished the Townsend Depot from other improvised hospitals in the city.

Young women who were invited to Baggot Street 'as to their home' were not only to be given skills to fit them for future employment, but they also became practiced in prayer and meditation, were prepared for the sacraments and guarded against the dangers that surrounded them.[11]

Foundations:

Conditions of deprivation which were so prevalent in Dublin in the early 1830s were reflected throughout the whole of Ireland and it wasn't long before the services of Sisters of Mercy were sought from their Dublin Convent. The pattern for the new foundations was based on life as lived at Baggot St. Each house became autonomous and the appointed superior took responsibility for the formation of novices who came in great

---

[6] *The Rule and Constitutions of the Religious called Sisters of Mercy,* Browne and Nolan Ltd., Nassau Street, Dublin, pp. 4-16.
[7] Ibid., p. 11.
[8] Ibid., p. 5-6.
[9] Derry Manuscript, as quoted in Bonaventure Brennan, RSM. *It Commenced with Two,* published by the Sisters of Mercy, Northern Province, 2001, p.22.
[10] Ibid., p.38.
[11] Degnan, M. Bertrand, RSM, *Mercy Unto Thousands,* Browne and Nolan Ltd., Dublin, 1958, p. 59.

numbers. She also was responsible for establishing schools, arranging for visitation of the sick poor and in most cases setting up a House of Mercy and/or Orphanage.

Educating the young in the schools, visiting the sick in their homes and in hospital, requesting permission to instruct inmates of workhouses and gaols took a lot of dedication and courage especially in the period prior to, during and after the 'Great Starvation' (1836-1850).

There was a lot of controversy among most of the bishops about the Education System, set up in 1831, but Archbishop Murray (Dublin) and Bishop Murphy (Cork) were in favour of giving it a chance to prove itself, so Catherine McAuley applied to be affiliated with the new Board in 1834. Among the reasons she gave for doing so was that:

> *There was an important apostolic challenge for her in a system which she felt could be permeated with Gospel values by her involvement with it.*[12]

It was not until November 14, 1839 that Baggot Street was accepted into the National School plan;[13] by then several foundations had been made and schools were placed under the authority of the Board of Education. While religious education could be taught for only one half hour a day the Sisters made the most of this time and within a few months of arriving in a new area the fruit of their instruction was evident. In Tullamore the first formal reception of the Sacrament of First Holy Communion since the Penal Days was held with great pomp. After Mass the children came in procession to the convent where they were entertained to breakfast.[14] Two years later:

> *More than 930 children received the Sacrament of Confirmation from the hands of the Lord Bishop Dr.Cantwell, who was delighted and gratified at the answers of the children, showing how well they had been prepared by the Sisters.*[15]

It was the same in all foundations but the inspectors kept a close eye that no deviation from the rules was permitted. One school visitor reports:

> *Commissioners require that the prayer called the 'Hail Mary' be recited but once during the ordinary school hours and only at the time notified, or set apart for religious instruction. On similar grounds they object to the repetition of the 'Angelus' at 12 0'c and direct that it shall only be repeated under the limitations specified....*[16]

Several outbreaks of cholera devastated Ireland in the mid to late 1830s and the sisters of Mercy were on hand at every crisis, nursing the victims and bringing them spiritual comfort. Some bishops thought that the Sisters were foolhardy to endanger their own

---

[12] O'Tuathaigh, G., *Ireland Before the Famine, 1798-1848* (Dublin, 1972) p. 103ff, where distrust of the new system is discussed.
[13] P. R. O. Register of Schools, Co. Dublin, vols 1 and 2, 1835-43, dealing with Roll 2018, the official number of Baggot Street School.
[14] Tullamore Annals, 1836.
[15] Tullamore Annals, 1838.
[16] Education Archives, Dublin, Ed. 24, Folio 169.

lives in this way, but the only thought the visiting Sisters had was to bring relief, comfort and support to the sick and dying.

Workhouses, which gave preference to 'the aged, the infirm, the defective and children,'[17] sprang up throughout the country in the early 1840s. With so many poor people crammed into one space the presence of the Sister of Mercy was sorely needed but not always welcomed. Nevertheless when permission was sought, 'to give instruction to all classes there, and to visit and console the sick in the hospital adjoining,'[18] it was granted.

By 1855 the 'beneficial results the pauper inmates (of the workhouses) derived from visits of the Sisters of Mercy in carrying out their works of charity'[19] caused them to be *invited* and *welcomed* by the Board of Guardians. One of the medical officers, Dr. Elliot, paid them this glowing tribute:

> *No doubt there is something wonderful in your religion. It astonished me to see ladies, of such social position and refined education such as you are, so devoted to the sick poor and to witness the calm resignation of the poor people and the spirit of faith with which they leave the world. I can see nothing like it in Protestantism.*[20]

In these early years the Sisters also attended to the spiritual needs of prisoners even when the parish priest thought it 'inexpedient' for them to seek permission to visit the gaol on a regular basis:

> *They always got permission to visit convicts in order to instruct them and prepare them for death, which often occurred during these troubled times, they were always consoled by the eagerness with which these poor outcasts received their instructions and prepared themselves to meet their Eternal Judge, and there has never been one instance of one of these poor culprits dying unrepentant in Tullamore gaol.*[21]

The foundation made to Birr was a special challenge. 'The Catholic population took sides in a long-running and bitter disagreement between a curate and his parish and bishop.'[22] Fr. Theobald Mathew preached in Birr in 1840 and, sensing 'the bitterness that lingered on after fifteen years of dissension,'[23] recommended to the parish priest, Fr. Spain, that 'the establishment of a community of Sisters of Mercy would prove an effective means of counteracting the sad effects of the schism.'[24] The Sisters of Mercy had little or no experience in this kind of healing ministry, but they were willing to go to Birr, depending

---

[17] Brady, John, *Riocht na Midhe, Social Welfare in Meath,* published by *Meath Chronicle,* p. 60.
[18] Tullamore Annals, 1841.
[19] O'Brien, Pius, RSM, *The Sisters of Mercy of Kilrush and Kilkee,* published by the Congregation of the Sisters of Mercy, Clare Champion Printers, Ennis, 1997, p. 48.
[20] Ibid., p. 49.
[21] Tullamore Annals, 1845.
[22] O'Brien, op. cit., p. 9.
[23] Ibid., p. 12.
[24] Ibid., p. 13.

as usual on 'Divine Providence.' Their presence bore fruit, as moving gently and prayerfully among the people, spreading peace wherever they went, reconciliation was eventually achieved. We are reminded of Catherine's own words: *'there are some things the poor prize more than gold, though they cost the donor nothing: the kind word, the gentle compassionate look and the patient hearing of their sorrows.'*[25]

2. Long Period of Mainly Institutionalised Ministry

The next phase of the life of the Sisters of Mercy was to be the longest when, like most apostolic institutes, things became stabilised, institutionalised and 'respectable.'

Sisters of Mercy were now being *sought* for a growing number of both primary and secondary schools throughout the country. With the passing of the Intermediate Act (Ireland) of 1878, government-sponsored secondary schools replaced the Pension School system, and guaranteed that children were under the spiritual influence of the Sisters of Mercy long into their teens.

From 1860 the Baggot Street Sisters had conducted a private Training College. This was replaced, in 1903, by a larger college at Carysfort Park, Blackrock, Dublin. In 1898 the Mary Immaculate Training College was opened in Limerick. Lectures in Sacred Scripture, Moral and Dogmatic Theology and Liturgy were included in the curriculum. The extent of the influence of these colleges on the Christian formation of young teachers, and the subsequent impact of this training on thousands upon thousands of Catholic children are inestimable.

Catholic Voluntary Hospitals:

The Sisters of Mercy opened the Mercy Hospital in Cork in 1857, the Mater Misericordiae Hospital in Dublin in 1861, and the Mater Infirmorum Hospital in Belfast in 1883.[26] In 1861 the congregation took charge of the nursing at Jervis Street Hospital, Dublin.[27] One can only imagine the difference this made for Catholic patients who now could receive spiritual comfort from the Sisters on a daily basis, especially in the case of seriously ill patients.

Training Schools for nurses became attached to these hospitals in the following decades,[28] thus extending the sphere of influence in the training of Catholic nurses.

Not long after this Sisters of Mercy were welcomed on staffs of the Workhouse Hospital and also invited to undertake management positions in these institutions. As a result conditions for spiritual as well as physical well being improved:

---

[25] *Familiar Instructions,* p. 138.

[26] O'Connor, John, *The Workhouses of Ireland – The Fate of Ireland's Poor,* Anvil Books, Dublin, 1995, p. 267.

[27] Kelly, Patricia, RSM, *From Workhouse to Hospital –The role of Irish Workhouses in Medical Relief to 1921,* M.A. Thesis in Modern History, Coláiste na hOllscoile Gaillmh (National University of Ireland Galway), p. 64.

[28] Ibid., p. 64.

Incessant labour for months brought order and cleanliness to the sick poor; the chapel was cleaned and adorned; the inmates attended daily Mass and Rosary in the evening. All the solaces which only religion can bring were brought into their daily lives…. At this time devotion to the Eucharistic Hour was spreading and nowhere was it adopted with more spirit than at the Mater as the hospital was called.[29]

The Irish Republic:

With the establishment of the Irish Free State in 1922 the ethos of Catholic schools and hospitals was further enhanced. Departments of Education and of Health had new standards and the values espoused by the Catholic Church were enshrined in the new government's documents. In primary schools the time allotted to religious instruction remained at one half hour per day but the whole ambience of the school changed. All the old customs of the early Sisters of Mercy were now able to be freely practised: prayer before and after class; Angelus recited at midday; the Hail Mary recited silently when the clock struck the hour; processions in honour of Our Blessed Lady during the month of May; devotion to the Sacred Heart; aspirations, etc. The local bishop was permitted to appoint a priest as Catechist-*cum*-Inspector. In secondary schools religious education included the study of Scripture, Church History, Apologetics etc. and an annual examination was set by the diocese. The 'Bishop's Prize' for excellence was a coveted honour.

In the hospitals regular prayers, especially the daily Rosary, were recited in the wards. Visitation of patients in hospitals by the sisters and clergy of all denominations was encouraged. Ministry to the spiritual needs of the patients brooked no interference. Special emphasis was placed on care of the dying, especially the administration of the Sacrament of Extreme Unction (as it was then called). Wards were placed under the special patronage of a variety of saints and religious images such as the crucifix, pictures and statues lined the corridors – all creating an uplifting ambience for patient and visitor alike.

The 1950s and 60s were marked by a remarkable increase in vocations to religious life and the number of Sisters of Mercy reached an all-time high. This was providential, as the same period saw a growth of new Catholic parishes in the United States needing sisters to help staff the local Parochial Schools. Some pastors turned to Ireland when religious in the United States could not keep up with the demand. Numerous groups of Sisters of Mercy in Ireland responded to the call, anxious to ensure that children in the United States had the same opportunities for education in the Faith as their Irish counterparts. The Irish Sisters of Mercy benefited from this new experience of working side by side with lay colleagues and being part of the general life of the parish.

Visitation of the sick poor and distressed at home and abroad continued, bringing consolation and spiritual richness to the house-bound and those in hospitals and nursing homes.

---

[29] O'Brien, Pius, RSM, *The Sisters of Mercy of Birr and Nenagh,* published by the Sisters of Mercy, Diocese of Killaloe, Clare Champion Printers, Ennis, 1994, p. 86.

In this era of stabilisation sodalities such as the 'Holy Angels' and 'Children of Mary' flourished under the guidance of some Sisters of Mercy, as did the junior branch of the 'Pioneer Total Abstinence Association,' and the Irish Catholic Nurses' Guild which aims at promoting Catholic ethos and values in our hospitals.

During this time Ministry of Spirituality on a more personal basis was confined to the instruction of converts. This was done discreetly in the convent parlour by certain of our sisters who had a special charism for it; and parents brought their new-born children to the convent to have the Sisters consecrate them to the Sacred Heart and dedicate them to our Lady. Prayers for these occasions were included in the *Little Companion of the Sisters of Mercy.*

3. Post Vatican II Diversification

Vatican II called religious to take a closer look at

1. the Gospel,

2. the spirit of the foundress, and

3. the signs of the times.

The Charismatic Movement, which swept the world after Vatican II, brought many of us a new way of praying with Scripture and devotion to the Holy Spirit. It also brought Sisters of Mercy a greater freedom to move out and share prayer with others. Talking about one's prayer life and hearing the experiences of others were found to be enriching for all involved.

Care of young adults was manifested through programmes such as JIL (Jesus Invites us to Love); and SEARCH, which brought young people together in a relaxed setting to deepen their relationship with God and one another. Adult teams included lay people (lay and religious) and clergy – Sisters of Mercy were enthusiastic about this new method of highlighting God's love.

'Parish Renewal' was another collaborative approach to ministry which Sisters of Mercy became involved in at this time. Small groups of clergy, religious and lay members of the community came together to share their response to God's call in their lives, thus creating a greater understanding of the various vocations within the Church and the need for mutual support.

Up until now retreats were preached to the whole community, but now individually-directed retreats were on offer, an appreciation of which soon paved the way for Sisters of Mercy themselves becoming trained as spiritual directors and retreat givers.

Irish Spirituality in all its richness, especially that of 'finding God in all things,' was revitalized – some aspects of the Irish Spiritual Tradition are reflected in our own Mercy Spirituality. Perhaps it was a refocusing on the Irish missionary outreach that inspired our response to the needs of developing countries in the 1970s. With it came a new understanding of mission – we were not called 'to *bring* the Word of God' to distant lands, but to *find* God present there and, by living among the people, help them, and ourselves, to interpret the events of our lives in the light of the Gospel.

Gradually, too, we were being alerted to our responsibility for 'care of the earth' and the conservation of its riches for future generations. This in turn introduced a Spirituality of the Cosmos emphasising the inter-relatedness of all of God's creation.

During this period two things happened simultaneously that had bearing on our ministries, including the Ministry of Spirituality: a decline in religious vocations and the urgent call of emerging needs. This necessitated a move from some institutional ministries in order to address issues which no one else seemed to be attending to. It also required retraining and sabbaticals to equip us for this.

Vatican II had recommended that: *Throughout their lives religious should labour earnestly to perfect their spiritual, doctrinal, and professional development. As far as possible, superiors should provide them with the opportunity, the resources and the time to do this.* [30]

As far as the Ministry of Spirituality was concerned – Regina Mundi (Rome) and Milltown Park Institute (Dublin) became favourite places for more in-depth study of Theology and Scripture. St. Patrick's College, Maynooth opened up to lay theological students (1966); in the same year Mater Dei Institute for the training of Catechists for Post Primary Schools was established – later this programme was extended to include training of School Chaplains (formerly a prerogative of the clergy). Mount Oliver Institute of Religious Education opened in 1969 providing retraining as catechists for both primary and secondary teachers, and also put a strong emphasis on Adult Religious Education. Some Sisters attended Corpus Christi Institute in England for their up-dating in catechetics. Religious Education became a more specialised subject. A great number of Sisters of Mercy availed of these courses in order to become more professional in their approach to the Ministry of Spirituality. With regard to spiritual care of hospital patients a new course CPE (Clinical Pastoral Education) was offered for training of Hospital Chaplains. This, too, was open to laity and Sisters of Mercy were among the first recruits. The Irish School of Ecumenics, at both its Dublin and Belfast campuses, offered opportunities for those wishing to advance the process of *Peace* and *Reconciliation*.

An increasing number of sisters were invited by their bishops to become Diocesan Catechetical Advisers at both primary and secondary levels. Diocesan Pastoral Centres were placed under the directorship of Sisters of Mercy, and Sisters of Mercy began to appear on the staff of some major seminaries as professors of Theology and Scripture.

Another innovation was the introduction of the 'Parish Sister.' This is one of the ways where collaboration between clergy, the parish sister and parishioners is most effective. Pre-baptism and pre-marriage courses are a genuine expression of Adult Faith Development linked with significant moments in their lives, and those of their children.

---

[30] *Perfectae Caritatis,* n. 18.

Sisters have been able to provide Eucharistic Services when necessary, and Visitation is enriched by being free to bring Holy Communion to the sick and house-bound.

Religious art down the years has played a distinct role in focussing attention in prayer. Now, in the tradition of the Eastern Church, *Iconography* began to attract some of our gifted artists, as a means of deepening their own spiritual lives and enriching those with whom they shared this new understanding of 'Praying with Icons.'

The most significant impact of Vatican II on religious was the call to renewal of their own lives and, for Sisters of Mercy, the resulting better understanding of our status as an Institute of Apostolic Right. With the revision of our Constitutions we had a clearer view of our place in the Church at this point in our history. Under the heading *Apostolic Life* particular apostolates were redefined against the background of Catherine McAuley's original concern for the 'poor, sick and ignorant':

> *In particular this concern is reflected*
> *in our commitment*
> *to the spiritual welfare of people,*
> *through catechesis,*
> *through sharing prayer,*
> *and through building Christian community.*[31]

4. A Present-Day, More Collaborative Approach to the Ministry of Spirituality

In the nineteen eighties more and more Sisters of Mercy in Ireland were answering the call to become spiritual directors – some were trained overseas and others closer to home at Manresa House, Dublin. Availing of training in the art of supervision further enhanced their own spiritual development and honed their skills for this ministry.

Sisters of Mercy also became members of teams at existing Retreat Houses throughout the country. These retreats were varied, from the traditional individually-directed retreat, to creative retreats; retreats centred on Irish Spirituality, to those which explored a deeper understanding of the universe and our place in it; contemplative retreats and those which use art, music and movement as prayer forms – to name but a few.

In the 1980s retreats for small groups were brought to parishes in the form of 'Siol' (seed) Retreats (presented by a sister and a lay person) and 'Neighbourhood Retreats.' The Week of Guided Prayer/Directed Retreat in Parishes was also introduced at this time, based on the one-to-one Ignatian style retreat, devised by John Veltri, S.J. and adapted with his permission. The latter was introduced into Ireland by Dervilla Byrne, RSM, when she was a member of the Manresa House Team.

Since it wasn't always feasible for some people to avail of training at recognised centres of spirituality, Sisters of Mercy were involved in setting up training programmes at parish

---

[31] *Constitutions of the Sisters of Mercy of Ireland,* 1985, n. 43, pp. 22-23.

level. These were more accessible and affordable. The teams were made up of sisters and other lay people.

This partnership in the Ministry of Spirituality has grown from strength to strength. To guarantee accountability to the Faith Community, supervision of Prayer Guides was introduced by adapting (with their blessing) methods of Individual and Peer Supervision drawn up by Rosemary Dougherty and Susan Jorgensen for Spiritual Directors.[32] As the ministry grew, the more experienced Prayer Guides were trained as Supervisors, the aim being to have each diocese, or area, become independent. Companion manuals, *Teach us to Pray* and *Let There Be Light*, were prepared for Prayer Guides and Supervisors respectively.

In 1994 the Sisters of Mercy of Ireland and South Africa formed one congregation, sharing of personnel being one of its riches. Two spiritual directors from each of four provinces formed a Spirituality Commission which met regularly with Dervilla Byrne, then Congregational Leader. From this group Sisters of Mercy and their partners in the Ministry of Spirituality were provided with a Code of Ethics by 2000.[33]

In recent years prayer groups are going strong in most parishes – with Sisters of Mercy as leaders or participants. This Small Christian Community experience is much valued, especially by those who for one reason or another cannot participate fully in the Institutional Church.

Pilgrimage is so much a part of Irish Spirituality that it is not surprising that some of us find ourselves caught up in organising and leading pilgrimages to the holy places of our tradition. Our Lady's Shrine at Knock is probably the most frequented, but Lourdes, Fatima and Medugorje are also reasonably accessible from Ireland. The places associated with St. Patrick such as Lough Derg (popularly called St. Patrick's Purgatory) and the steep climb up Croagh Patrick keep us in touch with the penitential aspect for our own journey. Catherine McAuley's advice that imitation of Jesus meant 'walking the very same path He trod,' is taken literally by Sisters who organise pilgrimages to the Holy Land. In recent years Mercy International Centre holds a strong attraction for Sisters of Mercy and their associates and colleagues, especially for the experience of *Walking and Praying with Catherine*.

In several dioceses in Ireland Sisters of Mercy have been invited to manage Pastoral Centres. In these centres the focus is mainly on ongoing adult religious formation. People are also prepared as Special Ministers of the Eucharist and Ministers of the Word. The *Forward in Faith* extra-mural course from Maynooth College has been very popular and well-attended. Programmes such as Myers Briggs and the Enneagram offer participants a deeper understanding of themselves, and others, as human beings.

---

[32] Salem Institute of Spirituality.

[33] *Ministry of Spirituality – Principles of Good Practice: A Liberating Source*, published for private circulation for Sisters of Mercy and their Associates. Compiled by Josephine O'Grady Walshe, RSM, Noeleen Reilly, RSM, Breda McFadden, RSM, and Helen Kennedy, RSM (2000).

Perhaps the most compassionate work of these centres, and the most urgent, is the provision of bereavement support, and the training of parish groups to offer this compassionate service in their local area.

- The rise in the number of deaths by suicide, especially of young males in their late teens and early twenties, has severe traumatic effect on the loved one's immediate family, and also extends to friends, and the wider community, who are bewildered by this growing phenomenon.

- Road-accident fatalities are another great trial. Notwithstanding increased Government strategies, and more stringent penalties for 'road rage,' and drink-driving accidents, too many innocent people are losing their lives on our roads.

- Abuse of drugs results in many premature deaths.

- Murder is now an everyday occurrence, the most recent form being murder-suicide where whole families are wiped out in violent, irrational, and often retaliatory actions.

- Gang warfare in some of our cities is on the increase, governed by a 'shoot to kill' policy.

There is so much scope here for the Ministry of Spirituality, where specially trained listeners can create space for the sharing of all the hurt and anguish in a safe, non-judgemental setting.

'Welcoming the stranger' is becoming more meaningful for us in Ireland as more and more foreign nationals come to live among us, either by choice or of necessity. There is a new challenge here for us (especially in light of our Mercy tradition of hospitality) to establish meaningful relationships with these stranger-friends which will enable mutual understanding of our diverse beliefs.

In this technological age media resources are part and parcel of the Ministry of Spirituality. The Congregation of the Sisters of Mercy are among the Trustees of RNN (Religious News Network), one of our sisters, Marie Stuart, RSM, being Director from 1994 to 2004. RNN supplies over 30 local community and hospital stations reaching an estimated audience of 300,000. Topics are of a religious and social nature, including Faith/Spirituality. Local radio is also a medium for Sisters of Mercy to be involved in 'A Thought for the Day' and retreats for special seasons of the year.

An important resource for us Sisters of Mercy is the multi-award-winning interactive CD-Rom, *Mercy and Justice Shall Meet,* a Fraynework Production commissioned by MIA. Looking at present social issues across the world, in the light of the Gospel and the Spirituality of Catherine McAuley, helps us, and those with whom we minister, to make connections which up until recently would be unthinkable. Print resources which inspire and inform us for ministry are the *MAST Journal*[34] and *Presence.*[35]

Many Irish Sisters of Mercy are members of SDI (Spiritual Directors International), and recently AISGA (All Ireland Spiritual Guidance Association) has been established here for the support of all who are engaged in the Ministry of Spirituality.

Spirituality of Catherine McAuley – Fanning the Flame:

The Bi-centennial of Catherine's birth (1978); the international gathering in Dublin of Sisters of Mercy for *Trocaire* (1981); Catherine declared Venerable (1990); establishment of Mercy International Association (1992) with its Centre in Catherine's first House of Mercy (1994); celebration of the 175th anniversary of the founding of the Sisters of Mercy (2006) all helped us, and our associates and colleagues, to touch into the spirit of our foundress in life-giving ways. Recently, one such experience is 'Going Deeper with Catherine,' a reflective retreat aimed at helping us deepen our understanding of Catherine's spirituality and appreciating our own experience of Mercy in the light of it.

Mercy Associates have been working and praying with Sisters of Mercy in many parts of Ireland for many years, especially in areas now known as the Western Province and the South Central Province. These groups are presently finding new and more meaningful ways of relating with each other in ministry. The same is true in our South African, Kenyan and United States Provinces.

None of the individual congregations which formed the Northern Province (in the new united Congregation) had a history of 'Mercy Associates,' so a new model of collaboration between Sisters of Mercy and other compassionate people has emerged and has been developing over the past ten years.

In this model, which the Sisters in the Southern Province have also adopted, there are several distinctions from the more traditional Mercy Associate movement. We call it the 'Circle of Mercy.' (See Appendix A)

5. The Future

The 2006 Congregational Chapter Statement asks us, among other things, to consider, 'How will we nurture the hunger for God?' Each Provincial Chapter discerned its response (see Appendix B). These responses, culled from *Reflections on the Chapter Season – as we embrace new beginnings.... 2007,* will be our guidelines for the next six years. In this *Year of the Word,* wish us well as we embark on a new phase of our journey!

---

[34] *Journal of the Mercy Association in Scripture and Theology,* published by the Sisters of Mercy, USA.
[35] *Presence—An International Journal of Spiritual Direction,* published by Spiritual Directors International.

Appendix A

Some of the differences between the 'Circle of Mercy' model of Associates and the more traditional form of Mercy Associates:

- The 'Circle of Mercy' is open to Sisters of Mercy and lay women and men as *equal* members. To underscore this equality we refrain from using the term 'associate.'

- Commitment is made to each other in the local Circle of Mercy, 'to live the Gospel according to the spirit of Catherine McAuley,' rather than making commitment to the Province/Congregation of the Sisters of Mercy.

- Members formally commit themselves to Prayer, Mutual Support and Compassionate Service for one year. This commitment is renewable.

- The 'Circle of Mercy' exists alongside, and in harmony with, the Congregation and has the potential to carry the charism of Catherine McAuley independently in the future should the occasion arise.

- Local circles are small in number and reflective in nature. They may be connected with each other in neighbouring clusters, and through regular meetings held for representatives from each circle.

- Fundamental to each circle is a collaborative and flexible way of working that maximises the contribution of each person, and that gives expression to an aspect of Mercy appropriate to each group.

- A Core Group is the hub of co-ordination and inspiration.

Appendix B

How do we nurture the hunger for God?   (Congregational Chapter 2006)

The responses from each of the seven Provincial Chapters (2007):

- We commit ourselves to nurture the hunger for God in ourselves, each other and the wider community as we: deepen our Spiritual Life; open ourselves to be enriched by the experience of others in our common search for meaning as we share our own experience of God; pray together; open our space and spiritual resources to the wider community.

- We will nurture the hunger for God by: taking Sabbath time regularly and participating in ongoing formation; availing of retreats, seasonal prayer services, and media resources; journeying with others in prayer and compassion.

- Centred in the God of Mercy, we nurture the contemplative dimension of life, joining with others in the search for meaning. As we nurture the hunger for God we will: engage in courageous conversations about our understandings of God, our spiritualities and the diversity among us both personally and in community; create healing rituals; avail of centres and spaces for quiet and reflection, in different parts of the Province, for Sisters and others; expand our website to include a database in the spirituality section to provide information for those seeking meaning in life.

- We will nurture our prayer life together and maintain an ethos of mutual compassion and caring as community; Sisters are encouraged to take time and space with their own hunger for God and to be open to sharing their experience with one another, with associates and with others who are searching for meaning.

- We re-commit ourselves to the practices as recorded in the statutes and statement of Chapter 2000, pages six, seven and nine; we call local communities to come to an agreement regarding communal prayer (statutes, p.3); we call ourselves to make a concerted effort to use inclusive language in our prayer and liturgies.

- We acknowledge both the hunger for God and the malaise in our society. Respectful of the unique and diverse ways of expressing faith, we promote faith development, pastoral renewal, inter-faith dialogue, and nurturing of spirituality.

- We recommend that the Provincial Leadership Team organise assemblies on such topics as the Constitutions, Mercy values and charism, Mercy life of Catherine McAuley, different methods of prayer, sharing our ministries; we call ourselves to personal responsibility for our own growth in spirituality and to continue our efforts at reconciliation and conflict resolution, so that our actions and lifestyle reflect the heritage of Mercy.

A U.S. Sister of Mercy Dialogues with Tradition

Dolores Liptak, RSM

Our identity as Mercy Sisters is fundamentally based upon a shared history that began in Ireland and has been extended to many continents. This brilliant record not only conveys "who we were" but it also makes possible our asking the more pressing question: "who are we today"? It brings us into what some have called the deep tradition of the charism from which we derive our sense of belonging as Sisters of Mercy. In this paper I want to explore, through history, the U.S. experience as it has been focused through the lens of one collective portrait. This singular image, I believe, can become the foundation for grasping what American Mercies can contribute to the conversation about how we can rekindle a spirit to serve as "fire cast on the earth-kindling."[1]

Because the U.S. Mercy community was immensely blessed by the tremendous gift of having Mother Frances Xavier Teresa Warde as the preeminent American founder, I believe that we are in a privileged position to use her as the means by which we can not only describe our story but also guide our future course. Choosing Mother Warde as a prefigure and personification of Mercy in our quest for identity and purpose first occurred to me as I looked back to the essential sources that tell us of this great woman's amazing contributions to the U.S. Mercy history. During the course of that research, I began to realize that the specific role that she played could serve as an excellent means by which all Mercies can visualize the future possibilities of their Institute.[2]

A careful study of Mother Warde's years of service in the United States reveals how central her role was to the development of the U.S. Mercy tradition. Invited to serve God's people in a pioneer land, this remarkable woman determined the goals she and her fledgling community needed to fulfill. Instinctively she understood that America was a perfect place to accomplish the singular mandates of their congregation. There, the Sisters could respond to their God as missionaries who wished to witness to God's deep desire for mercy. There they, too, could "proclaim the glad tidings," especially by instructing their fellow Irish exiles in the teachings of a Church considered alien in a Protestant land. Furthermore, in America, her Sisters could bring the passion they felt to provide comfort, solace, and assistance to God's beloved poor, in other words, to slake the hunger of both soul and body that plagued America's Catholic communities. Being witnesses as they stood in solidarity beneath the cross of Christ, sheltering and supporting those for whom Christ died, and doing this within the institutional, albeit pioneer U.S. Church—these were the daily goals that she knew her community could assume. Even

---

[1] See Margaret Susan Thompson, "Charism or Deep Story? Toward a Clearer Understanding of the Growth of Women's Religious History in Nineteenth Century America," *Review for Religious*, 1999.
[2] Three principal sources on Frances Warde are Kathleen Healy, *Frances Warde: American Founder of the Sisters of Mercy* (New York, 1973); [Sister Mary Austin Carroll], *Leaves from the Annals,* Vol. 4, (New York, 1895); and Mary C. Sullivan, *The Correspondence of Catherine McAuley: 1818-1841* (Washington and Dublin, 2004). After first giving the entire name of a Sister of Mercy cited in this paper, I will use the simpler designation, namely, her title and last name, throughout the remainder. Thus, Mother Warde, after first designation.

more, in this wild, raucous America, she also encouraged her Sisters to respond in extraordinary ways, in effect, to offer their service as first responders whenever crises or disaster confronted Americans or where the weight of social sin bore down. Leading her community in attending to these goals as well, Mother Warde helped create an admirable, unified depiction of women who were filled with faith and ready for action—of women whose love for God was primed to spill over abundantly into the chaotic world they encountered.[3]

What, indeed, had inspired Mother Warde to provide us with such a vision? Who helped her realize what she could accomplish by serving the American Church in this multi-dimensional, apostolic way? In the first place, she was a true daughter of Ireland. Like her people, she had been greatly influenced by Ireland's "devotional revolution," re-awakened after the enactment of the 1829 Catholic Emancipation Act. This spiritual renewal emphasized Ireland's glorious past, personified as it was by its ancient and heroic missionary Saints, Patrick and Columbanus. Had not it been Mother McAuley's devout hope to follow their example as she reached out to God's beloved beyond Dublin, even beyond Ireland? Had she not founded ten foundations of the Order in Ireland and two in England in her brief ten years as superior of the Institute? Clearly, her desire to hear and respond to needs that were at the very heart of the Church became Mother Warde's preoccupation as well. Like so many other Sisters who entered Baggot Street during Catherine's lifetime, Mother Warde had learned at Catherine's feet that one's encounter with Christ was the main challenge of being a Sister of Mercy. She, too, wanted to find Him and to follow Him—if need be, to the ends of the earth.[4]

Mother Warde's personal call to become a foreign missionary had, however, become crystallized only after an American bishop approached the St. Leo's community in Carlow, Ireland. On that fateful evening in 1843, Bishop Michael J. O'Connor, who had previously translated the first Mercy Constitution for Roman officials, made a startling request. Having just been appointed first Bishop of Pittsburgh, Pennsylvania, the eager bishop appealed to the Sisters to join him as he took up work among the members of his impoverished American diocese. What he told them was that, in frontier America, there were souls to be saved and that the purpose of the vowed lives of witness and service that had been articulated in their Constitution fit perfectly the needs of the Irish immigrant people he had been called to serve. Just as Catherine had once enjoined her Sisters to "find Jesus Christ to love and serve with their whole heart," the bishop now begged them to fulfill that same injunction in this pioneer Church.[5]

Accepting Bishop O'Connor's offer, the Mercy Sisters at Carlow became the first Irish community of nuns to commit their congregation to missionary foundations in the United States. This courageous step proved, in itself, to be revolutionary. By their response, the Sisters declared that they wanted to join in the official missionary enterprise.

---

[3] See Benedict XVI, *Deus Caritas Est,* 2006. Scriptural passages are from Matthew 9: 9-13; Luke 4: 16-30; on wilderness, see Katherine Burton, *His Mercy Endureth Forever* (Tarrytown, 1946), p. 69.
[4] Mary Peckham Magray, *The Transforming Power of the Nuns: Women, Religion, & Cultural Change in Ireland, 1750-1900* (New York and Oxford, 1998), p. 4; Carroll, p. 540.
[5] Healy, *passim.*

Furthermore, they made it known that they understood themselves to be co-partners, even co-adjutors, in the charismatic ministry of the Church. While they admitted that the responsibility of the clergy necessarily lay with the conferral of the sacraments and the celebration of liturgical action, the Sisters imagined another empowering role for themselves. In America, they hoped to be capable partners on a great missionary journey.[6]

Through their willingness to accept the bishop's request, the Carlow Sisters demonstrated their desire to be united in spirit with the intentions of Mother McAuley. More, they indicated the training that they had received from her disciple, Mother Warde, who had served as both their first superior and novice director. Like her, they wanted to imitate the zeal of St. Francis Xavier in his burning desire to "convert souls"; like her, they wanted to adhere to the Ignatian motto, *Ad majorem Dei gloriam.* As Mother Warde had taught them, so they were willing to act on the belief that witnessing to Christ's love was the only aim in life worth striving for—the *raison d'etre* of their lives. Another renowned American founder, Mother Mary Baptist Russell, would later echo the same Mercy resolution that gave Mother Warde purpose, namely, to live one's life solely to fulfill God's provident will on behalf of souls. "Let us then leave ourselves humbly and confidently in the Hand of Divine Providence," she wrote, "do all we can to glorify Him, by living as true religious, real Sisters of Mercy…" An early California missionary captured this same intention when she wrote back home: "Pray a great deal, please, for us and our mission. Bear in mind, beloved Sister, that in your quiet convent home you may convert thousands in America."[7]

From the time of the Carlow Sisters' departure for America until their superior's death in Manchester, New Hampshire in 1884, Mother Warde remained the primary spokesperson of the Mercy Sisters' intentions. More, she functioned as the compass point around which the Sisters came to understand their own particular mission. In whatever burgeoning area of the United States in which the Sisters began to settle, her missionary spirit seemed to inspire and lay the foundation for grace. Note the deep respect that Mother Russell expressed to Mother Warde about the place she held even in that early period. In a letter written five years after Mother Russell founded the San Francisco community, this intrepid missionary from Kinsale, Ireland, acknowledged Mother Warde's special role among the American Sisters. In her words, "Every house in America with very few exceptions claims the honor of being founded by Mother Warde…"[8]

Under Mother Warde's careful watch, in fact, thirty-six American foundations were established throughout the United States; seventeen of these would become motherhouses

---

[6] Quoted from a 19th century Chicago Mercy manual, in Eileen Mary Brewer, *Nuns and the Education of American Catholic Women* (Chicago, 1987), p.36. On missionary zeal beginning in Ireland, see Suellen Hoy, "The Journey Out: The Recruitment and Emigration of the Irish Religious Women to the United States, 1812-1914" in *Journal of Women's History* 6 (Winter, 1995), *passim.*

[7] See Healy, pp. 97-119, on the compilation of the *Spiritual Maxims of Mary Frances Warde,* used in Carlow, Naas and Wexford; on Mother Mary Baptist Russell, see Kathleen Doyle, *Like a Tree by Running Water: The Story of Mary Baptist Russell, California's First Sister of Mercy* (Nevada City, CA, 2004), pp. 177-178. On California mission, 1859 correspondence, see Carroll, p. 25.

[8] Doyle, quoted letter is on p. 202; see also pp. 207-215. See also Healy, p. 206.

or centers of enduring significance. Furthermore, by her death in 1884, these original foundations had grown to include more than one hundred houses and apostolates. Even the few houses that Mother Warde did not directly establish reflected her influence in complicated, yet palpable ways. No other American founder, Mercy or otherwise, approximated such a record of prodigious accomplishment. An excellent organizer and administrator, she was the one who oversaw what was happening under the Sisters' care during the formative years of their American adventure. Through her, most bishops made direct requests and often negotiated contracts in order to establish a community of Sisters of Mercy in their dioceses. At other times, bishops enlisted the help of other prelates to accomplish the same effect. Through it all, Mother Warde remained the central figure as Sisters were acquired—whether from American motherhouses or directly from Ireland.[9]

As Mother Warde neared her death, New York's Archbishop Michael Corrigan was among those bishops who acknowledged the remarkable leadership she had provided—both her ability as founder and her phenomenal power to attract new members to the Mercy community. Even as the Mercy community expanded beyond his jurisdiction, he suggested that she was "still the religious superior." So powerful did her influence linger in the minds of those who had early come to experience the quality of her leadership, moreover, that Providence Bishop Thomas Hendricken actually referred to the Mercy community as the one "which she almost founded." Back in London, Mother Mary Clare Moore, an outstanding missionary in her own right, struck the right chord when she suggested that Mother Warde should be known as "Mother Exodus" since she was continuing to lead others, in Moses-like fashion, toward the "Promised Land." Just as Christ had invited the apostles to "go, sell all you have and come, follow me," Mother Warde urged her Sisters to see their Mercy vocation as an opportunity to be disciples of Christ and partners in the American mission. As one priest noted, it was clear that the Mercy unity of purpose and charity had been shaped by this clear goal. True discipleship bestowed the badge of honor that Mother McAuley desired for them and made them "one heart and soul in God" in their religious pursuits.[10]

Mother Warde's goal, however, was not to be seen as founder, but as missionary. She wanted to spread the message of God's love as clearly enunciated by the Scriptures. Enlivened by the spirit of the founder who had been so motivated by Gospel values, Mother Warde always urged her Sisters to exhaust themselves as Catherine had. This meant that they were united to Christ in mission—easing the path of the "neighbor in need," supporting "God's dear little ones," standing by those who suffered. In no time, young women began to follow her example and joined the community. Little wonder that impoverished Irish immigrants, in particular, turned to this new, faith-filled community and became the first recipients of their determined energy. Rapidly, the Mercy Sisters "...won their way into the hearts of the people, whether in the hospitals of plague-

---

[9] Healy, "Institutions of Mercy Founded by Frances Warde," pp. 518-522; see also p. 59. For number cited (36), see Carroll, p. 261. The matter of contracts was routine; for almost every bishop signing a contract was routine. See Bernard O'Reilly's contract with the Sisters of Mercy, 1851, Archives of the Sisters of Mercy of Hartford, CT, as one example.

[10] See Carroll, on Corrigan's opinion, p. 247; Hendricken, p. 263; and Moore, p. 161. On Fr. Dean, see Healy, p. 164.

stricken cities or in the prisons, by the couch of the dying or the cradle of the orphans." From city to city, they began Sunday Schools and adult education classes, usually conducted at night. These became the surest way the Sisters had to fulfill the first intention of their Constitution to "draw souls to God." At the same time, within their convent homes, the Sisters renewed their strength through prayer and, in their spare minutes, brought peace and comfort to orphans and women who had shelter among them. Always, the sick, homeless, and elderly were tenderly served.[11]

Because of episcopal priorities, the Sisters soon became more involved in the specific works of the diocese. These efforts became organized as they cooperated with the clergy in developing parish schools, local hospitals, and health care facilities. In the midst of this variety of organized services, however, the Sisters continued to focus upon immediate concerns and remained especially alert to news of sudden disasters or crises. For a religious community that had scarcely earned the right to be "walking Sisters" in Ireland, the irony was clear. In America, the Sisters had discovered that there was no boundary to the works of mercy, no restrictions to their passion for the poor. In effect, the Sisters could fulfill the fondest hopes of their founders. As American Sisters, they could be all things to all persons: instructors in the faith, teachers, hospital workers, first responders, and, yes, even fellow mourners should tragedies befall God's people.[12]

Mother Warde's encouragement that the Sisters engage in such broad-scale ministries remained the pattern set for all subsequent U.S. Mercy endeavors. Perhaps this is the reason why, in the fourth volume of Mother Mary Austin Carroll's *Leaves from the Annals of the Sisters of Mercy*, Mother Warde's name recurs repeatedly—even when the stories of other foundations are recounted. In chronicling the flurry of activities that constantly transpired in the second half of the nineteenth century, for example, Mother Carroll continued to mention how influential Mother Warde remained in setting the pace of missionary zeal. This is true, too, of those foundations begun by Irish Sisters from Dublin, Naas, Ennis, or Kinsale. In some way, it appears that Mother Warde was always considered some part of the entire enterprise. Although Mother Patricia Waldron had been originally recruited by Mother Warde from the Diocese of Tuam, Ireland to work as her novice director in Manchester, for example, she remained her faithful disciple after being reassigned to take over the duty of superior in Philadelphia—a responsibility Mother Waldron maintained magnificently for another fifty-five years. In the case of far-off California, Fr. Hugh Gallagher successfully used Mother Warde's influence when he sought Sisters from Kinsale in 1854. Years later, Mother Warde was of even more direct assistance when she replied affirmatively to Grass Valley (CA) Bishop Eugene O'Connell's request to establish a mission at Yreka, California. In this way, two Mercy foundations were soon well established in the distant gold-rush fields of California, once again with Mother Warde's knowledge and help. Because of both clergy and benefactors

---

[11] Carroll, p. 517; Doyle, *passim*. Quote from *Souvenir of the Centenary of the Sisters of Mercy, Savannah, Georgia: 1845-1945*, p. 11.

[12] The term "first responders" has become the common one to designate emergency workers. It appears to be the best term to designate the Sisters of Mercy of any age. See Edna Marie Leroux, RSM, "In Times of Socioeconomic Crisis" in Ursula Stepsis and Dolores Liptak, RSM (eds.), *Pioneer Healers: The History of Women Religious in American Health Care* (New York, 1989), pp. 118-143, as one example of this phenomenon.

who admired the work of Mother Warde, Cincinnati, Little Rock, and the Connecticut communities of Middletown and Meriden were also begun, from Ireland, during the same period.[13]

The New York Mercy community is an apt example of a foundation deliberately initiated because of the first impression that Mother Warde had made when she arrived in the United States in 1843. After meeting Mother Warde when he hosted her first stopover, the famed Bishop John Hughes immediately realized that he, too, wanted Sisters of Mercy for his diocese. Three years later, he personally managed to convince Mother Agnes O'Connor to leave the new ministry she was pursuing in London in order to serve New York's Irish immigrants. Joining her in this mission would be Sister Mary Camillus Byrn, Mother McAuley's beloved godchild and Mother Warde's close friend. According to accounts, she was the one who put the entire American Mercy mission into an unique perspective. She wanted to go to America, she told them, so that she could then truly take "my godmother's place, for I know how she would have loved to go." For many of the Sisters, the desire to reflect Mother McAuley's spiritual quest to be a missionary proved as inspirational as it had for Mother Warde. Perhaps this willingness to go to unknown lands, as Catherine would, in order to witness to, and sacrifice their lives for Christ, is best captured in a simple word picture composed by an Indian chief and written fifty-four years after Mother Warde had established a mission among the Indians of Maine. In this letter, Chief Louis Nicholas proclaimed: "The Sisters of Mercy, who know no home but the Heart of Our Lord, have labored untiringly among the Penobscot Indians... Many sacrifices were made by them for the education of our children...many weary hours were spent visiting the sick and the dying."[14]

Because of their desire to be at the heart of the Church's missionary work, however, the Sisters were to have an unexpected, and perhaps forgotten, impact upon the larger American culture as well. In the first place, the uniqueness of the Sisters' vocation and the various ministries they performed played into the hands of those American Protestants who already feared the power of the Catholic Church. Freed because of their vows in religion from Victorian restrictions, the Sisters inadvertently threatened the dominant social view that women should be wives and mothers and that the family was the proper sphere for women's activities. How were Protestants, then, to deal with women who lived celibate, communal lives of prayer and service and, furthermore, saw

---

[13] Mother Austin Carroll (New Orleans), Mother Angela Fitzgerald (Hartford), and most other founders represent perfect examples of Sisters who both admired and feared Mother Warde yet saw her as their guide. On Mother Austin's perspective, see Sister Mary Hermenia Muldrey, RSM, *Abounding in Mercy: Mother Austin Carroll* (New Orleans, 1988), p. 222 ff. On Mother Fitzgerald's, see Carroll, pp. 518-519. The interactions of bishops and priests with Mother Warde showed much evidence of the respect and trust she used to build upon in order to extend Mercy communities. See also Healy, pp. 352-390 re Bishops de Goesbriand (Burlington); Bacon (Maine); Bayley (New Jersey); Purcell (Cincinnati); Kenrick (Baltimore), etc. On Mother Waldron, see S. M. Eulalia Herron, *The Sisters of Mercy in the United States: 1843-1928* (New York, 1929), pp. 249-254. For Cincinnati's and Little Rock's beginnings, see Carroll, pp. 286-296; on Little Rock, see Herron, pp. 71-74. On Ennis, see S. Pius O'Brien, *The Sisters of Mercy of Ennis* (Killaloe, Ireland, 1992), pp 27-32.
[14] For quote by Sister M. Camillus Byrn, see Katherine Burton, *His Mercy Endureth Forever* (Tarrytown, NY, 1946), p. 69. For quote on the Indians of Maine, see Healy, p. 422.

parish, convent, and church ministry as the primary centers for passing on the faith? Anger over what contradicted their tradition of dispensing faith "from the hearth" complicated the good intentions apparent in the Sisters' ministry to the poor, sick, and ignorant, and, for a while, caused the Sisters great suffering. In 1855, Mother Warde became the first Sister of Mercy to directly confront this particular problem when the Mercy Motherhouse at Providence, Rhode Island came under attack by a mob alleging that they were unlawfully confining a Sister. Although Mother Warde, the bishop, and the Irish workmen who assembled around the convent building on the night of the proposed reprisal were successful in turning away the wrath of the rioters, she never failed to be wary of the reality that the lifestyles of the Sisters could be used to do them harm.[15]

Because of such encounters, moreover, Mother Warde came to realize that the Sisters were perceived as threats not only because of their Catholic faith but also because of their independent way of pursuing the organized ministries of teaching and serving the sick poor—rights actually being denied nineteenth century Protestant women. That women religious worked closely with clergy in order to contribute to the development of schools, in particular, proved so alarming, in fact, that the famed Yankee educator, Catherine Beecher, declared openly her suspicions over the propriety of such interaction and suggested that the cooperation that Sisters maintained with priests was proof of an ongoing Catholic conspiracy to "take over America." At one point, Beecher published her views, arguing, ironically, that nuns held "posts of competence, usefulness and honor for women of every rank and of every description of talents." While she begrudgingly admired this development as supportive of women's rights, she resented the "privileged independence from certain societal norms" and the power that Sisters wielded. Thus, Mother Warde became a target of Catherine Beecher's attack on the independence of nuns just as women religious, in general, suffered because of their adherence to the tenets of the Catholic Church. Yet, as Mother Warde indicated, this kind of suffering could only be counted as gain. Here, in America, the Sisters had been called to be witnesses, through whatever means, of God's desire to save souls.[16]

Ironically, such threats and mistreatment were to dissipate more quickly than Mother Warde imagined. In fact, within the very next decade after the Providence affair, the fact of the Sisters' independence was to take on a far more positive connotation. As the Civil War erupted in 1860, the Sisters found themselves in a perfect position to offer their services—this time as first responders in the greatest crisis that ever befell American society. Had it not been, in particular, for the immediate opportunity seized upon by the Sisters of Mercy, in Washington, DC and Baltimore, MD, to volunteer their facilities and their service and later to become involved in the work of army hospitals, on the battlefields, and in hospital ships, they could never have been able to prove to such a wide audience of Americans that their lifestyle of service was not only worthwhile but

[15] The Protestant ethic and the antagonism that occurred because of it are discussed in numerous books; with respect to the implications regarding women see Marie Anne Pagliarini, "The Pure American Woman and the Wicked Catholic Priest: An Analysis of Anti-Catholic Literature in Antebellum America," in *Religion and American Culture*, 1999, pp. 97-128.
[16] For quote on Beecher see Kathleen A. Brosnan, "Public Presence, Public Silence: Nuns, Bishops, and the Gendered Space of Early Chicago," in *The Catholic Historical Review* (July, 2004), p. 486.

genuinely and immensely productive for all involved. Indeed, the Sisters' participation in wartime service proved that vowed, celibate women were highly capable of making significant contributions to the shaping of American culture.[17]

In fact, the Mercy Sisters' reaction to the Civil War became the most dramatic example they could employ to show their fellow Americans what had always been—as almost one hundred thirty of the 650 sisters who eventually nursed on both sides of the conflict were Mercy nuns. Though the Sisters had already amazed other citizens by their immediate involvement in periods when epidemics or disasters struck, the Sisters' services during this war became the greatest proof of their desire to proclaim God's love through deed. In a letter sent to Propaganda Fide, Hartford's Bishop Francis McFarland was perhaps the only American bishop to note the religious impact of the Sisters as they responded to war. He wrote: "…[T]he abnegation of the Sisters of Charity & Mercy …have commanded respect and have brought about the conversion of a large number of unbelieving and heritical (*sic*) soldiers who had not been able to avoid admiring the heroism of those Sisters on the battlefields and in the hospitals." His remarks explained the essence of the Mercy vocation. The Civil War had provided the ultimate means for them to prove their purpose, and, thus, their most important victory.[18]

What must be remembered, furthermore, is that there is no record that the Sisters ever acted under the belief that they needed official Church approval to become involved in tragic times. Instead, they responded as if it were their very birthright and the driving force that had brought them to America. Well into the twentieth century, Mercy Sisters were among the first to rush to every emergency whether this involved epidemics that plagued the urban ghetto or accidents and disasters that occurred in the mining or lumber camps of the west. They were prepared when floods or earthquakes destroyed whole cities or towns. Free to respond to any crisis, they consistently drew the admiration of those in charge. What seemed like ordinary work to them became, for outside observers, extraordinary service. This continual willingness to rush to those who were suffering became, in fact, the crowning glory upon which the U.S. Sisters of Mercy dispelled any doubts about their proper place in American society.[19]

In the twentieth century, the Sisters of Mercy continued to give the same special impression both within the institutions of the Church and on society in general. No longer feared because of the impact of differing lifestyles, they perfected their educational

---

[17] Wartime service for the Sisters of Mercy is detailed in numerous monographs regarding local communities. See in particular, Carroll, pp. 66-105 on both Northern and Southern fronts; and *passim*. On the change of attitudes that resulted whenever Sisters faced challenges in society, Carol Coburn and Martha Smith, *Spirited Lives: How Nuns Shaped Catholic Culture and American Life, 1836-1920* (Chapel Hill and London, 1999), touch on this theme with respect to American nuns in general.

[18] On Sisters of Mercy during the war, see Sister Mary Denis Maher, *To Bind Up the Wounds: Catholic Sister Nurses in the U.S. Civil War* (Baton Rouge, 1989), p. 70. Maher distinguishes among local groups; her numbers are 18 Mercy Sisters from South Carolina; 18 from Vicksburg, 11 from Cincinnati, 22 from Baltimore, 15 from New York, 34 from Pittsburgh, and 10 from Chicago (approximately 130 sisters). For Bishop McFarland's assessment, see correspondence of Bishop McFarland, Hartford, to Propaganda Fide, Paris, 12/29/1863, Archives of the University of Notre Dame.

[19] See chapters by Edna LeRoux and Judith Metz in Stepsis and Liptak, *Pioneer* Healers, pp.39-68; 118-144. Also see Maher, *passim*.

expertise, assisting in the professional development of diocesan schools and establishing academies and colleges. By the mid century, for example, the number of Mercy colleges organized was second only to those begun by the American Jesuits; in 2007, there are still eighteen Mercy colleges. On both secondary and primary levels, outstanding Sisters educators acted as *de facto* supervisors of schools or planners of nation-wide curricula. Many Sisters achieved national prominence in both educational and health care professions. In particular, Sister Mary Josetta Butler, then of the Chicago province, was honored for envisioning the broader picture of creating educational possibilities. Not only was she a college president, but later she initiated and directed the international Better World Movement, collaborated in establishing the North American Sister Formation Movement, the Overseas Education Program, and the Mercy Higher Education Colloquium —all amazing proofs of her Mercy vision, especially regarding improving the lives of women. The healthcare profession would also benefit from excellent Mercy leadership. Sister Mary Maurita Sengelaub, a Detroit Mercy, brought her pre-eminent skills to the field of health care. Early in her career, she oversaw the progress of the twenty-seven hospitals of her province and later worked as consultant to administrators in every Mercy province. Her career was crowned by her becoming an administrator for the Division of Health Affairs of the United States Catholic Conference and, later, as first woman president of the Catholic Health Association. Finally, from the time that Mother Carroll founded a Mercy community in Belize, Central America before the turn of the twentieth century, various Mercy congregations would continue to respond to the founders' convictions about becoming God's messenger of the Good News. Because of the efforts of U.S. congregations, Mercy Sisters have today remained involved in the development of some twenty branches of the Mercy Order in the Caribbean, as well as Central and South America.[20]

To this day, Sisters have addressed immediate social problems. Freed, during the 1960s, in particular, from certain restrictions imposed by the 1918 Canon Law revisions, and in conformity with new legislation developed by both Church officials and community chapters, they have become public witnesses. They have often organized or joined protest marches, especially ones that demonstrated against racial injustice. They have sought out opportunities to live and work among the most disadvantaged in society. They have created numerous national organizations aimed at making fundamental changes. They have led movements on behalf of those politically oppressed or victimized by the latest scourge of disease, often becoming the solitary spokespersons or accepting leadership positions in order to lead the fight for social justice. Their accomplishments, at the very center of human need, would encompass several full-length monographs.

In recent times then, the U.S. Sisters have taken two well-worn pathways in order to follow in the footsteps of their founders. They have responded to the words of their

---

[20] For statistics of Mercy colleges in 2000 (since then one college, Trinity College, Burlington, Vt. has closed) and re S. M. Josetta, see Mary Jeremy Daigler, *Through the Windows: A History of the Work of Higher Education Among the Sisters of Mercy of the Americas* (Scranton, 2000), pp. 19 and 119-121. During its first year, S. Josetta's Overseas Project, organized in 1960, located 30 colleges to host 83 Sisters from 28 foreign communities. See Angelyn Dries, OSF, *The Missionary Movement in American Catholic History* (Orbis, 1998), p. 205. Re S. M. Maurita, see Stepsis and Liptak, pp. 239-249.

Constitution that required them to use every means to live out Christ's challenge to "Follow me." They have remained bearers of the Gospel, missionaries, first responders, women who have stood by the Cross with Christ. What, then, should be said of us and of our intentions for the future of Mercy? Our outreach will bear little fruit unless we see that every project that we engage in today continues to be done with the same hopes and dreams of Mother McAuley in mind. As U.S. Mercies, we must remember what motivated Mother Warde and those who followed her. We must recall their passion.

A recent news article suggests that such a vision of Mercy's future is, indeed, very much alive. It announces the desire of the Burlingame (CA) regional community to put their full power into a massive effort to change lives through Mercy. In the words of the creators of this plan, their "passion for the poor" has impelled them to make "poverty history." Their initiative, called Mercy Beyond Borders, is reminiscent of many other Mercy national organizations that have already proven their worth, including such highly successful initiatives as Mercy Housing, Inc., and the McAuley Institute, both of which have responded, for some twenty years, to the issue of finding affordable housing for the poor. The Burlingame initiative is a logical outgrowth of such efforts, It goes one step further since it desires to address global poverty. For Sister Marilyn Lacey, RSM, its present spokesperson, what is needed for the Mercy community is to reflect the same passion that drew all Mercy founders beyond Ireland to embrace God's beloved poor. It asks that we become part of a "million-nun movement" that connects U.S. Mercy resources with projects already established in developing countries. Embedded in the plan, however, is the same desire, expressed from the time of Mother McAuley, that our Sisters continue, by their lives, to testify to, to witness to, God's incredible Mercy.

Such ambitious hopes remind us of the words of Cardinal Leon Joseph Suenens, whose groundbreaking book, *The Nun in the World*, first published in English in 1963, launched a generation of American Sisters toward what he referred to as "salvific activity." Then he argued that Sisters had to be at the very center of the drama of human salvation and that it was their responsibility to break through the restraints of the past to follow Christ's example through active mission. Sister Lacey's words—that we must "mobilize our Mercy passion"—are in harmony with this view. They are also strangely reminiscent of the ones that compelled Mother Warde to lead a band of Sisters across an ocean. Every Mercy Sister would do well to remember what impelled our first missionaries to cast the fire for the first kindling and made the Sisters "mobilize" their efforts to "give God to the world." Such remembering, indelibly marked as it is upon the soul of the U.S. Mercy community, can help us recall who we were and can be again. In this way, we, too, can cast the fire of our passion and, thereby, proclaim the glad tidings of the Good News.[21]

---

[21] Leon Joseph Cardinal Suenens, *The Nun in the World*, is quoted in Amy L. Koehlinger, *The New Nuns: Racial Justice and Religious Reform in the 1960s* (Cambridge & London, 2007), pp. 38-39. Re the Burlingame proposal regarding global poverty, see Catholic News Service, USCCB, August 31, 2007.

Mercy Fire Kindled In Guyana—April 1894; Still Burning—2007

Mary Noel Menezes, RSM

1. MERCY IN GUYANA – Beginnings, 1894

On 23 April 1894 three Sisters of Mercy, two from Midhurst, West Sussex, England and a Guyanese postulant, enkindled with the fire of Christ's love and zeal, landed in British Guiana bringing with them Mercy unto thousands. The country into which they arrived was a land of "many waters," of vast forests, a land of indigenous peoples, the Amerindians, a land of many needs. This was a land which through the beginnings and development of the sugar industry had brought to its shores African slaves, Portuguese, East Indian and Chinese indentured servants. After the Abolition of Slavery in 1834 and indeed even before that time, efforts had been made to educate the people. Throughout the nineteenth century missionaries from the Society for the Propagation of the Gospel, the Church Missionary Society, and the London Missionary Society were active in the interior of the country, Christianising and educating the Amerindians. In 1847 the Ursuline Sisters arrived and ten years later, the Jesuits, both of whom opened Secondary schools. The need for education was acute and Bishop Anthony Butler of British Guiana invited the Mercy Sisters, who had first gone to Barbados in 1892, to work in the schools. They settled in a poor area in Charlestown, Georgetown, and, in true Mercy fashion, immediately carried out one of the chief functions of the Order, that of teaching.

They began teaching in the government school, later named Carmel R.C. School and shortly after opened a private school for girls in the centre of the city. The school blossomed and later became a grant-in-aid school, later one of the leading elementary schools in the country, Sacred Heart R.C. School. In 1897, in the community room of their Charlestown convent, the Sisters offered four classes in secondary subjects. This marked the beginning of St. Joseph High School which was to become one of the leading Secondary Schools in the country. Many a future vocation to the Sisters of Mercy was nurtured in that school; many future leading citizens of the country received their education from the Mercy Sisters who, as well as providing first-class education, imbued the students with a lasting love of the poor.

With the arrival of more Sisters from the British Isles, the Sisters branched out into other government-aided schools, St. Mary's, Brickdam in the city, Victoria and Kitty on the East Coast, Henrietta, Essequibo and, in the interior, Santa Rosa and Morawhanna. In the 1920s a number of local women joined the community in Charlestown. In 1910 at the request of the Bishop, three Sisters left Charlestown to establish a mission among the Amerindians at Takutu, Rupununi, in the far south of the country near Brazil. One of the Sisters of the Takutu foundation was the later well-known and respected Sr. Teresa Fernandes, M.B.E.

In the 1930s as the educational work increased and the number of Sisters remained constant, the Charlestown community requested permission to join the Sisters of Mercy of the Union in the USA. The Scranton province generously accepted the GUYANA

MISSION as part of their province, and in October 1935 ten Sisters arrived in the country to work in the schools and at the Mahaica Hospital which cared for patients suffering from Hansen's disease. Between 1936 and 1946, nineteen more Sisters arrived to work in the schools, St. John Bosco Orphanage, Mahaica Hospital and St. Joseph Mercy Hospital, Georgetown. They injected new life into the Mercy community and consequently there was a spate of vocations between 1935-1970 when young Guyanese women entered the Mercy Novitiate in Dallas, Pa. and returned after their First or Final Vows to work in their country's schools and orphanage. I can proudly attest to the fact that I was one of those Sisters, working first in the elementary schools, then the High School in Georgetown and later at the University of Guyana. Other Sisters worked at the Government Training College and in a Government Ministry—the latter being an Amerindian trained by the Sisters of Mercy in Santa Rosa.

But education was not the only avenue of mercy. In 1902 the Sisters were asked to take charge of the St. John Bosco Boys Orphanage, at Plaisance, a village 8 miles from the city. One hundred and five years later this work, so dear to the heart of Catherine McAuley, is still under the care of the Sisters, though presently there is a lay administrator trained by the Sisters. Hundreds of boys have experienced the loving care of the Sisters—many return to visit, to remember and show their appreciation.

In 1945 the Mercy Sisters were asked to administer a hospital founded by the Sword of the Spirit Movement. Today, in its 62nd year, St. Joseph Mercy Hospital is one of the leading hospitals in the country, still with a Mercy Sister as its Administrator.

Work Among the Indigenous People
Yes, the major ministries of the Sisters of Mercy were in the service of the poor, sick and uneducated. It is impossible to indicate the breadth, width and extent of the works of Mercy carried on by the Sisters—the visitation of the sick, the comforting of the sorrowful, the compassionate listening, the material and spiritual help offered to so many of our people in every walk of life. But a very special ministry was that among the Amerindian people, numbering approximately 50,000.

Three quarters of the county is forested—indeed Guyana possesses one of the last pristine forests in the world. In those forests and along its many rivers (numbering over 100) and in the savannahs live our Amerindian people of various tribes: the Arawaks, Caribs, Warraus, Patamonas, Macusi, Wai-Wais and others. The hardships shared with these people, living in the "bush" as it was called, *sans* the necessities of life, coping with various insects, being wary of the wild life, the jaguars and other animals, were gladly borne by the Sisters. The saga of this history has been written by one of those Sisters who served for years among the Amerindians. The Santa Rosa Mission in the north-west of the country was first settled by Spanish Arawaks who had been Christianised by the Capuchin missionaries, and during the Bolivarian revolutions in Venezuela had fled for safety into the Guiana territory. Today the majority of Catholics in Guyana are in the interior among the various Amerindian tribes. There is sadness among our 15 Sisters today that we had to leave that mission field in the 1970s due to lack of personnel.

Independence of Guyana

In 1966 when Guyana gained independence the country experienced a period of intense Guyanisation with its by-products of anti-foreignism and, unfortunately, racism. Dr. Robert Moore rightly stated: "In the early 1960s as Guyana approached independence Indians and blacks came into conflict over who would inherit the British mantle of government. The conflict in some parts of the country became intense and brutal."[1]

By the end of the 1960s and into the 1970s large numbers of people migrated to Canada, the USA and the UK. Socialism, under the government of Prime Minister, Linden Forbes Burnham, became the order of the day. Businesses were nationalized; in 1976 so too were the schools. Surprisingly, the Sisters were still encouraged to teach in them. But these Sisters were few, and according to government regulations, due for retirement. The future was, however, not all bleak. There were some vocations and some new vistas, a small school started under the convent's chapel blossomed into the Stella Maris Preparatory School supported by a large number of parents who wanted their children to have the benefit of religious as well as sound education. A Night Shelter for Homeless Women was started, but now, due to scarcity of our Sisters, it is being administered by the Missionaries of Charity.

2. PRESENT MINISTRIES IN THE MIDST OF STRESSES AND STRAINS IN COMMUNITY AND COUNTRY

In Guyana the social fabric of our society is severely eroded. Family life is dysfunctional. The gap between the rich and the poor widens; over 80% of the population exists below the poverty line. Many continue to emigrate. Recent statistics show that 83% of our University graduates migrate in search of greener pastures and away from the ever-increasing violence within the society; those who remain seem to lose the battle with the high cost of living and lack of employment opportunities; they turn to illegal trade in guns, drugs, sex. The drug scene has paved the way for an increase of violent crimes; daily one reads in the media of murders, robberies, and rape. Many young people are in jail; others are walking the streets and begging.

Many agree that much of this deterioration has been the result of the breakdown of the educational system. Guyana, from once boasting the highest rate of literacy in the Caribbean, now has shamefully reached a low. After the government take-over of the schools in 1976, there has been not only an educational, but a moral decline to which most Guyanese attest. Morale among the teachers, not only at the elementary and secondary schools but also at the University, is low. The University, in particular, has suffered from such a malaise.

The concern of the Sisters of Mercy regarding this collapse of the educational system made them consider new avenues where they could especially help the young.

---

[1] Robert Moore, "Colonial Images of Blacks and Indians in Nineteenth Century Guyana" in Bridget Brereton and Kevin A. Yelvington, *The Colonial Caribbean In Transition* (Gainesville: University of Florida Press, 1999), p.126.

They started a Saturday school for young children in the premises of one of the convents in Georgetown. The concern was, above all, for the youth—the youth who had neither the ability nor the funding to attend Secondary Schools. Thus, at the beginning of the twenty-first century in 2000, a Mercy Wings Vocational Centre was opened in one of the poorest areas of the city, to train young men and women in various subjects, above all, Home Economics, Child Care, carpentry, masonry, etc. In the same year a Mercy Boys' Home was established to provide accommodation and continuing support to boys leaving our Orphanage at 16 and having no one and nowhere to go to. Here the boys continue their education at Secondary School or move into various jobs. Some are studying at colleges in the U.S.A. A small school connected to the Orphanage assures the young boys of a solid and basic education—most of the boys at the Orphanage have been abandoned at birth by mothers either unable or unwilling to support their offspring. All these works are generously supported by many benefactors, both from within the country and overseas who were once Mercy students. Much financial help is also given by members of the diplomatic corps and local businessmen. The Sisters have always subscribed to Catherine's dictum that one must connect the rich to the poor. In no other way could we help the many people within our care.

Guyana ranks third in the world after Africa and Haiti in the high incidence of HIV/AIDS. Programmes and projects are in place at St. Joseph Mercy Hospital to give positive help and medical support to those suffering from the disease. A Mobile Clinic, operating from Mercy Hospital and with the service of its doctors and nurses, serves the poor and sick in the outlying areas of the city. Recently, a new project to help sick and disabled Amerindian children, who are flown in from the interior, has been started.

Previous mention was made of the work of the Sisters of Mercy at Mahaica Hospital among the patients suffering from Hansen's disease. In 1970, due to rabid Guyanisation (the Sisters were American) as well as lack of Sister personnel, the Sisters of the Baltimore Province in the USA, who had administered Mahaica, had to withdraw. It was a sad day for the patients for whom the Sisters were not only nurses, but also friends, comforters and confidantes. After the Sisters left the Hospital, Sisters Noel and Celine Marie continued to visit the patients, supporting them and, with the help of benefactors, assisting them in their needs. Over the past few years, other Sisters, among them the Administrator of Mercy Hospital, have also visited the patients.

Since 1970 the needs of the patients have increased. As successive governments became more and more strapped for cash, the Mahaica Hospital has been low on their priority list. Above all, the government, as well as most of the Guyanese population, still have the biblical concept of leprosy and do not visit the compound. Thus the patients rely on the Sisters, and have done so, over the past years, for basic supplies, bandages, pain killers, various needed flashlights, thermos flasks, even wheelchairs, refrigerators and TV! The Sisters help to finance hospital bills and funeral expenses. Another work of mercy here is to literally bury the dead as the patients are unable to assist. Most of the patients are immobile, blind and generally helpless. This work is a key one which, undoubtedly, must continue throughout the twenty-first century as long as these wonderfully patient people need comfort, hope and joy.

Nevertheless, the patients have a wonderful philosophy of life and are cheerful. For us Mercies it is a tonic to visit these people, "the outcasts of society" as they are considered, who have nothing of the world's goods, the forgotten ones in our society, yet who show us how to be grateful to God for blessings received through friends. Bereft of home, of family, of sight, of limbs, they look for Mercy in its every expression.

3. MERCY HOPES AND PLANS INTO THE TWENTY-FIRST CENTURY; CHANGED SCENES; UNCHANGING MERCY

Every day one reads in the headlines of the world's newspapers of torture, rape, and death in every shape—the massacre of the old, the brutal killing of children, the destruction of hundreds of villages leaving thousands of refugees and homeless people:

Nations at war	Families at war
Tribes at war	Individuals at war
Classes at war	

Millions are without food, water, shelter, work, medicine, schools, and without a future, without a chance, without a hope. Never before was Mercy needed more in every area of life, in every country where we live and serve. Never before in Guyana where the trends of violence, drug-related crime, dysfunctional families, street children, the escalation of HIV/AIDS and racial and political disunity are rife, a microcosm of global trends, were people so looking for Mercy.

The future of any country lies with its youth. Thus Mercy must, above all, reach out to the youth of Guyana. As we no longer work in the schools per se, we have tried to reach them and are still trying to reach them through the work at the Mercy Wings Vocational Centre, at the Mercy Boys' Home, involving our Mercy Volunteer Corps, young people from the USA, who give immeasurable help in counseling, retreats, working with the boys at the orphanage, bringing a breath of "fresh air" and hope to our youth. Extremely conscious of the drug environment in the country and peer pressure on the youth, Mercy sees the needs of youth as crucial. With only 15 Sisters, and of the 15 only 5 in active ministry, we have to have a realistic approach to the varying needs. But those few of us can, at least, teach our young people to reach out to the other with open hands, not clenched fists, not hands holding knives or guns.

In trying to show others the way to peace we Mercy Sisters have to be in the forefront of helping to stop domestic violence and violence in general. Some of us belong to various organizations, among them the Guyana Human Rights Association and Women in Black, which protest peacefully in street demonstrations against violence, especially against the abuse of women and children. In dealing with Ministers of the government, with educators, with businessmen, we Mercy Sisters still find ourselves in a position to influence them in some small way, particularly as many of them had been educated in our Mercy schools and by Mercy at University level.

In Guyana there are multitudinous religious sects, apart from the main Christian ones. Sisters are involved in the ecumenical movement in the country, working with groups and attending ecumenical prayers and working sessions. Political and racial disunity is rife. Because of a personal relationship with members of the various political parties, a few of the Sisters serve on national committees and, in a very small way, help to bring peace in those pockets. If peacemaking belongs to the heart of our Christian vocation, how much more does it belong to our Mercy vocation? As Henri Nouwen so strongly states:

> When I listen to the sounds of greed, violence, rape, torture, murder and indiscriminate destruction, I hear a long, sustained cry coming from all the corners of the world. It is a cry of a deeply wounded humanity that no longer knows a safe dwelling place but wanders around the planet in a desperate search for love and comfort.[2]

Such a cry is being heard in our country today, and this is the challenge for Mercy there, to listen and respond to the many cries of anguish, to speak out against injustice, to bring hope, comfort and, above all, peace to our people in the schools, the orphanage, the hospital, the leprosarium, continuing the mandate of Catherine McAuley who always stressed "the kind word, the gentle compassionate look, the patient hearing of sorrows."

Indeed, the multitudinous needs throughout the world as noted in all the papers submitted are staggering. No group of people, no matter how well-disposed and willing, could hope to apply the bandages to every wound in their society. Again, we are in no position to stop a nuclear holocaust, but each Sister of Mercy in every single corner of the globe, enkindled by Christ's love, can continue to share that love as He did, in healing both mental and physical wounds, feeding the hungry, comforting the sorrowful.

How well Mary Sullivan captured the essence of these goals:

> If I were to summarize in the broadest terms Catherine McAuley's embrace of cultural diversity and her legacy of hospitality to strangers....I think Catherine McAuley would say: This is the way we must do it—one person at a time; one answering of the figurative doorbell, one opening of the figurative door, one embrace of the stranger, one welcoming of the other, one sharing of our bread and milk—one person at a time.[3]

The nineteenth century of Catherine McAuley differed in many respects, but the twenty-first century is no different in the need for Mercy at every turn, for Christ continues to come to our door in many guises. The fire enkindled by those three Mercy Sisters in British Guiana in 1894 still burns brightly in the country, though not as widely spread.

---

[2] Henri Nouwen, *Peacework: Prayer, Resistance, Community* (New York: Orbis Books, 2005), pp. 28-29.
[3] Mary Sullivan, RSM, "Welcoming the Stranger: The Kenosis of Catherine McAuley," *MAST Journal* 6, no.3 (Summer 1996), p. 17.

Each Sister has to ask herself continually: "What is the Gospel according to me, a Sister of Mercy?" Do I always show by my life that the Gospel is GOOD NEWS?"[4]

May I conclude by quoting Article 7 of our Mercy Constitutions in the Americas:

> We carry out our mission of mercy guided by prayerful consideration of the needs of our time, Catherine McAuley's preferential love for the poor and her special concern for women, the pastoral priorities of the universal and local church and our talents, resources and limitations.

What an agenda for Mercy in any century!

---

[4] Mary Noel Menezes, RSM, "Fostering Faith in Caribbean Culture," *Cultures and Faith*, Vol. II, No.1 Pontificum Consilium de Cultura, Citta del Vaticano, Rome, 1944, p. 43.

The Political Ministry of Women: An Australian Perspective

Sophie McGrath, RSM

Response to Social Analysis papers from an Australian historical perspective

This paper is an historical response from an Australian perspective to the statistics Elizabeth Davis quotes in her paper concerning the proportion of seats held by women in the following parliaments: Canada 20.8%, Australia 24.7%, the United Kingdom 19.7%, the United States 16.3%, United Nations 9.4%.[1]

While all of these figures are small, among the countries cited Australia has the greatest percentage of women in parliament at the national level. This is not unexpected since, while New Zealand was the first country in which women won the right to vote (1893), it was in South Australia in 1894 that women first won the right not only to vote but to be voted for, and this ultimately led, after the federation of the Australian states, to Australian women being granted the right to vote and be voted for at the national level.[2]

The Australian Pioneers

Across the centuries there is evidence of men who supported women in various ways, especially with regard to obtaining an education and who valued women as spiritual counselors. On the whole, however, men have resented women assuming power beyond the family. This was the experience of a significant group of women in Australia, many of whom were Catholics, who had worked for the vote. Anxious to promote their social welfare agenda they chose to align themselves with the Labor Party whose policies they considered resonated with theirs. The Labor men, however, foiled their attempts to become equal members, and it was with difficulty the women established what was called the NSW Labor Women's Organising Committee in 1904, the first of its type in Australia and, one could safely say, the world.

On the occasion of their Silver Jubilee this Committee produced a brochure in which they recalled: 'Recognition of our worth in the political world was slow within our own (Labor) movement and we were five years working before the Annual Conference (which controls our forces) granted us a Constitution.' By 1909 the Committee had been recognized as a constitutional portion of the ALP and granted representation at the annual Conference. Indeed on the occasion of the celebration of their Silver Jubilee, J. H. Scullin, the Prime Minister of Australia at the time, acknowledged that it was the women who had been largely responsible for the first national success of the Labor Party. The women recalled: 'Many days were spent in walking from door to door – a task which oftentimes meant covering a whole electorate in order to place the policy of Labor in the homes of women of the city. In the country our noble band of women went forth with little or no provision made for their comfort.'[3]

---

[1] Elizabeth M. Davis, 'How Can We Dare Wisdom and Mercy in the Mosaic of Our Realities' Mercy International Research Conference, 2007.

[2] A. Oldfield, *Woman Suffrage in Australia – A Gift or a Struggle?* (Melbourne: Cambridge University Press, 1992), 59 et seq.

[3] NSW Labor Women's Organising Committee, Silver Jubilee Brochure (1929), 9.

The women rejoiced in their achievements: 'What a reward we have reaped – and how hopeless the task looked when we set out! Without money, and with the whole of the press against us – what a handicap! The overcoming of these handicaps has realized for us full citizen's rights in all walks of life, the organization of women in every industry: the Early Closing Act, the Minimum Wage Act, the 44 hour working week, shop and factory legislation, the appointment of inspectors to guard awards, old-age and invalid pensions, the Maternity Allowance Act, widows' pensions and family endowment. Still there is much left undone. That is for the future workers to undertake. The task is noble and self-elevating. The CAUSE is ever worthwhile. Carry on the work handed down by the pioneer women!' [4]

The first President, Kate Dwyer (married, a dedicated Catholic and lifelong member of the NSW Catholic Women's League) exhorted the women of 1929 in her Silver Jubilee message: 'As women are the home-makers they should be given every encouragement and scope to become nation builders, for the interests of home and nation are so interwoven one cannot be separated from the other . . . . Women of the Labor Movement, remember that whilst progressing you must look to securing your rightful place among the councilors and legislators of your country. You have ability, capacity and grit.' [5]

Annie Golding, also a dedicated Catholic and a leading pioneer in the campaign to attain the vote for women in Australia, declared: ' ...it is fitting that a few remarks should be made by me – one of the pioneers who aided in that strenuous struggle to bring women on to the political horizon. There is no apology needed for them being there. The world sent out a 'S.O.S' – and they responded. The only regret is that they are still on the outer rim of political life. Some should be in both the State and Commonwealth Parliaments, as legislation controls every phase of human existence from the cradle to the grave. Under its administration come marriage, health, food, housing, education and hours of labor, also recreation and leisure.'

Among other things she added: 'Remember, in the past our colossal emporiums were partly built upon unpaid child labor, and lessons should be learned from that bad old past. Pioneer women of the Labor Movement throughout Great Britain and the Commonwealth, undeterred by the bogeys of convention and tradition, bravely blazed the track, and infused a soul into Labor by their onward march, and raised a standard for other women to follow.' [6]

Women Into Politics, Inc
Despite all the valiant efforts of these pioneer women, their successors in Australia a century later are gravely concerned and took the initiative in 1998 to organize the group Women Into Politics (WIP), Inc. They explained:

---

[4] Silver Jubilee Brochure, 9.
[5] Silver Jubilee Brochure, 10.
[6] Silver Jubilee Brochure, 10.

Women have had the vote for nearly 100 years. As yet this has not been translated into political power, nor has equal representation been achieved. Women do not have control over public matters which govern their social and economic well-being. Women have little influence on public policy or public decision making on the great matters of the day – on economic management, employment, war and peace, the environment, social welfare measures, foreign affairs or foreign aid. Women continue to rely on the good will of men in high office for their well-being.[7]

WIP lamented: 'Until those in power are persuaded to reform our political institutions, and until women are approximately half of our parliaments and decision makers, Australian women will continue to be lobbyists, not main players.'[8]

It is significant that WIP, in the healthy tradition of its pioneer forebears, cooperates across political parties and religious affiliations, pointing out: 'One of the strengths of the (our) organization is that it is accepted as non-partisan by women in and out of the political parties, and we are able to have the benefits of a range of ideas.'[9]

WIP concluded their Report on the eve of the 21st century:

The growing discussion of how to both retain or regain civil society and accommodate powerful financial markets, how to do the research that will show that social capital is worthwhile, that social gain can benefit business, will no doubt continue and develop, if only because women recognize the necessity for balance in the world of affairs. We will all have to develop new ways of operating to gain for women what is our right, and perhaps to re-invent old strategies. We still do live in a community, not an economy![10]

Alas, in its most recent Report (2006-2007), WIP regretted:

The increase in numbers has slowed .... this has been a cause of frustration to women's hopes that the influence of women would become more equal.... The number of women on the boards of the top 100 corporations remains abysmally low. Meanwhile the 2006 – 2007 year has seen ongoing decline in standards, as Australian politics grows unashamedly more ruthless, less reliant on merit or on rational argument, research and consultation, and more related to self-interest, caprice and public relations 'spin', as it is now called, than to intelligent policy development.

---

[7] http://www.womenintopolitics.org.au/object.html.

[8] WIP website, Objectives and Rationale, 2.

[9] Edith Stein, a strong feminist, was most insightful in her analysis of the nature of man the male. She noted from experience in her own country that women parliamentarians from opposing parties could work together more effectively than the men on projects for the common good. See E. Stein, *Woman – The Collected Works of Edith Stein* Vol.II, translated by Freda Mary Oben (Washington: ICS Publications, 1987). For a statement of strong feminist commitment see E.Stein, *Life in a Jewish Family – An Autobiography*, edited by Dr L.Gelber and Romaeus Leuven OCD, translated by Josephine Koeppel OCD (Washington: ICS Publications, 1986).

[10] WIP Annual Report, 1998-1999, 3.

Some columnists have written openly critical pieces about abuses of parliamentary process that appeared in the major newspapers.[11]

A challenging reality

A significant development in the saga of promoting the political influence of women in Australia was the resignation from parliament of three very capable, successful women for family reasons, all had young children.[12]

It is pertinent at this stage to draw attention to the fact that there is much in the news in recent years concerning the problems associated with infertility and the problems which arise from women having their babies at a later age as well as the trauma involved with IVF fertility treatments.

Relevant historical background

As we look through the historical lens in connection with these developments our attention is drawn to Betty Friedan and her 1963 publication *The Feminine Mystique*. Many women throughout the western world resonated with the central thesis of this seminal publication: '…our culture does not permit women to accept or gratify their basic need to grow and fulfill their potentialities as human beings, a need which is not solely defined by their sexual role.'[13] At that time Betty Friedan held that women should not have to choose between marriage and a career, it was merely a matter of setting up a new life plan in terms of one's whole life as a woman.[14]

It is significant that, though Betty Friedan's *The Feminine Mystique* is well known, little attention has been given to her publication, *The Second Phase,* in which she assessed with great honesty and insight developments in the women's movement from 1960 to 1980.

In this latter publication Friedan explained that she had gradually become aware that something was 'off', 'out of focus', 'going wrong' in the terms by which the rising generation were trying to live the equality for which she and her associates had fought. She explained that those who had established the women's movement had already had their families, but young women starting out on promising but demanding careers found that they barely had time to develop a relationship let alone care for a family. Friedan observed that she 'sensed the exhilaration of "superwomen" giving way to a tiredness, a certain brittle disappointment.' She also deplored the fact that many married women were often forced by economic circumstances to work and were not free to have a child.[15]

Friedan admitted that she and her conferees had been naive; they had not realized the complexity of the task ahead of them. She also lamented that too many women politicians

---

[11] WIP, Annual Report 2006 – 2007.

[12] Federal Parliament: Natasha Stott-Despoja (Democrat), Jackie Kelly (Liberal); NSW Parliament: Carmel Tebutt (Labor). The latter two are Catholics with a strong Mercy component in their education.

[13] B. Friedan, *The Feminine Mystique* (Penguin, 1965), 68.

[14] Friedan, *Feminine Mystique*, 297.

[15] B.Friedan, *The Second Stage* (London: Michael Joseph Ltd, 1982), 21, 22, 26 -29.

submitted to the male political machinery. But what else could they do when they did not have the numbers? She observed: 'I believe it's over, that first stage of the women's movement. And yet the larger revolution, evolution, liberation that the women's movement set off, has barely begun.'[16]

Friedan held that the central thesis of *The Feminine Mystique* still held, i.e. that women had to have scope for developing their talents and serving humanity beyond the home, but she considered:

> ... the second stage cannot be seen in terms of women alone, our separate personhood or equality with men. The second stage involves coming to terms with the family – new terms with love and with work. The second stage may not even be a women's movement. Men may be at the cutting edge of the second stage. The second stage has to transcend the battle for equal power in institutions. The second stage will restructure institutions and transform the nature of power itself . . . .[17]

Betty Friedan summed up the situation: 'How do we transcend the polarisation between women and women and between women and men to achieve the new wholeness that is the promise of feminism and get on with solving the concrete, practical everyday problems of living, working and loving as equal persons? This is the personal and political business of the second stage.'[18] She recognized the fear of women which many men have and which damages the relationship between men and women. To illustrate her point she quoted the comment of a West Point man looking for more in life. He had confessed: 'Men are jealous and afraid of women, maybe envious of their power. It may sound corny but there is power in women's ability to create life, closeness to life, that men don't have, always chasing power, in the company, in the army . . . .'[19] Friedan also declared:

> I believe that 'masculine' leadership with its emphasis upon competition and a clear win-lose is not appropriate to the second stage of human liberation. Rather I advocate a leadership style generally perceived as 'feminine' but open to use by either men or women. It is based on synthesizing, intuitive, qualitative thinking and a contextual, relational power style.' I advocate its use because its concern is with presenting the whole picture rather than concentrating on a given task; growth and the quality of life,

---

[16] Ibid., 30 -33.

[17] Friedan, *The Second Stage*, 34. Friedan also explained that the emergence of sexual politics in the women's movement in the 1970s was a product of the experience of the younger liberated women of the 1960s, which was in many ways destructive. She held that these women were reacting against the early male leaders of the radical student and countercultural movements of the sixties, who were more blatantly male chauvinist 'pigs' than their conservative fathers – 'Man' became 'the enemy'. Friedan also lamented Kate Millett's attitude to motherhood and family life in her influential publication, *Sexual Politics*, in which 'man' is portrayed as 'the oppressor' driven by 'metaphysical cannibalism'; he is a 'natural predator' and pregnancy is 'the temporary deformation of the body for the sake of the species' and the foetus is a 'parasite' and 'uninvited guest', 54 -56.

[18] Friedan, *The Second Stage*, 47.

[19] Friedan, *The Second Stage*, 167.

rather than fixed quantities and the status quo; the sharing of internal resources and the establishment of interdependent adaptive relationships of support.[20]

In her honest critiquing of the 1960s women's movement Betty Friedan was not alone.[21] In recent times a worthy successor of Betty Friedan has emerged—Naomi Wolf, who published the insightful *The Beauty Myth* in 1990.[22] This young woman, after experiencing the stresses of the life of a successful, politically engaged, married woman, discovered for herself the wisdom of Betty Friedan, sharing it in her 2005 publication *The Treehouse*. In this she concluded: ' Not that there is no value in politics; but I was finding out in my own daily struggles – to be a good wife and mother, to be a decent teacher – that if politics was not based on the heart's wisdom, it was arid.'[23]

What Now?

This brings us back to the three young women in Australian politics who recently retired for family reasons and leaves us facing the problem of the dearth of women in politics in the English speaking western world where the Sisters of Mercy have ministered and continue mainly to minister.

In Australia it leaves us still challenged by the words of the pioneer suffrage worker Annie Golding in 1904: '... the world has suffered through want of the dual influence. Only the masculine was cultivated. In all lands property, military glory, and lust for power were the highest ideals. The humanizing influences – sentiment, family love, and other domestic virtues – were relegated to an inferior place.'[24]

It was the great old USA suffrage worker, Elizabeth Cady Stanton, who asserted at the end of her long life: 'I consider the hey-day of woman's life is the shady side of fifty, when the vital forces, heretofore expended in other ways, are garnered in the brain, when their thoughts and sentiments flow out into broader channels . . . .'[25]

---

[20] Friedan, *The Second Stage*, 250.

[21] There is a surprising amount in Germaine Greer's 1970 publication, *The Female Eunuch,* which resonates with many aspects of Betty Friedan's 1980 *Second Stage.* Alas, the somewhat outlandish behaviour and statements of Germaine Greer have distracted and detracted from that which is intrinsically valuable in her work.

[22] N.Wolf, *The Beauty Myth,* first published, London: Chatto & Windus, 1990; London: Vintage, 1991. In this she exposed the exploitation of women by the marketing industry. She acknowledged that though there has always been a degree of 'beauty myth' in the lives of women it 'grows ever more influential and pervasive because of what is now conscious market manipulation.' She went on to name the multi-million dollar diet, cosmetic, cosmetic surgery, and pornography industries which have 'arisen from the capital made out of unconscious anxieties, and are in turn able, through their influences on mass culture, to use, stimulate, and reinforce the hallucination in a rising economic spiral,' 17.

[23] N. Wolf, *The Treehouse* (London: Virago Press, 2006), 251.

[24] A. Golding, 'The Evolution of Woman and Her Capabilities,' *Proceedings of the Australasian Catholic Congress* (Melbourne, 1904), 562.

[25] Cady Stanton, *Eighty Years and More of Reminiscences, 1815 – 1897,* first published London: T. Fisher Unwin, 1898; reprinted New York: Schocken Books, 1971,447. The Australian, Annie Golding, stated in her 1904 paper 'The Evolution of Women and Their Possibilities' : 'America led the way in the higher education of women .... Later ideals of rights and privileges were pioneered by Lucretia Mott, Susan B. Anthony and Mrs Cady Stanton.' *Proceedings of the Australasian Catholic Congress (*Melbourne, 1904), 563.

As we ponder the problem of increasing the influence of women in parliament, it is suggested that we give attention to this reality in the life-cycle of women highlighted by Elizabeth Cady Stanton over a century ago. Most women want to marry and have the love and companionship of a man and family, and they are most likely to be able to do this if they marry in their early 20s. They also have the need and the responsibility to serve the community beyond the family. For most women major responsibilities in the wider community can best be undertaken in middle-age. With solid initial and appropriate ongoing education, which accommodates family demands, and with husbands genuinely involved in the family, these middle-aged women will bring to their political service invaluable lived family experience, which the Australian Catholic married suffrage worker Kate Dwyer extolled in 1929, as mentioned previously.

There is a heartening ray of hope in Australia in connection with men to facilitate this development: Morris Iemma, the present Premier of NSW, who has young children, earlier in 2007 announced to his cabinet that he wanted to organize certain meetings around his family commitments. This was an historically significant incident. Predictably, it caused a stir among some older men politicians who questioned Iemma's commitment to his job. Also many men in Australia are attending the birth of their children, and it is noted that the Tressillian Movement in Australia is now including fathers in the sessions concerning problem babies where previously they had given these only to mothers. There is, too, a growing movement in Australia to encourage and support fathers, initiated by Warwick Marsh, the founder of the Fatherhood Foundation.[26]

Where do the Sisters of Mercy stand in relation to this? Clearly Catherine McAuley was concerned for the welfare of society and saw women as playing a crucial role in this. They needed to be empowered by the acquiring of skills to become economically independent as single women and thereby in a position to make more free choices. As is well known, Catherine saw the education of women as fundamental to the welfare of the family, the building block of society. The Mercy Sisters were noted from the beginning for being prepared to do what was necessary in particular circumstances to promote the common good[27] and they therefore became involved in health and social welfare work in addition to teaching. But always education was seen as the basic means of promoting long term solutions to problems in all areas of ministry.

In Australia it is clear that women religious generally and the Sisters of Mercy in particular have made a significant contribution in the educational field. It was noted in the 1980s that almost all the women who has risen to high leadership positions in the public service in NSW and at the Commonwealth level in Australia were 'convent educated.'[28]

---

[26] Added to these 'signs of hope' are the Men's Shed movement, the establishment of the Fatherhood Foundation (see www.kairos.com.au) and developments in men's spirituality. See David Tacey, *Remaking Men – the revolution in masculinity* (Melbourne: Viking, 1997) and books by Richard Rohr.

[27] A. Fahey, 'Female Asceticism in the Catholic Church: A Case-Study of Nuns in Ireland in the Nineteenth Century', PhD thesis, University of Illinois at Urbana-Champaign, 1982.

[28] Carmel Niland (President of the Anti-Discrimination Board of NSW), *SHMA*, Vol 2, No 1, 1984, 4. The Mercy 'convent schools' were noted among those mentioned.

Presently in Australia in the forthcoming federal election the Prime Minister is being challenged in his electorate by Maxine McKew, a 50 year old highly successful political journalist and TV presenter, an ex-student of the Sisters of Mercy's All Hallows College in Brisbane. It is relevant to note that though married she has had no children. The sample polling gives her a high chance of success.[29]

Thinking about fostering and providing for the political service of women in their middle-age leads to the raising of the following issues and challenges:

* The development of the mentality among the wider community generally and women in particular that such an evolution is natural, organic and to be encouraged.
* The development of a theology that will inspire and sustain a spirituality of service at the leadership level especially in politics.
* The involvement of both men and women educators in this process.
* The working for family-friendly parliamentary structures.

Some current resources of the Sisters of Mercy in Australia to be used to promote the above:

* The Mercy Secondary School Association which functions both nationally and internationally.
* Influence in primary schools through promotion of the Mercy charism in former Mercy schools as invited by the principal and encouraged by the Diocesan Education Offices, e.g., involvement in staff education days.
* Influence in Management Boards of secondary schools, and involvement in staff formation.
* Influence at a tertiary level through involvement in teacher and nursing education.

While this paper is necessarily limited in scope and has dealt directly with only one aspect of Elizabeth Davis's paper, it is considered that the issue being addressed is basic to the addressing of many other problems raised in the social analysis papers, e.g., Anne Itotia states that the main cause of Kibera's dire state is 'international and national policies.'[30] Presently Australia's foreign aid budget is abysmally low and the prevailing economic policy of the government supports exploitive international policies in relation to developing countries. It is expected that with more women involved in political decision making this situation would be redressed. It is pertinent to note that Pius XII declared after World War II:

---

[29] Maureen McGuirk, RSM (North Sydney) knows this political candidate well and reports that she attributes a lot of her success to her education at All Hallows and cites a particular sister who was especially influential.

[30] Anne Itotia, 'Africa Urbanisation and Proliferation of Slums – A Case Study of Kibera, Nairobi,' International Mercy Research Conference.

If more attention were paid to the anxieties of feminine sentiment, the work of consolidating peace would move ahead more rapidly. Those nations which are well-supplied with the goods of this world would be more hospitable and more generous toward those who are in want. Those in charge of public property would be more cautious in their dealings. With women in charge certainly the organizations set up to take care of community needs in the fields of housing, education, hospitals and employment would get more done and be more foresighted.[31]

---

[31] O. M. Liebard, *Official Catholic Teachings: Love and Sexuality* (Wilmington, N. Carolina: McGrath Publishing Co., 1987), 188.

Mercy Embodied/Embodied Mercy as Justice, Wisdom and Holiness

Elaine Wainwright, RSM

The theme of the conference, "Fire cast on the earth—kindling" is an evocative one. Catherine McAuley draws language and imagery from the Gospel of Luke to capture the power of mercy as it is cast onto the earth like a fireball, and to turn our attention to the one who casts it. She juxtaposes this with the word 'kindling' which shifts the mood of the metaphor from power to the imperceptible catching alight, the initial bursting forth of a flame, the tending and nurturing that the fire might take hold. Imperceptibly indeed, she has nuanced the Lukan verse in which Jesus says: "I came to bring fire to the earth, and how I wish it were already kindled!" (Luke 12:49), so that the Lukan text now echoes through Catherine's text and through us and our texts as we gather to reflect on "being mercy into the twenty-first century". It echoes, however, with the nuances Catherine gave it for her times and it has echoed and will echo through us in our times as we engage this theme, informed as we are by all that is our world as we have sought to describe and analyze it and all that we have focused into our articulations of the call to mercy into the twenty-first century.

Circles and Spirals of Storytelling

We are drawn into circles and spirals of storytellers and storytelling. We are being animated by, becoming aglow with passion[1] as we draw into the spiraling process of our meaning-making, the lives and commitments, the passion and the pain of women and men of mercy—in the barrios of Brazil; in the 'informal settlements' of Boksburg, South Africa; in the high-rise United Nations buildings of New York City; on the islands of Tonga, Samoa, New Zealand and Australia where silenced voices seek to be heard and justice to be done for the *tua*, for the first peoples, and for those who are diaspora in this region; among those living in poverty and dying of AIDS in Kibera, Nairobi, and across the African continent; beside those working with and on behalf of the planet; and with those educating for justice and change anywhere in our world. Mercy has been kindled, mercy is kindling, mercy seeks re-kindling as it is cast anew on the earth in this new century with its poverties and its potentialities, with its powers and its perversities.

We have heard and we will continue to hear the voices of our sisters, the voices of our partners in mercy, the voices of all those with and among whom we live and work. It is this that calls forth a new storytelling as did Catherine's time. We carry all of this with us in our consciousness, as we have heard it articulated in our initial paragraphs describing how we hear the call to mercy, as we heard it particularized in the papers of Elizabeth Davis, Anne Itotia, Senolita Vakatā, Ana Maria Pineda, and Elizabeth McMillan. We will do as Catherine did as we tell our sacred story anew, letting that story echo in our re-

---

[1] Among the meanings that *The Australian Concise Oxford Dictionary* (J. M. Hughes, P. A. Mitchell and W. S. Ramson, eds; 2nd ed.; Melbourne: Oxford University Press, 1992), 620, gives to the word 'kindle' are "arouse or inspire" and "become animated, glow with passion."

telling, letting traces of that story intersect in wonderfully creative ways to shape a new tapestry of texts, a newly woven story or stories.[2]

With all this consciousness, I want to dialogue in this paper with the gospel of Matthew,[3] to explore *embodied mercy/mercy embodied*. I will draw into that exploration mercy's intimate connection with wisdom as seen in Elizabeth Davis' paper and as is evident in the gospel of Matthew.[4] I will investigate mercy's connection with justice as the gospel of Matthew connects them and as that connection echoes through Ps 84 and the prophetic literature as well as through much of our theologizing as women of mercy over recent decades. I will also indicate the connection between mercy and holiness, a connection made recently by Joan Chittister in one of her lectures in Auckland and which can be drawn into the fractal imaging of embodied mercy as we know it and seek to live it.[5]

Encountering Embodied Mercy

The Jesus of any one of the gospels can be imaged in multiple ways. Each of the evangelists/storytellers sought to tell Jesus' story and their community's story as they intertwined. We now re-tell that story as our story, as the Jesus story, the Matthean story, and our story intertwine. As we dialogue with our tradition in and through the Matthean gospel story, we can encounter the Jesus of this story as mercy embodied or as embodied mercy.

One of the earliest metaphoric namings of Jesus is Emmanu-el or G*d with us.[6] That G*d who can be imagined in many ways, is called *Rachamim*, the Womb-compassionate one

---

[2] One of the images that I wish to use not only to inform this paper but to inform our process of theologizing in a postmodern age, described as it has been by Elisabeth M. Davis, "How Can We Dare Wisdom and Mercy in the Mosaic of our Realities," 22-24 of this volume, is that of the fractal or the Mandelbrot Set. From a foundational imprint, multiple spirals emerge going in different directions forming the most wonderful patterns as modern computers image a mathematical formula that seeks to explain aspects of our universe. In the same way, from the foundational imprint of the gospel, multiple ways of theologizing and living mercy will emerge – this may be one way of celebrating the "prophetic spirituality of life" (Davis, "How Can We Dare," 23) rather than a neo-totalitarianism that would seek to make all the same. For further exploration of these fractal images see http://www.math.utah.edu/~pa/math/mandelbrot/ mandelbrot.html#applet (Accessed 3.9.07) and for examples of the design see http://images.google.co.nz/ images?q=Fractals&svnum=10&um=1&hl=en&ie=UTF-8&start=20&sa=N (Accessed 3.9.07).

[3] I am very conscious of the extremely limited aspect of this paper in which I have had to choose to engage with the Gospel of Matthew in a very limited way and through that the biblical tradition in an even more limited way. Our theologizing could engage with and needs to engage with the manifold threads of mercy and justice that weave their way through our sacred story.

[4] Davis, "How Can We Dare," 13-26.

[5] Joan Chittister used the phrase "keepers of mercy's flame" which resonates with the imagery of this conference as she explored holiness in today's world in a paper delivered recently in Auckland. See also Nico Koopman, "Confessing and Embodying the Holiness of the Church in the Context of Glocality. A Rage for Justice," paper delivered to the ANZATS Conference, Canberra, 8 – 12 July 2007, in which he used the phrase "a holy rage for justice" which he takes from the Danish theologian Kaj Munk.

[6] One of the ways which Elisabeth Schüssler Fiorenza has proposed to interrupt our familiarity with the naming of the divine and its accompanying male imaging is to write that name in this way: G*d (see Elisabeth Schüssler Fiorenza, *Jesus—Miriam's Child, Sophia's Prophet: Critical Issues in Feminist Christology* (New York: Continuum, 1994), n. 3, 191. I will use this nomenclature throughout this paper to invite us as women of mercy to be/come deeply aware of the power and pervasiveness of dominant male images in our consciousness, woven into our spirituality and theology and given expression in our language

in the Hebrew Bible (Ex 33:19, 34:6; Is 30:18; 49:13, 15; 54:10), the one who called a people out of Egypt (Matt 2:15, quoting Hos 11:1-4, a poem replete with female images of the divine).[7] But such an early naming of G*d's *rachamim* as embodied in Jesus is in anticipation. Indeed, as a newly born baby, Jesus, with his parents, is under threat politically from a puppet king, Herod. Like so many children around our globe today, Jesus is displaced at birth. His parents must flee with him for their very lives. We are not told of the reception these refugees received in Egypt. As readers, however, we fill in the gaps in the story, recognizing that the survival of this family and their capacity for choosing to return to their homeland as its political climate changed points to a possible favourable reception in Egypt. What this story does, therefore, is to situate embodied mercy in a context of political upheaval and its incumbent displacement of peoples.[8] It is a context that calls out for the fire of *rachamim* to be cast on the earth and for the G*d who called "his [sic] son" out of Egypt (Matt 2:15 quoting Hos 11:1) to call all the displaced of our world out of their exile through those who today embody *rachamim*.[9]

A second aspect of the fire of *rachamim* cast on the earth and made visible in the birth of Jesus is embodiment and materiality.[10] Jesus, while being of a spirit that is holy (1:18, 20), is of the body of Mary, his mother (Matt 2:11, 13, 14, 20, 21). She, in her turn, stands in a line of women who give birth from their bodies—Tamar (1:3), Rahab and Ruth (1:5) and Bathsheba (1:6) and the many unnamed women—birth to sons as the story's emphasis suggests but also birth to daughters. The embodiment of mercy turns attention to the material—the materiality of bodies but also the materiality of the universe. The story of embodied mercy is not only located in human persons. It is also located in place—the place where the child was [2:9], the star that guided the wise ones to this place (2:2, 7, 9, 10), a place which is then called *oikos* or house (2:11). The wise ones then return to their own country or region (their *chōran*). One cannot tell the story of embodied mercy, one cannot be embodied mercy, kindling the fire cast on the earth, apart from location, apart from the materiality of all that makes up that location. Mercy into the twenty-first century means that this materiality needs to be honoured and valued as is the

---

and symbol systems. I believe that unless we shift patterns of thought and language, we will not be able to change structures and systems of power on behalf of all those, especially women and children, whom such language marginalizes and renders invisible and hence of no account.

[7] For one exploration of this imagery, see Elaine M. Wainwright, "The *Rachamim*/Womb compassion of Israel's God: Shared," paper given at the 2006 conference of the Australian Health and Welfare Chaplains Association, Brisbane, Australia, 9-13 July. This can be accessed at http://www.centacarebrisbane.net.au/ pastoral_ministries/hospital.php. This paper demonstrates how *rachamim* intersects with many other ways of naming the G*d of womb-compassion, one of which is *chesed* or covenant fidelity.

[8] Anne Itotia, "Africa: Urbanization and Proliferation of Slums: A Case Study of Kibera, Nairobi," 33-35 and 38-40, shows the complex history of colonization and displacement of peoples that characterizes not only Kenya but much of Africa. This theme of displacement of peoples is also at the heart of the Visioning Statement of Mercy International (http://www.mercyworld.org/projects/index.asp, accessed 31.8.07) and hence is a central call to us into the twenty-first century.

[9] Many women of mercy today work with displaced peoples either in their diaspora context or as they return to their homeland through Mercy and Jesuit Refugee Services as well as with other organizations.

[10] I want to draw our attention to the pervasiveness and multiplicity of materiality in our sacred story in order both to raise awareness of the other-than-human which we have so often overlooked in our focus on the human/divine encounter and to encourage us to learn to read anew for embodiment and materiality so that we might develop an ecological consciousness necessary for saving our fragile planetary home.

human, protected from political and economic domination as the newly born Jesus is protected from the political machinations and destructive intentions of Herod.[11]

And before leaving the opening stories of the *Rachamim* that is cast on the earth and is the with-us G*d, it is important for us to note that this embodied *rachamim* is located in family (*whanau*) and genealogy (*whakapapa*).[12] It is located in culture, the Jewish culture of first century Palestine, an occupied country whose people's religious and other cultural traditions were being shaped by the colonizer as well as being held to firmly by the colonized. Embodied mercy today is likewise located in cultures, cultures being colonized by globalization with its development of a global culture that consumes the local, the indigenous. Reading the Jesus story with the lens of embodiment, materiality, and the centrality of family, genealogy and culture is to read with the Jesus of history, with the Matthean community of the first century Roman empire and with the daughters and sons of Catherine kindling the fire of mercy in our day in all the varieties of their locations and cultures. It is to hear, to experience the winds that blow from our shared sacred story through our many realities and to know the shared call to mercy.[13]

Wisdom-shaped Embodied Mercy

One of the characteristics of today's world that impacts on all of our contexts is globalization.[14] We may do well to examine it in dialogue with the pervasiveness and power of the Roman empire in the first century. Jesus proclaimed an alternative *basileia* [empire] to that of Rome, a *basileia* characterized by righteousness or right ordering, not the unjust *pax Romana*, a peace or ordering won by power and might rather than justice and love.[15] Jesus proclaims that this new *basileia*, the *basileia of the heavens,* the *basiliea of G*d*, is near at hand, is indeed embodied in his ministry of preaching/teaching and healing (Matt 4:17, 23-25 and 9:35 which frame Jesus' ministry of preaching, teaching and healing). It is this *basileia* that also frames the beatitudes (5:3-10), woven through as they are with challenges to do righteousness (*dikaiosynē* or right ordering) and mercy (*eleos*). The wisdom Jesus teaches in the beatitudes and throughout the Sermon on the

---

[11] Our storytelling also needs to take account of the "male children of Bethlehem", the children for whom Rachel weeps, who are not saved as Jesus is saved [Matt 2:17-18]. Who are the ones that our storying and our living of Mercy leave to annihilation by the political oppressors (as the Matthean storying of embodied mercy does to the male children)? These are uncomfortable and challenging questions but ones which we must not avoid for to do so may lead us to avoid giving attention to who and what we leave to annihilation.

[12] I use here the two Maori words *whanau* and *whakapapa* because of their centrality in Maori culture and life and the awareness that this raises in New Zealand society (or at least segments of it) of the importance of family and genealogy and its connection to location and culture. For further exploration, see Tui Cadigan, "A Three-Way Relationship: God, Land, People. A Maori Woman Reflects," in *He Whenua, He Wāhi/Land and Place: Spiritualities from Aotearoa New Zealand* (Helen Bergin & Susan Smith eds; Auckland: Accent Publications, 2004), 27-43.

[13] I am drawing here on the imagery and language of the poem with which Elizabeth Davis closes her paper. See Davis, "How Can We Dare," 26.

[14] Davis, "How Can We Dare," 20-22.

[15] Warren Carter, *Matthew and the Margins: A Sociopolitical and Religious Reading* (Maryknoll: Orbis, 2000), reads Matthew's gospel in the context of the Roman Empire of the First Century CE. See also his *Matthew and the Empire: Initial Explorations* (Harrisburg: Trinity Press International, 2001) in which he explores that culture more fully and *The Roman Empire and the New Testament: An Essential Guide* (Nashville: Abingdon, 2006). See also Mary Ann Beavis, *Jesus and Utopia: Looking for the Kingdom of God in the Roman World* (Minneapolis: Fortress, 2006).

Mount is that of embodied mercy/justice or righteousness (5:6, 7, 10, 20; 6:1, 2. 3, 4, 33).[16] The healing action that Jesus undertakes in proclaiming the *basileia* (Matt 8-9) is womb-compassion.[17]

To stand in the gospel tradition, to continue to tell the gospel story of the *basileia* of G*d/the *basileia* of the heavens ought to engage us subversively but perhaps the fact that both socially and ecclesially, we now belong predominantly to the empire has obscured our commitment to the subversive. We are among the "haves" rather than the "have-nots", those possessing rather than distributing the world's resources for the alleviation of poverty. To become embodied mercy/justice and righteousness, we may need to proclaim that the *globalization of G*d is near at hand*. What would that mean— that just as Jesus sought to imagine, proclaim and work for an alternative to the *basileia* of Rome, we need to imagine, proclaim and work for an alternative to the *globalization* of today's Romes. This would not entail a denial of globalization but rather a seeking after ways in which we might critically analyze it, read or decipher the signs of our times with wisdom in order to determine what will not lead to the right ordering that is of G*d and those elements of the global networking which can be turned toward justice, mercy and fullness of life for all.[18] Such a task is not one that we can do alone but one in which we must participate with others across Christian and all faith traditions. This would be to continue the telling of a gospel that was subversive. This would be to embody the mercy that comes from wisdom sought out in our day as Jesus sought, proclaimed and lived it in his day.

Embodied Mercy – Seeking after Holiness
There are many stories, many aspects of mercy embodied or embodied mercy that we could explore in the gospel of Matthew with the many intertexts from the scriptures of the Matthean community that have been drawn into their storying of Jesus. I will, however, take up just two stories and explore them in a little more depth that they might contribute to our theologizing and open up ways in which different communities of mercy might theologize about the embodying of mercy in many different locations. The first story is that of the Canaanite woman in Matt 15:21-28. It is a story that one can

---

[16] I have explored this more fully in "The Spirit of Compassion of Jesus Healer: Shared," the second of four papers given at the 2006 conference of the Australian Health and Welfare Chaplains Association, Brisbane, Australia, 9-13 July. This can be accessed at http://www.centacarebrisbane.net.au/pastoral_ministries/ hospital.php.

[17] Immediately following the repeated summary of Jesus' ministry in 9:35 (see the parallel and framing aspect of 4:23/9:35), the narrator says that when Jesus saw crowds as he went on his itinerant ministry journey, preaching, teaching and healing, he had compassion on them – womb-compassion. The verb used is *splanchnizomai* which scholars suggest means moved in the depths of one's being, one's bowels, one's womb. For other uses of this same verb to describe Jesus' ministry of compassion, see Matt 14:14; 15:32; and 20:34.

[18] *Gaudium et Spes* called us to read the signs of our times in 1965. Also Elizabeth Davis, "How Can We Dare," 21-22, drew our attention to the statement of the Commission of the Bishops' Conferences of the European Community, *Global Governance: Our Responsibility to Make Globalisation an Opportunity for All* (2001) which is available at http://www.comece.org/comece.taf?_function=euroworld&_sub=_trade&id =4&language=en, and which makes a similar contemporary call in the face of globalization. The Commission lists the core values that are possible within globalization as respect for human dignity, responsibility, solidarity, subsidiarity, coherence, transparency and accountability.

return to over and over again and it will yield up new insights. As we place this story in its literary context (15:1-28; 14:13-16:12), we find contestation over holiness: is it found in the "tradition" or is it seeking to hear what is of G*d (15:3, 6, 8-9). Jesus, the wisdom teacher, challenges disciples: do you not understand that holiness is of the heart (15:17-20).

Following this exchange, the Matthean storyteller invites the listening community into a story in which Jesus is tested in relation to his embodying of mercy and holiness. This story is located on the border between Tyre/Sidon and Upper Galilee. It is a borderland story and it is not completely clear who is in whose territory as Jesus and the Canaanite woman meet: one has come out and one has gone to or into (Matt 15:21). The story is set, therefore, for the possibility of something new emerging from such a context and such an encounter as Gloria Anzaldúa indicates:

> At some point, on our way to a new consciousness, we will have to leave the opposite bank, the split between the two mortal combatants somewhat healed so that we are on both shores at once, and at once see through the serpent and the eagle eyes.[19]

The woman represents in this story the female-headed household of the outsider or the other, the one who crosses cultural boundaries to seek healing for her daughter.[20] She is named in the language of religious outsider (Canaanite) but she is also ethnic outsider (of the region of Tyre and Sidon). And her daughter/her household, she designates as demon-possessed. There are a number of ways in which the first-century Matthean community might have understood the designation 'demon-possessed'.[21] For our purposes, I want to explore just one of them, namely that the daughter bears in her body the dislocations associated with the social, economic and political conflict within the region where Tyre/Sidon and Upper Galilee met.[22] She represents the women and children trafficked across borders, the people of Kibera, especially the children of the female–headed households, all those whose lives are marred profoundly by the social, economic and political situations in which they seek to survive. The breakdown of human relations is visited on the body of this young daughter and on the land itself, the land which becomes the border across which healing mercy is negotiated: "Have mercy on me," the woman cries (Matt 15:22).

The shock for us in this story is that Jesus does not respond to the woman's cry for mercy in this boundary encounter. In fact, the Matthean storyteller narrates that he ignores her.

---

[19] Gloria Anzaldúa, *Borderlands/La Frontera: The New Mestiza* (San Francisco: Aunt Lute Books, 1987), 78.

[20] See Itotia, "Africa: Urbanisation and Proliferation of Slums," 35.

[21] See Elaine M. Wainwright, *Women Healing/Healing Women: The Genderization of Healing in Early Christianity* (London: Equinox, 2006), 125-127.

[22] Gerd Theissen, *The Gospels in Context: Social and Political History in the Synoptic Tradition* (trans. L. M. Maloney; Edinburgh: T & T Clark, 1992), 79, says that "[a]gressive prejudices, supported by economic dependency and legitimated by religious traditions, strained the relationships between the more thoroughly Hellenized Tyrians and the Jewish minority population living either in Tyre or in its vicinity, partly in the city and partly in the countryside. The economically strong Tyrians probably often took bread out of the mouths of the Jewish rural population, when they used their superior financial means to buy up the grain supply in the countryside."

This rejection is followed by a similar rejection from the disciples of Jesus, those learning embodied mercy through the teaching, preaching and healing ministry in which they are engaged with Jesus, who propose to send her away.[23] And as part of the construction of a three-fold barrier to this woman's cry for mercy receiving a favourable response, Jesus moves from the boundary encounter to the centrist religious position: I was sent only to the lost sheep of the house of Israel (15:24). Jesus like the Pharisees of 15:1-9 and like the disciples (15:23) must grapple with a new situation that calls for a new challenge. He knows and articulates the theology of "chosenness" as Leticia Guardiola-Saénz calls it,[24] a theology which would have been considered both 'word of God' and 'tradition' (Matt 10:5; Is 53:6; Jer 50:6; Ezek 34 and Gen 18:19; Deut 7:6; 14:2; Is 41:8 by way of example) in Jesus' context. Faced with this woman who is 'other', who is from across the border, whatever that border might be, Jesus is challenged to discern what it means to be the embodied *rachamim* of the G*d of Israel, the prophet of the "spirituality of life" in this situation which is new, this situation in which it is not "one's own" but the "other" who begs for mercy. This is the discernment required of one who seeks the right ordering, the justice and the holiness which is of G*d.

The boundary-walker, the woman who is "other," refuses to accept the construction of insider and outsider that Jesus began in v. 24 and continues in v. 26 in response to her second cry for help (v. 25). Rather she tentatively proposes a new household that would enable herself and her daughter to share the same bread with Jesus and his disciples – even if partially, like the dogs who eat the crumbs! Her courageous and persistent engagement in this situation of challenge with and of Jesus enables Jesus to move back to the margins where he recognizes what she desires as being of G*d.[25] Healing/holiness is effected in this encounter as the cry of mercy is heard "where the cry of the poor meets the ear of God"[26] when the one who seeks to embody mercy can allow that G*d will be

---

[23] The Jerusalem Bible translation of this verb is "give her what she wants" but this is questionable given the use of the same verb, *apoluein*, at 14:15 when the disciples propose to Jesus that he send the hungry crowds away to buy food for themselves and 15:32 when Jesus does not want to send the crowds away hungry lest they collapse on the way. The two stories of multiplication of loaves/bread form a frame around the story of the Canaanite woman. It seems strange, therefore, that the verb would be used with a different meaning in this context, especially when there is no indication in the story itself that the disciples want Jesus to respond to her need. Rather their response is in line with Jesus' initial ignoring of the woman's request.

[24] Leticia Guardiola-Saénz, "Borderless Women and Borderless Texts: A Cultural Reading of Matthew 15:21-28," *Semeia* 78 (1997): 72, who, from her position of Mexican-American interpreter, challenges that "[i]f the ideology of chosenness has proven to be fatal and exploitative to the two-thirds of the world, then it is an ideology that needs to be challenged by all liberative readers."

[25] The language of what she desires/wills in v. 28 echoes that of what G*d desires in the prayer of Jesus (Matt 6:10). For a variety of approaches to this Matthean story, see my *Towards a Feminist Critical Reading of the Gospel according to Matthew* (BZNW 60; Berlin: de Gruyter, 1991), 102-116, 217-247; "A Voice from the Margin: Reading Matthew 15:21-28 in an Australian Feminist Key," in *Reading from This Place: Volume 2—Social Location and Biblical Interpretation in Global Perspective* (Fernando F. Segovia, & Mary Ann Tolbert, eds; Minneapolis: Fortress, 1994), 132-153; *Shall We Look for Another? A Feminist Rereading of the Matthean Jesus* (Maryknoll: Orbis, 1998), 84-92; and *Women Healing/Healing Women*, 153-155; and 123-130 for the Markan parallel.

[26] Sandra M. Schneiders, *Finding the Treasure: Locating Catholic Religious Life in a New Ecclesial and Cultural Context* (New York: Paulist, 2000), 141, describes the prophetic aspect of contemporary religious life as wanting to be "where the cry of the poor meets the ear of God."

always new in the cry of the one most in need. Tradition, word of G*d, and holiness, justice and right will always need to be negotiated in the face of human need both within the congregation as we explore some of our centralist hermeneutics—whiteness, western-focused-ness, resource richness and other perspectives which we must name together—and more broadly as cultural and religious traditions of our world call us beyond what is known and safe. The G*d/*Rachamim* with us will be always new, asking new embodiments of mercy of us in the new situations we encounter. Displacement of peoples, trafficking in women and children, the rape of the earth and the solidifying of traditions of holiness/spirituality into authoritarian demands for conformity—all these cry out for new embodiments of mercy.

Mercy Ever Embodied Anew

The final story I wish to explore is one which points to the "going away" of one embodiment of mercy in the person of Jesus but the remaining of that embodiment in those who come after. It is the story of the woman who pours out healing ointment over the head of Jesus. In exploring her story, I want also to demonstrate that in this story, the threefold aspects of the Matthean right-ordering or justice spiral: right-ordering of resources/Earth; right-ordering of community relationships; and right-ordering of the human/divine relationships.[27] But this is not all. In looking briefly at the different ways in which this tradition of the woman with the ointment spirals through the other gospels, I will suggest that notions of a meta-narrative seem to be foreign to the origins of our Christian traditions. This in its turn might provide us with ways of understanding how we might hold "the integrity of multiple traditions while living in harmony."[28]

The ministry of Jesus prior to his arrest and crucifixion as told within the Matthean community closes with a great parable in which those who follow after Jesus are separated out into those who feed the hungry, welcome the stranger, clothe the naked, and visit the sick and the imprisoned and those who do not (Matt 25:31-46).[29] And through the parable, Jesus proclaims that "as long as you did it to the least, you did it to me" (Matt 25:40). Embodied mercy as Jesus was for the hungry, the stranger, naked, sick and imprisoned (Matt 11: 4-5 and passim) will now be continued in those who belong to the Jesus' movement and it will be as if they are doing it for Jesus, their teacher, healer and friend, the one whom they saw embodying compassion.

This parable is played out before the listeners/readers almost immediately when a woman with an alabaster flask of very expensive ointment pours it over the head of Jesus while he is at a meal in Bethany at the house of Simon the leper (Matt 26:6-13). There are many ways in which this story has been understood and I have no wish to contest these, but I want to suggest another reading which is important for our theologizing. The reader, at this strategic moment in the unfolding of the Jesus story, is drawn into a web of

---

[27] Michael H. Crosby, *House of Disciples: Church, Economics, and Justice in Matthew* (Maryknoll: Orbis, 1988), explores such intersections in much more detail than is possible here through the metaphor of *house* which he claims as being central to the Matthean gospel story. This could warrant further exploration in our theologizing mercy.

[28] Davis, "Can We Dare," 25.

[29] This parable is so often used to refer to the "corporal works of mercy."

relationships. Jesus is introduced as being in a particular space, a space into which a woman comes with an alabaster flask of costly ointment of pure nard that she pours over his head.

In Matthew's gospel, the house is a place of teaching and healing, the ministry of embodied mercy.[30] The naming of the house as that of Simon the leper focuses particular attention on healing and Bethany is also a place of refuge (Matt 21:17). The materiality of village and house give a significant context to the action of the woman. It is in this space that attention is drawn both to the woman, to the alabaster jar of ointment of pure nard which she has, and to her action which brings her into relationship with Jesus. The naming of the *alabastron* turns our attention toward Earth and the stalagmitic deposits from which this transluscent marble called *alabastros* was obtained. Earth has given of its resources to provide the woman with an appropriate container for the costly ointment or perfumed oil. Earth and the material of Earth are drawn into relationship with the human and invite the human person to be attentive to the gift.[31]

Into the *alabastron* has been placed very costly ointment [*myron*] of pure nard. *Myron* is a general word used to describe a wide range of perfumed ointments or oils both of which are prepared from plant substances grown in the Earth. The woman's breaking of the stem of the flask and pouring out of the ointment on the head of Jesus is an act of giving. She is the instrument of the giving, of the gifting, through her identification with the ointment but the ointment is the gift (it has been received by her as gift and will be given to Jesus as gift). Jesus as recipient freely receives the gift that will strengthen him to give the ultimate gift, his life. As Anne Primavesi says:

> *These interactive relationships between giver and receiver, between giver and gift and between gift and receiver link them openly, materially, sensually, with the link made tangible (usually) in some object passed by one to the other, chosen by one for the other and received by one from the other.*[32]

Power is in the gift, in the *myron*, a power to bestow something that is lacking, to respond to the cry, the need. The context, Matt 26:1-5, points readers toward the lack: it is two days before the Passover and the chief priests and scribes are seeking to arrest Jesus and kill him. Jesus is facing into death with all the emotional turmoil that would entail. *Myron* poured over the head would put "good odours to the brain" Athenaeus says in the *Deipnosophistae* and this, he affirms, is "a highly important element of health" (XV.687 d). He goes on to say that "the sensations of the brain are soothed by sweet odours and cured [or healed] besides" (XV.687 d). The healing power of the *myron* of pure nard, this *pharmakon*, remedies the lack in Jesus so that he is able to face death: in pouring out the

---

[30] For teaching see Matt 5:15; 7:24, 25, 26, 27; 10:12, 13, 14; 12:25, 29; 13:1, 36, 57; 17.25; 19:29; 24:17, 43 and healing 8:6, 14; 9:10, 23, 28.

[31] Anne Primavesi, *Sacred Gaia: Holistic Theology and Earth System Science* (London: Routledge, 2000), 160, says that "[t]o see life as a gift event is to see that I am alive because I am continuously gifted with what I need to live. I am gifted because other organisms and species have not evaded or ignored the demands I make on them. Ultimately, this fact does not allow me to evade or ignore my dependence on the earth. Or to ignore my responsibility to return it, at the very least, the gift of gratitude."

[32] Primavesi, *Sacred Gaia*, 156.

ointment, she has prepared my body for burying (26:12). His need has been met by the merciful generosity of the woman and the power of the ointment. Had the gift been withheld as the indignant ones would have wished, the deficiency in Jesus would have been felt more acutely. And what she has done, her good work, is gospel and is to be proclaimed, to be enacted in the whole world (Matt 26:13). It rightly orders the human-to-human, the human-to-other-than-human and the human-to-divine relationships. Mercy will be embodied in each new enactment, beyond the ministry of Jesus, beyond the death of Jesus, beyond the work of Catherine and all those who remember her story. Mercy will be ever embodied anew when such gifting takes place and where such right-ordering is enacted.

And this story that is told similarly in the Markan community (Mark 14:3-9), spirals out in other extraordinary ways in different communities' telling. In the Johannine community, Mary of Bethany anoints the feet of Jesus with the ointment/*myron* of pure nard and wipes them with her hair in an action which parallels that of Jesus' washing the feet of his disciples and wiping them with the towel with which he girded himself (Jn 12:1-8 and in particular Jn 12:3; and cf 13:5b). This paper does not allow me the space to explore the characterization of Mary of Bethany in any detail but it can be shown that the sexually suggestive nature of her action indicates that it is the type of act that would normally be performed by a courtesan or prostitute. Since Mary is nowhere else presented as a courtesan, then her action would seem to be symbolic like that of Jesus, who is not a servant but who washes the feet of his disciples as would a servant. The action of both Mary and Jesus is that of crossing boundaries and entering a state of liminality; and it is the urgency of the time that calls forth such radical actions of boundary crossing. Mary's extreme act seems to be expressive of her extraordinary friendship in the exigency of the moment and its impending danger both for Jesus and those associated with him. Dangerous times call for courageous actions, symbolic actions, which might convey the depth of feeling, the depth of meaning of those times. This, it seems, is how the story of the alabaster jar of pure nard is woven into the tapestry of the Johannine narrative. And what an extraordinary story it provides for us as we explore the exigencies of embodied mercy into the twenty-first century and their continuing beyond our current embodiment.[33]

To conclude this section, I note ever so briefly how the Lukan community re-shaped this story (Luke 7:36-50). Reading against the grain of the Lukan characterization of women in that gospel, we encounter an anointing woman who embodies love (Luke 7:41-43). She knows herself forgiven by G*d[34] and she gives expression to her recognition of

---

[33] For further exploration of this story from this perspective, see Elaine M. Wainwright, "Anointing/Washing Feet: John 12:1-8 and Its Intertexts within a Socio-Rhetorical Reading," in *"I Sowed Fruits into Hearts" (Odes Sol.17:13): Festschrift for Professor Michael Lattke* (Pauline Allen, Majella Franzmann and Rick Strelan, eds; Sydney: St Pauls Publications, 2007), 203-220. See also Charles H. Cosgrove, "A Woman's Unbound Hair in the Greco-Roman World, with Special Reference to the Story of the 'Sinful Woman' in Luke 7:36-50," *Journal of Biblical Literature* 124.4 (2005): 675-692, for the symbolism of unbound hair.

[34] Jesus' description of the woman's being forgiven in v. 47 is in the perfect passive tense – she has been forgiven – and because of this she shows great love to Jesus as the one who represents the G*d whom she knows has forgiven her. The same tense of the verb is used in v. 48 when Jesus says to her: your sins have

embodied compassion in the person of Jesus. Within the three opening verses of the narrative (vv. 36-38), this woman acts in a highly erotic and excessive manner in relation to the body of Jesus,[35] taking the initiative, doing actions intended to give pleasure to Jesus, sexual pleasure, not just once but continuously. Intimately woven into and through her actions is the materiality of the human body, its substances and fluids, and the material of Earth, its substances and fluids. Jesus in no way interrupts her actions that catch him up in the interplay of bodies, Earth, fluids and substances. Rather he receives her ministrations. Her actions transgress both the physical space of the house of the Pharisee as well as the culturally gendered politics encoded in the text in and through the material that the text evokes.

Engaging intimately with the materiality of body and Earth, she has shown the hospitality that Simon failed to show to Jesus who is a prophet. Jesus demonstrates his prophetic insight not by stereotyping the woman but by recognizing in this woman of outrageous love expressed in and through powerfully erotic materiality, the great love of one who has been forgiven. She knows herself forgiven before she acts. She has not waited for the men in this context to tell her she was forgiven whatever her sins were that have been hidden from the readers of this text. She has a relationship with the Loving Forgiving One quite separate from that affirmed or denied by either the Pharisee, or the one whom the gospel names as Teacher. Having been drawn into the intimate and erotic experience of the forgiven woman, Jesus the prophet recognizes in her great act of love that Loving Forgiving One whom she acclaims through all that we have seen caught up in her actions. The permeating *myron* infuses and is infused by the radical incarnationality manifest in the woman, in Jesus and in the erotic intimacy of their encounter which is caught up into divinity. This is embodied love, holiness, wisdom and justice—it is radical and situational and invites ongoing storying in our different contexts of incarnationality.

Exploring these three iterations of an early Christian tradition of embodied mercy reminds us that stories and traditions of mercy will be multiple in our day. Like the early emerging communities of faith and love, we too are being invited to embody mercy and tell our stories of mercy in the many different modes and manners that characterize our contexts. And as we who have carried these stories in the vessel of religious life engage with and give way to others who will carry the stories in the vessels of different life choices, as did Jesus, embodied *Rachamim*, we will receive the ministrations of mercy of others as Jesus did as life is handed over. The storytelling will go on and it will go on in extraordinarily rich and new ways as did the telling of the story of Jesus, the *Rachamim* of G*d with us.

---

been forgiven [he does not say that he forgives her sins]. This very significant insight for the interpretation of Luke 7:36-50 is discussed in detail in Evelyn R. Thibeaux, "'Known to be a Sinner': The Narrative Rhetoric of Luke 7:36-50," *Biblical Theology Bulletin* 23 (1993): 151-160. On the basis of the perfect passive of the verb, Thibeaux skillfully demonstrates (p. 152) that "the woman's sins have been forgiven before she performs the loving actions in vv. 37-38" and that the words of Jesus are simply "his offering her *assurance* (sure knowledge) that God has forgiven her sins and salvation is hers."

[35] 'Erotic' is used here to connote love generally together with its most typical implication, sexual love.

Conclusion

What I have been able to trace in this short paper is like the finger pointing toward the moon. It indicates what is possible, it opens up potential. It will, however, be the ongoing storytelling in our different contexts in dialogue with the multiplicity of our situational questions and issues and with our sacred traditions and texts that will enable us to embody *rachamim*/mercy as wisdom, justice, and holiness in today's world and into the twenty-first century.

Enkindling Mercy in a Multicultural Context: Focus on Jamaica

Theresa Lowe Ching, RSM

Introduction

In a 2005 *MAST* article entitled, "The Development of Caribbean Theology: Implication for Mercy Re-Imagining/Reconfiguring Project",[1] I identified four of the key issues that can be said to characterize the postmodern world context and to have significant impact on the Caribbean region. They are: globalization, fragmentation, cultural and religions pluralism and increased vulnerability. Elizabeth Davis' social analysis paper on the present world context[2] certainly testifies to the continued imperative of considering these and other issues in order to understand our present world reality and to point the way towards a Mercy response more in keeping with the authentic living of the Christian message towards the creation of an alternative vision in service of the coming Kingdom of God.

Within the limits prescribed for this paper, I will discuss the issue of cultural and religious pluralism specifically in relationship to the multicultural reality of the Caribbean region with a special focus on Jamaica. Given Mercy's commitment to embrace our multicultural/international reality, it seems a fitting topic to discuss the challenge of "Enkindling Mercy in the Twenty-first Century." Moreover, multiculturalism is, indeed, a significant postmodern issue that speaks directly to the necessity of seeking truth as it is revealed, though always partially, in particular contexts.

I will proceed by considering, firstly, the formation of the Caribbean multicultural society with special focus on Jamaica and the Mercy community experience in Jamaica as typifying that reality. Secondly, I will consider briefly the development of Caribbean Theology as a postcolonial, liberationist enterprise with an almost exclusive emphasis on the African experience. Thirdly, I will suggest the lineaments of a more adequate multicultural theological response. And finally, I will identify some specific challenges for Mercy as we endeavour to own and live our multicultural reality as a very significant aspect of our effort to "Enkindle the Fire of Mercy in the Twenty-first Century."

The Caribbean Context: Focus on Jamaica
Formation of a multicultural society
Colonialism, beginning in the fifteenth century and continuing for more than five hundred years in the Caribbean, initiated the migration of persons of numerous nationalities and ethnic origins into the region, thus creating a distinct multicultural society. Europeans from Spain, Portugal, Holland and Britain, and subsequently from

---

[1] Theresa Lowe Ching, R.S.M., "The Development of Caribbean Theology: Implications for Mercy Re-Imagining/Reconfiguring Project", *MAST,* Vol. 15, no. 2.
[2] Elizabeth Davis, "How Can We Dare Wisdom and Mercy in the Mosaic of Our Realities?" Paper delivered at Mercy International Research Conference, November 9-13, 2007, 13-26 in this volume.

North America vied for control of the various islands and territories in order to gain access to the natural resources and to develop a lucrative transatlantic trade.[3] This would eventually result in the "persistent poverty"[4] and continued underdevelopment of most of those countries in tandem with the increasing wealth and development of the colonizing powers of Europe and North America.

With the establishment of the plantation economy in the Caribbean, African slaves whose presence had already been well known in Iberia, were bought mainly from the West Coast of Africa and transported, under the most heinous conditions, to Jamaica and other Caribbean countries. They were brought to provide the necessary labour force to replace the native Indians who all but disappeared due to diseases caught from the European colonizers and the horrendous conditions to which they were subjected. However, there still exists a sizeable minority of indigenous persons, particularly the Amerindians in Guyana who are often forgotten but cannot be ignored.[5]

The story of the slave trade and the inhumanity of plantation life to which the African slaves were subjected need not be repeated here. With our limited focus on the formation of the multicultural society in the Caribbean and particularly in Jamaica, we need only note the vast numbers that were forced to make the "Middle Passage." From the fifteenth to the nineteenth century it is estimated that twenty million African slaves were transported to the Americas, two million of whom landed in Jamaica.[6]

Following upon the abolition of slavery in the Caribbean, beginning with Haiti in 1804 and ending with Brazil in 1888, and specifically in Jamaica in 1834, new challenges, both political and economic, arose regarding the insufficiency and unpredictability of the labour supply. A solution was sought by encouraging a new wave of migration, starting with Europe and gradually more so from India and China, the countries that were under imperial rule at that time. According to Look Lai, it was an "age of unprecedented economic expansion in the Americas and elsewhere, and correspondingly unprecedented movements of peoples."[7] Thus, "Europeans, Maltese, Portuguese-speakers from Madeira, Cape Verde and the Azores, Africans 'liberated' from slave ships of foreign countries, African-Americans, Chinese and East Indians" were imported into the Caribbean and particularly into the countries most depleted of their regular labour force, viz., British Guiana, Trinidad and Jamaica. Eventually, British India became the main source of immigrants for the plantations and this lasted until 1918 when the indentured labour

---

[3] See Verene Shepherd & Hilary McD. Beckles, editors, *Caribbean Slavery in the Atlantic World* (Kingston: Ian Rabdle Publishers/ Oxford: James Curry Publishers/ Princeton: Marcus Wiener Publishers, 2000).

[4] See George L. Beckford, *Persistent Poverty: Underdevelopment in Plantation Economies of the Third World* (Jamaica/Barbados/Trinidad and Tobago: University of the West Indies Press, 1972). This is the classic Caribbean publication re this phenomenon.

[5] Mary Noel Menezes, R.S.M., "Mercy Fire Kindled in Guyana – April 1894; Still Burning – 2007." Paper delivered at Mercy International Research Conference, November 9 – 12, 2007, 124-130 in this volume.

[6] Hilary Beckles, "Reparations: Taking Forward the Caribbean's Case." Paper delivered at Mona Research Conference, August 31 – September 2, 2007, Kingston, Jamaica.

[7] Walton Look Lai, *The Chinese in the West Indies 1806-1995: A Documentary History* (Kingston, Jamaica: The University of the West Indies Press, 1998), 2. Cf. Shepherd & Beckles, *Transatlantic Trade.*

experiment ended. The numbers and distribution of these immigrants are succinctly reported by Look Lai:

> Between 1838 and 1918, just over half a million new immigrant labourers (536,310) had entered the British West Indian plantation system, 80 percent from India alone, 7.5 percent from Madeira, and 3.5 percent from China. British Guiana received 56 percent of the total immigration, 55.6 percent of the 430,000 Indians, and 76 percent of the approximately 18,000 Chinese. Trinidad received 29.4 percent of the total migration, 33.3 percent of the Indians, and 15 percent of the Chinese. Jamaica received 10 percent of the total migration, 8.5 percent of the Indians, and 6.4 percent of the Chinese.[8]

Besides, during this time the lucrative exploitation of Caribbean resources and new trade opportunities also brought other settlers from the Middle Eastern countries, particularly Syria and Lebanon, and Jews from Italy and elsewhere. All came to swell and diversify even more the immigrant population of the Caribbean region. Thus the multicultural/multi-racial society of the Caribbean with all its plurality and diversity was established and continues to exist up to the present, only becoming more plural and diverse with the influx of other immigrants from other parts of the world, with all the attendant problems that such cultural dislocation would naturally engender.[9]

The complexity of the region and of the Jamaican society understandably defies description and full understanding. Nonetheless, it cannot be ignored and perhaps even more, it offers fertile and privileged soil for analysis of many of contemporary issues and postmodern concerns including "multiculturalism", the specific focus of this paper.

The Multicultural Community of Mercy in Jamaica
The story of Mercy's arrival and development in Jamaica is presumably well known in our international community of Mercy. Hence, a summary glance will suffice to highlight, in particular, the multicultural nature of the community throughout its long history of more than one hundred and twenty-seven years.

The origins of Mercy in the island date back to December 12, 1890 when at the request of Bishop Charles Gordon, then Bishop of Jamaica, seven Sisters of Mercy arrived from Bermondsey, England. They had been recruited for the purpose of bringing stability and sustainability to the works of Mercy that had been initiated ten years previously, in 1880, by a native Jamaican, Jessie Ripoll, and two co-workers. These three creole[10] women subsequently joined the order and became the first Jamaican-born Sisters of Mercy.

---

[8] *Ibid.,* 4f.
[9] See Brinda Mehta, *Diasporic (Dis)locations: Indo Caribbean Women Writers Negotiate the Kala Pani* (Jamaica/Barbados/Trinidad & Tobago, 2004).
[10] "Creole" refers to persons of mixed ethnic heritage. For a discussion of the creolization process and the issue of Caribbean identity see Carolyn Allen, "A Mi: Revisiting Caribbean (Cultural) Identity", *Groundings,* Issue 11 (July 2003), 4-14.

Over the ensuing years, the works of the Sisters of Mercy continued to focus on the service of the poor and underprivileged in the society, specifically in child care homes, first for boys and then for girls, and in educational institutions. The rapid spread of these works of Mercy to various parts of the island bears witness to the critical needs that were being met by the Sisters. Membership in the community also grew, at first mainly through the recruiting of missionaries from England, Ireland and Malta. During those early years, in accord with the missionary mentality that prevailed at that time, native Jamaicans, especially those of African and Asian descent, were not considered fit candidates. Gradually, however, Jamaicans of various ethnic and cultural heritages were accepted into the community. Among these were creole women of mixed heritage, European and otherwise, second generation Chinese and women of African and East Indian descent. Missionaries from the United States, Canada, Cuba and Belize also came to swell the ranks of the Sisters of Mercy. Thus a multicultural/international community was established and continues as such to this day, albeit with no further addition of life-long missionaries from Europe or elsewhere. However, in more recent years missionaries from the United States and one Sister from New Zealand have been serving for specific periods of time in Jamaica. Presently, a new wave of missionaries, mostly from Africa, India, the Philippines and other Pacific islands, are coming to the island to serve the Church in various parts of the island. It is, therefore, not unlikely that the Mercy community in Jamaica will again be welcoming persons from one or another of these countries. Thus the multicultural/international nature of the community will likely continue into the future.

The Development of Caribbean Theology[11]

The origins of Caribbean theology can be traced back to the seminal publication in 1973 of *Troubling of the Waters*,[12] a collection of papers delivered at two theological conferences in Trinidad, edited by Idris Hamid. Similar to other liberation theologies, it can be characterised, as Matthew Lamb suggests, as the "religious correlate" of the other liberation movements that erupted in the 1960s in the post-Enlightenment turn to the victims of society.[13] It had become apparent by then that the liberal quest for freedom and equality for all, to be achieved through the primacy of reason and the reliance on science and technology, had eluded the majority of peoples, especially those in the underdeveloped countries. The gap between the wealthiest and the poorest nations continued to widen and the extent and degree of the dehumanizing poverty that existed among the marginalized persons and countries became an affront to the Christian sensibilities of many.

Like their Latin American counterparts, Caribbean theologians subsequently employed the praxis-centred method of doing theology to first of all identify the causes of the socio-economic, cultural, political and above all, religious forces of oppression that accounted for the persistent poverty, inhuman conditions and denigration that created persons

---

[11] See Theresa Lowe Ching, R.S.M., "The Development of Caribbean Theology: Implications for Mercy Re-Imagining/Reconfiguring Project" for a more thorough treatment of this topic.
[12] Idris Hamid, ed., *Troubling of the Waters* (San Fernando, Trinidad: Rahaman Printers, Ltd., 1973).
[13] Matthew Lamb, *Solidarity With Victims: Toward a Theology of Social Transformation* (New York: Crossroad, 1982), 28-60.

lacking a real sense of identity and self worth. The colonial experience was thus judged to be the primary source of the problem. As Hamid puts it:

> Imperialism of the spirit is the most final subjection that any people could experience. This imperialism has done and is still doing its work among us. Yet it has not completely conquered. The human spirit in the quest for wholeness bounces back in myriad ways. In the Caribbean, the search of the human spirit for freedom, wholeness and authenticity has expressed itself in various ways.[14]

Strident critique of the Church's complicity with the colonial masters in equating civilizing with Christianizing called into question the adequacy of the missionary activities, and specifically the use of Scripture, in communicating the message of Jesus of Nazareth. The need to reinterpret Scripture from the perspective of the oppressed within the Caribbean societies became an urgent imperative. Even more, the oppression of Africans and people of African descent under slavery became a focal point of theological reflection, in view of the devastating effects that still lingered in the region, affecting the majority black population in particular. Hence, the redemption that was sought would be intimately linked with liberation from all that still held the black population in bondage, in body, mind and spirit. The Exodus was interpreted as the paradigm of God's liberation and Jesus Christ became imaged as a black Messiah.[15]

Authentic interpretation and living of the Christian faith was thus to be sought in reaching back into the depths of African traditional religious experiences in order to retrieve the lost riches of that heritage. It was deemed that many of its values still persisted in the society and could contribute to the fashioning of a more meaningful and authentic Caribbean religious response. Even a cursory look at the various religious practices in the Caribbean will, indeed, reveal the tenacity of many African traditional beliefs and ritual practices that slaves from Africa no doubt brought with them. These, even to the present, coexist and are lived, oftentimes in tension with Christian beliefs and practices.[16] An exploration of some of these values could, therefore, be instructive.

---

[14] Idris Hamid, *Troubling of the Waters,* 6. Cf. Brian L. Moore & Michele A. Johnson, *Neither Led nor Driven: Contesting British Cultural Imperialism in Jamaica, 1865 – 1920* (Jamaica/Barbados/Trinidad and Tobago: University of the West Indies Press, 2004.
[15] See Kortright Davis, *Emancipation Still Comin': Explorations in Caribbean Emancipatory Theology* (Maryknoll, New York: Orbis Books, 1990); Lewin Williams, *Caribbean Theology* (New York/ Washington, D.C./ San Francisco: Peter Lang, 1994); Ashley Smith, *Real Roots and Potted Plants: Reflections of the Caribbean Church* (Mandeville, Jamaica: Mandeville Publishers, 1984); Noel Erskine, *Decolonizing Theology: A Caribbean Perspective* (Maryknoll, New York: Orbis Books, 1981).
[16] See Leonard E.Barrett, *Soul Force: African Heritage in Afro-America* (1974); George E. Simpson, *Black Religions in the New World* (New York: Columbia University Press, 1978); Maureen Warner Lewis, "The Ancestral Factor in Jamaican African Religions," in Kortright Davis and Elias Faraje-Jones, eds., *African Creative Expressions of the Divine* (Washington D.C: Howard School of Divinity, 1991), 68 – 80.

Aspects of African Religious Heritage[17]

It is to be noted here that undergirding these values are various aspects of a worldview that correlate in key instances with certain liberationist theological assumptions. Thus, firstly, the affirmation of the religious nature of the universe and hence the religious significance of the entirety of human existence sees no dichotomy between the material and the spiritual but instead the integration of both in one integral, earthly existence. A basic liberationist theological assumption affirms the unity of the history and rejects the separation of spheres that often marks traditional theology.[18]

Secondly, there is a decidedly this worldly focus in African traditional religions in the emphasis on life in the here and now. In this regard, the liberationist concern is to give due recognition to the value of life on earth and to be engaged in the transformation of persons and structures of society in the construction of the Kingdom of God, beginning here on earth and tending towards its fullness at the Eschaton.

Thirdly, traditional African religions' practical approach to God and the spiritual world again correlates with Liberation theology's emphasis on action rather than on theory, orthopraxis rather than orthodoxy.

Finally, the social, communal focus of African religions highlights the social view of the person, a cardinal point in African anthropology. As Mbiti expresses it, "I am because we are, and since we are therefore I am."[19] Again, Liberation theology's shift of focus from the individual to the social dovetails with this communal, corporate African stress.

Regarding particular elements of traditional African religions, it is generally agreed that many persist in various countries of the Caribbean. These can be seen specifically in certain present day Jamaican cults, namely, Kumina and Revival with its variants, Zion and Pukumina, all having roots in Myalism, a distinctive African retention.[20] In general these cults are marked by intense physical and psychic engagement, expressed in rhythmic ritual dancing and singing, and in communication with the world of spirits, both ancestral and otherwise. This experience of spirit-possession that often occurs is deemed to be the highpoint of contact with the other world, according to Allan Anderson.[21]

The Rastafarian movement likewise can be traced back to having its roots in Revival although the emphasis on spirit-possession is generally absent. According to Chevannes,

---

[17] The following is drawn from a research project that I started in 1999 while on the Dorothy Cadbury Fellowship at the Selley Oaks Colleges, Birmingham, United Kingdom. See Theresa Lowe Ching, "A Liberationist Spirituality in the Caribbean Context" in Philip L. Wickeri, ed., *The People of God Among All God's Peoples: Frontiers in Christian Mission: Report from a Theological Roundtable Sponsored by the Christian Conference of Asia and the Council for World Mission, November 11-17, 1999* (Hong Kong: Clear-Cut Publishing Company, 2000).

[18] See Theresa Lowe Ching, *Efficacious Love: Its Meaning and Function in the Theology of Juan Luis Segundo* (Lanham, MD: University Press of America, 1989), esp. 66-75; 129-134 for the liberationist assumptions and perspective referred to here and in the following paragraphs.

[19] John S. Mbiti, *African Religions and Philosophy* (London: Heinemann, 1969), 108.

[20] Barry Chevannes, *Rastafari: Roots and Ideology* (Syracuse University Press, 1995).

[21] Allan Anderson and Samuel Otwang, *Tumelo: The Faith of African Pentecostals in South Africa* (Pretoria: University of South Africa, 1993), 97.

African retentions can be identified in the movement along with certain Christian elements. Barrett also, classifying Rastafarianism as a "militant revolutionary" movement sees a link with Revival in its struggle against black oppression.[22] Its main objective is, indeed, to assert the dignity of the black person and to lay claim to the African heritage as self-defining in opposition to the imposed cultural values of the colonial legacy.

In addition to the above, a brief look at the Pentecostal movement could also offer further insights, bearing as it does such significant aspects of the African religious cults in the Caribbean as, for example, the prominence of the experience and action of the spirit, highly emotional engagement and a certain resistance to mainline churches. It is to be noted, however, that Pentecostalism is unambiguously Christian in its identification of the "spirit" with the "Holy Spirit" of Christian tradition.

Pentecostalism
In reflecting upon the rapid spread throughout the world of Pentecostalism, marked as it is by the experience and working of the Spirit, Margaret G. Kraft and others[23] claimed that the need for spiritual empowerment is a key factor. They contend that the movement, attracting as it does mostly the disadvantaged in many instances, seems to offer devotees a sense of dignity and self-worth and the communal support to cope with the harsh realities of life. Moreover, Harvey Cox goes even further to suggest that Pentecostalism reaches down into the primal depths of humanity indicating the perennial presence of the "*homo religious.*" His claim is that, "Pentecostalism is not an aberration. It is part of the larger history of human religiousness."[24] Thus he maintains that Pentecostalism in rejecting both "scientism" and "traditionalism" provides a third option in its return to the "raw inner core" of human spirituality capable of meeting the need of many for a different kind of "religious space."[25] Cox's question regarding the future direction of Pentecostalism (either towards "fundamentalism" and its emphasis on the "word" and doctrinal structures, or towards "experientialism" and the personal, subjective experience of the Spirit) still remains open and warrants further exploration.[26]

In conclusion, it is clear that there are values and assumptions drawn from the African heritage that are still operative in the psyche of the majority black population of the Caribbean. These ought not to be ignored, especially those that coincide with the

---

[22] Chevannes, 170. Cf. Leonard E. Barrett, *The Rastafarians: The Dreadlocks of Jamaica* (Kingston: Sabgster's Book Store, Ltd., 1977), 153.
[23] Margaret G. Kraft, *Understanding Spiritual Power: A Forgotten Dimension of Cross-cultural Mission and Ministry* (Maryknoll, New York: Orbis Books, 1995); Diane J. Austin-Broos, *Jamaica Genesis: Religion and the Politics of Moral Orders* (Kingston, Jamaica: Ian Randle Publishers, 1997).
[24] Harvey Cox, *Fire From Heaven: The Rise of Pentecostal Spirituality and the Reshaping of Religion in the Twenty-First Century* (London: Cassell, 1996), 83.
[25] *Ibid.,* 105. Cf. The postmodernist openness to the transcendent. The need for a balanced approach to the spiritual is obvious.
[26] In considering the above, it seems to me that a way forward might include a more thorough study of Spirit Christology that not only stresses the power of the Spirit as it filled and directed the life of Jesus of Nazareth but also the prophetic dimension of his actions as he confronted the structures of oppression operative in the concrete circumstances of his life and that of his people in Israel. This would hold both tendencies in creative tension and offset the dangers inherent in one extreme or the other.

liberationist theological perspective and with the more positive aspirations of postmodernity.

This said, the spread of Rastafarianism throughout the Caribbean region and to other parts of the world is a case in point of a movement growing out of a particular cultural context that has been proven to possess global appeal and relevance especially through the music of Bob Marley and others of the Rastafarian persuasion, touching as it does the universal yearnings of oppressed peoples for respect, personal dignity, equality, and freedom of spirit, mind and body. This is a clear indication of the significance of this religious movement and the promise that it holds for the creation of a world built on "peace and love." It attests moreover to the imperative of recognizing and addressing the implications of cultural particularity such as are present in this specific religio/cultural experience even as we work towards the creation of a new world order, a new humanity.

Towards the Development of a Multicultural Caribbean Theological Response
According to John B. Cobb, Jr., basic values and attitudes are transmitted more through culture as a whole than through religious traditions. As he puts it, "[a]lthough the religious traditions play a large role in shaping basic attitudes and values, it is through the whole complex of patterns of beliefs, values, and practices that make up a culture that these are chiefly transmitted."[27] Granted the truth of this statement, Caribbean theology needs to take more into account not only the various religious traditions that are present in the region but, perhaps even more directly, the contribution of the various cultures in which those traditions are embedded and which continue to influence, often unconsciously, Caribbean life and religious experience. Cobb rejects the option of allowing the values of the majority to be imposed on minorities, decentralizing into smaller units and having their values inform corporate acts and seeking to discover common values as the basis of action. Rather he suggests working towards "a new formulation of values, including multiculturalism itself that can be affirmed by members of most of the cultures involved."[28]

It seems to me that the last approach would not only be able to identify values that are already effectively operative in the growth of Caribbean persons but would also allow for the creative, dialectical interplay of seemingly contrary values in true recognition of diversity, even as we strive for unity in Christ Jesus.

It follows from the above that Caribbean theology must go beyond the almost exclusive focus on the African religious heritage, despite all its richness and challenges, to include the possible contribution that other cultural groups and religious traditions in the region are well poised to make.[29] Work now in progress at St. Michael's Theological College suggests that such an endeavour has the potential of pointing the direction towards a

---

[27] John B. Cobb, Jr., *Postmodernism and Public Policy: Reforming Religion, Culture, Education, Sexuality, Class, Race, Politics and the Economy* (Albany: State University of New York Press, 2002), 33.
[28] *Ibid.*, 64f.
[29] Cf. Mary Noel Menezes, "Mercy Fire Kindled in Guyana – April 1894; Still Burning – 2007."

much more adequate inculturation of the Christian message in the Caribbean.[30] The praxis-centred approach of Caribbean Theology to date would enable such a theology to directly encourage the collaboration of all in the creation of the new Caribbean person.

The Enkindling of Mercy in a Multicultural Context
What then are the challenges to Mercy seeking to enkindle the fire of God's compassionate caring for all in Jamaica and, indeed, in the entire Caribbean multicultural context? Given the multicultural composition of Mercy in the region, it seems to me that the recognition and exploration of the rich cultural heritages that inform the lived experience of its members promise much by way of a more respectful affirmation of one another and the courage to relate to "the other" with understanding and compassion. In order to do this, however, Mercy in Jamaica would have to reflect upon its past and present experience of being a multicultural community in service of a people of various cultural and racial backgrounds. It would have to examine the extent to which its founding and earliest members perhaps shared in the general missionary mentality and attitudes evident in the Church as a whole. It would have to ask what aspects of the critique of the colonial past as brought forward by Caribbean theologians might still apply today.

The endeavour to explore the Caribbean multicultural reality could also bear powerful witness and challenge to the entire Institute of Mercy, as we strive to enflesh our expressed commitment to embrace our multicultural, international reality as a strong imperative in the twenty-first century.

Understandably, there is in the making a monoculture that is being fashioned by the market economy on a global scale. The Institute of Mercy could offer prophetic challenge to this world divided on so many fronts, yet claiming to be one; a world affirming the postmodern recognition of diversity, yet driven by the exigencies of technocratic reason to bring order and control into play in order to achieve the unity that nonetheless remains elusive. Indeed, as Douglas Hall maintains, "it is the great paradox of the modern desire for mastery that in its quest for universalizing and totalizing comprehension, its system was obliged to *exclude* or *repress* that which lay outside it, thereby calling its universal and total comprehensiveness into question."[31]

After all, this postmodern context of our contemporary world does have positive elements capable of creating that alternative vision that we seek. A careful and self-critical use of many of its elements can contribute towards the creation of a new world of greater peace, justice and equality, such as we envision. Basic to the question of multiculturalism that is the immediate focus of this paper is the respect for particularity and difference that is rooted in the postmodernist acute awareness of the limitations and fragility of human

---

[30] The Centre for Caribbean Spirituality at St. Michael's Theological College conducts a yearly seminar to highlight the multiple ethnic and religio-cultural heritages of Caribbean peoples with the objective of developing a more adequate living of the Christian faith in the region and to promote constructive dialogue among the various faith traditions. The proceedings of the seminars are published in the St. Michael's Theological Journal, *Groundings.*
[31] Kevin J. Vanhoozer, ed., *Postmodern Theology* (Cambridge, UK: Cambridge University Press, 2003), 16.

existence that opens up human life more positively to the transcendent. As Douglas Hall expresses it, "Postmodernism aims to situate reason, reminding modern pretenders of a God-eye point of view that they are in fact historically conditioned, culturally conditioned and sexually gendered finite beings."[32]

Thus, as Mercy seeks to move forward in this direction (Cf. Direction Statement), it might be helpful to consider these constructs of cross-cultural hermeneutics suggested by Yeow Choo Lak in an article entitled, "Christianity in a Southeast-Asia Metropolis: Cross Cultural Hermeneutics."[33] They are as follows:

- A "situational construct" that "indicates one area of responsibility and concern in the midst of the varieties and dynamics of current realities."
- An "exegetical construct" that "suggests that we are to understand the Gospel and the Christian tradition vis-à-vis current givens."
- A "missiological construct" that "equips people of God with a missionary commitment that is informed by a theology that is capable of more than simply illuminating current givens with the flood light of the Gospel. It can also help manage and direct the changes currently taking place along lines more consonant with the Gospel and its vision for human life in God."
- An "educational construct" that "gives shape, content, direction and guidelines to our theological education" aimed at providing leadership in the field.[34]

Thus, he finally contends:

> In modest ways, cross-cultural hermeneutics endeavours to uncover and be convicted by the truth of our Christian faith – not as a collection of abstract doctrines but as a living tradition and heritage that is capable of illuminating our contexts and also of supplying motivations and directions for transforming them.[35]

In conclusion, the challenge to Mercy itself is to preserve the identity and integrity of all its members in promoting genuine respect for particularity and difference even as it seeks that union and charity that is the hallmark of the Mercy way of life. From this standpoint, it will be truly empowered to be and live Mercy in a broken, fragmented world, to be in solidarity with the truly "other", the poor, the underprivileged and the excluded. In this way, we will truly be empowered to enkindle the fire of Mercy in our very own times and to answer the "Call to Compassion" as expressed thus in poetry and in life:

> I listen to the agony of God –
> I who am strong

---

[32] *Ibid.,* 23.

[33] Yeow Choo Lak, "Christianity in a Southeast-Asia Metropolis: Cross Cultural Hermeneutics" in Mercy Amba Oduyoye and Hendrik M. Vroom, eds., *One Gospel – Many Cultures: Case Studies and Reflections on Cross-Cultural Theology* (New York/Amsterdam: Editions Rodopi BV, 2003), 13-37.

[34] *Ibid.,* 7.

[35] *Ibid.,* 36.

With health and love and laughter
     in my soul.
I see a throng
of stunted children reared in wrong
     and wish to make them whole.

I listen to the agony of God –
But know full well
That not until I share their bitter cry –
earth's pain and hell –
can God within my spirit dwell
to bring the Kingdom nigh.[36]

---

[36] Nancy Telfer, "The Journey," quoted in Iben Gjerding and Katherine Kinnamon, ed., *No Longer Strangers: A Resource for Women and Worship* (Milwaukee: Lutheran Human Relations), 49.

Fire Cast on the Earth:
Spiritual Implications for Mercy in the 21st Century

Janet K. Ruffing, RSM

Our conference theme evokes the apostolic zeal Jesus and Catherine McAuley shared: "fire cast on the earth, kindling," which continues to animate Mercy life into the 21st century. Luke captures Jesus' impatience at the resistance of his hearers to grasp and respond to the core of his teaching and his intensity, as he heads toward Jerusalem and exclaims, "I have come to cast fire on the earth and how I long for it to be kindled."(Luke 12.49, RSV) This is the same Jesus, who repeatedly responds with deep-felt compassion for the suffering of the excluded, the downtrodden, the poor, women, those ignorant of the Torah and of the relationship God desires to have with everyone, and, of course, for the sick and deformed. By so doing, he demonstrates God's universal love and concern for each person and evokes, in the recipients of his attention, healing, and compassion, a sense of their intrinsic human dignity. Jesus' saving, wholeness-making life, ministry, death, and resurrection bring about the fullness and abundance of a deeper and more all inclusive communion with God and solidarity with one another.

Catherine's letter to Elizabeth Moore in which she echoes these words of Jesus, expresses a similar urgency but a slightly different mood. Although Catherine was approaching the last year of her life, the arrival of the English women for the Birmingham foundation fills her with hope and consolation. She interprets an abundance of joy-filled candidates for Mercy religious life as "some of the fire he cast on the earth—kindling."(*Correspondence* 282) Catherine discloses her conviction that "the service of the poor for Christ's sake" (282) is at the heart of Mercy life just as it lies at the heart of Jesus' mission. Catherine's vision of religious life is profoundly Christological.

In an earlier letter to Frances Warde in which she comments on the arrival of the first of the five women, she shares how enlivening and animating it is for her to witness their generosity, admitting frankly that they were embarking on "a mission so contrary to our natural inclinations."(*Correspondence* 270) And she senses "the fire Christ cast upon the earth is kindling very fast" in this influx of desirable and accomplished candidates with solid vocations. (270) This consoles her in the face of many deaths within the community and the challenge of new foundations. Catherine expresses excitement and confidence about the future of the community which she anticipates will extend beyond her life-time.

These interior movements of zeal and confidence are the work of the Spirit. Vocations to a new form of religious life are clearly the Spirit's doing as well as the joy that animates both the English women and Catherine who chose "downward mobility"[1] in their solidarity with the poor and their dedication to their service.

IMAGES OF THE HOLY SPIRIT
I would like to connect this inspired interpretation of Mercy life with Hildegard of Bingen's plethora of images for the work of the Holy Spirit in individuals, in creation,

---

[1] See "Downward Mobility" in Dean Brackley, *The Call to Discernment in Troubled Times,* 90-104.

and in the human community. When Hildegard writes about the sacrament of confirmation she says: "The Holy Spirit is a burning and shining serenity that will never be depleted and which kindles fiery virtues so that, by the Holy Spirit, all darkness is banished." (*Scivias*, II.4.2) The Spirit is inexhaustible as a consoling presence and peace-giver. At the same time the Spirit "kindles" the specific strengths needed to hold the darkness at bay. In her sequence for Pentecost, Hildegard exuberantly addresses the Spirit in part:

> Fiery Spirit,
> Fount of courage,
> Life within life
> Of all that has being!
>
> Holy are you, transmuting the perfect into the real.
> Holy are you, healing the mortally stricken.
> Holy are you, cleansing the stench of wounds.
>
> O sacred breath O blazing love
> O savor in the breast and balm
> Flooding the heart with the fragrance of good,
>
> O limpid mirror of God
> Who leads wanderers home and hunts out the lost,
>
> Armor of the heart and hope of the integral body,
> Sword-belt of honor:
> Save those who know bliss!
>
> Guard those the fiend holds imprisoned,
> Free those in fetters whom divine force wishes to save.
>
> O current of power permeating all
> In the heights upon the earth and in all deeps:
> You bind and gather all people together. (*Symphonia* 149)

While it is impossible to comment on all the graces that the Spirit accomplishes within us, I note a few. The Spirit strengthens, encourages, transforms, and heals. The Spirit enlarges our capacities for love, infuses our hearts with appreciation and attraction to the good. As a consequence of this interior transformation, the Spirit works in the world interiorly as well, leading the lost home, searching out both those who know bliss, those in harmony with God's life but also those who are imprisoned by evil. Since the Holy Spirit permeates everything in heaven and on earth, the Spirit reconciles, binds, and gathers all people together. Ultimately, the Spirit intimately works within each person and through each person in community and the Spirit enkindles the fire, the reign of God among us that Jesus so desired.

Finally, in Hildegard's great cosmic vision, the Spirit is closely associated with love, with *Caritas* (feminine in Latin) who claims:

> I am the supreme and fiery force that kindled all living sparks and breathes forth no deadly things—though I suffer them to exist... I am the fiery life of the essence of divinity. I flame above the beauty of the fields and I glisten in the waters. I burn in the sun, the moon, and the stars. With an airy wind I stir up all things vitally through invisible life that sustains all things. (*B.D.W.* 1.1.2)

In these poetic texts, we discover an integral harmony within creation and the human community brought about by the Spirit of Jesus who enfolds us in Trinitarian life and who nudges us toward greater unity, greater inclusiveness, greater harmony, and greater compassion because this is the nature of who God is, and the divine life we are destined to share in a communion of interrelatedness. If we are to be Mercy in the 21st century, we depend on the Spirit's acting in us and our response to this divine initiative.

FIRST WORLD CONVERSION

From the perspective of spirituality, the situations analyzed or described in the social analysis papers, from extreme poverty to ecological degradation, require an interdisciplinary approach that includes the spiritual distress and deficiencies that we need to address in order to contribute toward the implementation of such world-wide consensus goals as the Earth Charter and the Millennium Development Goals as works of mercy for our times. These programmatic proposals are creative attempts to change the situation for the poorest and most disenfranchised persons in our global society. A massive change of heart is needed: a radical conversion of first world persons and communities toward the "downward mobility" of recognizing that the well-being of the entire earth community requires, not simply the voluntary actions of individuals economizing, but an intelligent reduction of our consumption of energy, goods, services, combined with governmental and non-governmental investment in the infrastructure needed to convert to a sustainable level of living that includes the well-being of the two thirds world as well as the first world. There is a spiritual malaise and captivity resulting from exaggerated individualism that leaves first world persons with great freedom of choice but also often lonely, anxious, and empty. Coupled with the consequences of this post-modern over-emphasis on the non-relational, non-contextual self is the massive effect on our psyches and spirits of living in what Mary Jo Leddy names a culture of "perpetual dissatisfaction"—the effect of the culture of money which so manipulates our desires that we incessantly crave for more. (*Gratitude* 14-32)

The "more" for which we crave can never satisfy the deeper longings of the human heart but creates a dynamic of "systemic distraction" and busyness that leave us harried, fragmented, driven to secure our self-esteem either through achievement or acquisition. Because we always need "more" of something—time, money, attention, experiences (even spiritual ones), entertainment, and "things," we become incapable of recognizing we are enough and even have enough and that we can make a difference in our world. We become incapable of living in an attitude of radical gratitude and awe, of receiving and being nourished by that which we actually have, are, and do. Such radical gratitude leads to or is supported by detachment, simplicity, and a sense of abundance. (*Gratitude* 38-42) It is ultimately radical interdependence with God's Spirit—an availability and a disposability to partner with the Spirit in our ministries and personal lives.

In Leddy's analysis, this culture of dissatisfaction is radically disempowering, because if we aren't good enough or don't have enough, or whatever we might do won't make a difference, we acquiesce in joining the ever expanding group of innocent victims and fail to do what we can in response to others in greater need. (*Gratitude* 79-81) Radical gratitude begins in an emotional economy of abundance and leads us to recognize and appreciate the most basic of all gifts—"our one precious and wild life."(Oliver, *Poems* 94) God sustains us, often gratuitously, if we stop long enough in our harried and driven lives to notice and respond to Creator God and the Spirit who strengthens, enlivens, inhabits, and invites us to move toward gratitude. In its core, this attitude of radical gratitude recognizes and responds to God whose life we share, in whose creative energies, and in whose inspired life we participate—all the activities of the Spirit evoked so poetically by Hildegard of Bingen.

Leddy proposes a spirituality that is an antidote to the learned habits of powerlessness and dissatisfaction fostered by our first world consumerist culture. She claims that for us, "authentic spirituality, genuine politics, and good economics arise from a spirit of radical gratitude." (*Gratitude* 4) Because we are subject to such pervasive social and cultural pressure to indulge our insatiable cravings and assuage our vague sense of guilt for not being or doing enough, we will need to adopt practices of resistance to our cultural expectations and claim the time we need for contemplative Sabbath, for prayer, for gratitude, for appreciating and consciously receiving the good gifts of God that fall daily into our laps. This critical disengagement from our all-pervasive cultural pressure can open a space for God, for the other, for a richer relational and communal life, and for our continued participation with God in the works of mercy we undertake for Christ's sake. This may open a new way of "being centered in God" in life and in ministry in 21st century conditions.

It seems to me that Mercy in the 21st century needs to focus as much, if not more, on the spiritual works of mercy than on the corporal. In most of the developed world, many basic needs are met, at least minimally, by governmental and non-governmental groups of different kinds. And while there is no truly just society which would obviate the need for most of the corporal works of mercy, the pressing need to respond to the spiritual hunger and perhaps spiritual bankruptcy of much that passes for religion and even spirituality in its self-centered, self-improvement mode is paramount.

Our social and economic discontentment leads us to plunder the earth's resources and to fail to recognize the two thirds world in the person of Lazarus lying at the gate of the one third world. The economic system of late capitalism depends on growth. This growth requires consumption increases in goods and services beyond sustainable levels for our planet if all peoples' most basic needs are to be met at a level commensurate with their human dignity. World-wide globalized, neo-liberal capitalism results in economic benefit for some but also in the diminishment of local cultures and the way people in those cultures construe meaning and foster community. In today's world, the rich never feel as if they "have enough" or "are enough" while the despair of the poorest of ever having even basic necessities deepens because technology and mass culture display to them the extravagant and wasteful consumption of the conspicuously affluent.

This cultural and economic situation is as much a spiritual issue for both the one third world and the two thirds world. In the one third world, we have the material resources and technological ability to end extreme poverty and to ameliorate the humanitarian disasters which result. In the two thirds world, there are also profound spiritual wounds inflicted by extreme poverty, forced migration, and the very gender specific violence and diminishment of the life potentials of women and girl-children. This situation requires intensive nourishment of authentic spiritual well-being, based on the Gospel which leans toward a preferential option for the poor, who in patriarchal systems are also always disproportionately women and their children.

In the one third world, a conversion is required at both the level of government action and in the lives of not just the extremely wealthy, but the ordinarily comfortable, to follow through on the commitments already made internationally and nationally to shift the expenditure of the funds from war and weapons to humanitarian aid and social development both within and beyond the one third world. This shift requires not simply individual voluntary action, but the investment of the promised minimal .07% of every country's GNP to relieve extreme poverty (MDG) and of even greater investment in systemic changes within the countries of the one third world to achieve sustainable development. Among the developed nations, the US is the stingiest and most recalcitrant in making and keeping these promises.

Living in harmony with the earth in a sustainable life-style will require a certain voluntary movement toward downward social mobility, consuming less of everything and assuming responsibility for the long-term consequences of our corporate greed and waste. Because the one third world is responsible for the current state of global warming and ecological disaster, we are responsible for cleaning up our enormous footprint on the planet even as more populous countries in the two thirds world, especially in Asia, seem bent on repeating our mistakes resulting in even greater planetary devastation.

SIGNS OF HOPE

Despite the overwhelming challenges on this level, there are also signs of hope and possibility. Albert Nolan has recently pointed out that on the spiritual level there is a growing process of "globalization from below." (*Jesus* 35) Our Mercy International Conference is one version of this movement. Because of the world's interconnectivity, Nolan suggests that compassion is now becoming globalized. A certain proportion of the human community now responds with compassion to all victims of injustice and affliction. While we remain challenged to overcome the racism of white privilege and intertribal and interreligious exclusion, nevertheless, more members of the world community recognize as brothers and sisters, people who are suffering anywhere in the world. The world responds to extreme need and disasters such as the Tsunami in 2004, the AIDS epidemic in Africa and elsewhere and in the depth and strength of the peace movement. Not only is a rather vicious economic system globalized, so too is a countermovement of peace-making, compassion, and justice. This is an engaged spirituality movement that is creating new ways of working for social change, empowering those who are most negatively affected in local situations, and discovering the need for new spiritual resources for resisting the "compassion fatigue" that can result by becoming personally overwhelmed by the world's needs.

SPIRITUALITY IN THE TWO THIRDS WORLD

The spirituality and the theology that grounds the two thirds world must function toward changing unjust conditions of oppression that limit the full flourishing of the life of the oppressed in every area of life, including in the churches. This requires a serious critique of a spirituality of the cross that reinforces alienation and that secures compliance with one's place in society (usually the bottom). This inauthentic spirituality of suffering is usually inculcated by the oppressor as good for the oppressed. It proposes a mysticism of suffering with the crucified Christ and looks exclusively beyond this life for any change or happiness in life,[2] while a robust spirituality of the cross can be an important spiritual resource in a perpetual condition of suffering, offering meaning and hope. Schillebeeckx names an inauthentic version of the spirituality of the cross "dolorism" (*Christ* 699) and points out that this theology never distinguishes necessary suffering (the human condition) from unjustly imposed suffering, and that it matters for our discipleship what causes we are willing to suffer for. Glossing over why Jesus was executed and by whom conceals the concrete circumstances that are likely to follow whenever anyone contests current power arrangements for religious reasons. It matters in terms of the Christian story what we are voluntarily willing to suffer for.

The spirituality called for in the two thirds world within a Christian context is a liberation spirituality. Liberation spirituality is unwilling to postpone all fulfillment of the reign of God to the next life, but requires a faith commitment here and now to work toward this vision in the present. Jon Sobrino identifies the Beatitudes and the Sermon on the Mount as the attitudes one discovers in men and women who express the values Jesus promotes in his life and teachings. But he asserts that prior to the Beatitudes is:

> ...a proclamation of mercy to the great masses that writhe in poverty, oppression, and repression—a proclamation that should fill us with mercy, and inspire us to a practice calculated to overcome these evils. But before all else, here is a mercy that ought to be maintained as something of ultimate value, and not trivialized in the name of eschatology or the plenitude of the Christian life. It is a matter, simply, of recovering, and especially of maintaining, that prior attitude of Jesus, "My heart is moved with pity for the crowd." (Matt. 15. 32) (*Liberation* 128)

This core response of mercy to the suffering masses which now floods our consciousness worldwide leads to an indignation that denounces the guilty, and a joy in the good news—the Gospel—and the corresponding relationship with God it offers. This is "the

---

[2] See Gebara, *Depths*, 104-108, and Schillebeeckx, *Christ,* 670-730, and my "Catherine McAuley's Spirituality of the Cross," *The MAST Journal* 2 (Spring, 1992): 14-19.

pearl of great price" for which men and women alive with the good news are willing to give their own lives if necessary.

For Jon Sobrino mercy, indignation, and joy are marks of a spirituality of liberation. Albert Nolan like Mary Jo Leddy shows that compassion and gratitude are not incompatible when we are moved to compassion in the face of seemingly intransigent evil. Nolan says Jesus "had a joyously grateful heart," and expands this view:

> Compassion and gratitude are not incompatible. When we allow ourselves to be moved by feelings of sympathy and compassion for others, we are imitating Jesus. In fact we are experiencing something that is divine. Jesus was compassionate because his Father was compassionate, and he taught his followers to be compassionate too—because God is compassionate. (Lk.6:36).

> Compassion is a gift from God, one of the most powerful of all God's gifts to us. We can therefore thank God for our feelings of compassion without in any way diminishing the reality of the suffering that evoked our feelings of compassion in the first place. We don't thank God for the suffering, but we are pleased to see people waking up gradually to the pain and suffering of others, and to the reality of human cruelty. Human cruelty, of course, is what happens when we humans have no compassion at all, when we lose all feeling for the other, when the ego reigns supreme. Compassion finds expression in prayers of intercession and in action. (*Jesus* 117)

In previous reflections on Mercy life, I began to understand freshly the connection between our charism of mercy and the gift of joy. This leads us to a deeper awareness that the compassion suffering evokes in our hearts is God's compassion expressing itself through us.[3] It is our joy to be gifted with the charism of mercy. But it will, as Nolan suggests, drive us deeply to prayer, to living in union with our Trinitarian God as intensely as it will drive us to action where we find the face of Christ in the poor.

ATTENTIVENESS TO GENDER
Throughout our Mercy world, we continue to claim Catherine's concern for women while at the same time eschewing feminist analysis or identification with Christian feminism as significant to our mission, or for that matter, to our own self-understanding. A religious variation of feminism takes gender into account as one explanation of the particular form of oppression that women experience in often quite different social contexts. Today there is no one feminism, but because we are women and because poor women suffer complicated effects of gender discrimination and gender-based violence, it is important from the perspective of spirituality to pay particular attention to the way in which the spirituality promoted within Catholic ecclesial life serves to legitimate and maintain sexism in a way that is detrimental to women's spiritual flourishing. There are many

---

[3] See my keynote addresses, "Proclaiming the New Dawn Centered in God" and "Living in the Mercy of God: Mercy Flowing Outward to the World," to the Mid-Atlantic Assembly, July 2006 and my presentation "Living in the Mercy of God: Our Joy and Our Bliss," to Sisters of Mercy of Aotearoa New Zealand, July-August 2007.

ways of understanding this relationship. I am currently finding the work of Brazilian philosopher and theologian Ivone Gebara and of American Beverly Lanzetta most suggestive and comprehensive in its approach to these issues. Ivone Gebara describes it this way:

> To say gender is to say male and female in their relation to social and cultural output, in the creation and learning of behavior, and in the reproduction of those same behaviors. To say man or woman is already to introduce a certain way of existing in the world, proper to each sex, a way of being the product of a complex web of cultural relationship. Female and male also have their effect on relationships between women and men exercised in private and in public. The notion of gender, bigger than biological sex, incorporates this relationship dynamic....
>
> ...distinct identities are established as habits through an immense and continuous work of socialization. (*Depths* 68)

This socialization leads men and women to perceive the world according to the dominant social structure which appears simply to be the unchangeable way things are. This social construction of gender is a major factor for maintaining fixed behaviors for each sex in each society.

In the current climate of insecurity in the face of world-wide economic and social change, one very harmful religious response to women's aspirations and flourishing has been the fundamentalist attempt to return to an idealized past. This movement is world-wide and across cultures and religions. "These efforts take different forms but have in common the attempt to control women's bodies, their ability to move freely, and their freedom to speak openly within their societies." (Ramdas, "Feminists and Fundamentalists" 102) Religious guilt becomes compounded with the "unrealistic guilt" women often feel when they contemplate attempting to change their circumstances or it is a feeling that pervades some women's consciousness in male-dominated situations. (Gebara, *Depths* 90-94)

WOMEN AND POVERTY
Every major international foundation and financial institution has empirically demonstrated that no development goals can be achieved in the two thirds world without investing in girls' education and the full and equal participation of women in their societies. (Ramdas, "Feminists and Fundamentalists" 102) "Where women are more educated and independent, societies tend to be much healthier than would otherwise be expected." (Epstein and Kim, "Power of Women" 39). Evidence is mounting world wide that poor women who benefit from micro-financing schemes and begin to exert more influence in their households, financially invest in education for their children and achieve a higher level of nutrition and health in their families. Poor men world wide spend a disproportionate amount of their meager resources on alcohol and male social activities, including prostitution. (Kristof, "Wretched" 34-6)[4]

---

[4] It is sobering to note that the educational level on which these assessments are based is primary school education for girls. Of the 920 million illiterate people in the world 600 million are women. Women and

EDUCATION

The implications for education are astonishing. Mercy sisters world wide already sponsor women's centers, garden projects, safe houses, affordable housing. Basic literacy for women of all ages is important as is education for girls throughout the developing world. However, it is important to recognize that education may also be related to women's full empowerment in the form of short term workshops and community groups. Ivone Gebara notes:

> It often happens that we have knowledge of what oppresses us but we do not have the means to change the rules of the game of oppression. Knowledge is certainly important in the process of transformation, but it is not enough to bring about actual change. To change the very conditions that produce relationships of domination, there must be a collective process of education. There must be agreement, a minimal consensus, a common analysis to intercept what has become habitual....there must be a change in the symbolic order and then change in actual practice, in the daily life of the culture. (*Depths* 69)

This change in the symbolic order has a spiritual aspect to it. The lens of gender allows an analysis of a particular woman's situation. An alternative vision is required to capture imaginations and to propose a hopeful alternative. Within Christian feminism, most describe a vision of humanity, men and women together trying to build better relations of justice and solidarity. It usually does not imply that women want to dominate men, simply reversing roles, but rather envision a new community of sharing, of mutual recognition of men's and women's values, embracing multiple cultures, peoples, and their values. This vision would be profoundly rooted in the life and experience of Jesus of Nazareth, especially his creation of a discipleship of equals and his vision of the reigning of God in our midst evoked through parables, the Sermon on the Mount, the Beatitudes and the parables that demonstrate the radical compassion of God and our solidarity with one another.

ATTENTIVENESS TO WOMEN'S SPIRITUAL WOUNDS

Finally, Beverly Lanzetta in her recent book *Radical Wisdom* calls for a contemplative feminism that heals and recognizes the soul wounds that women suffer as a result of patriarchal religion. There are profound spiritual dimensions to gender-based discrimination and violence from which we ourselves are not immune. Beverly Lanzetta proposes a feminist mystical theology or a contemplative feminism. Building on feminist theological, scriptural, and mystical studies in the last thirty years and the deepening understandings of the extensiveness and pervasiveness of the discrimination and violence that women suffer in every culture and region of the world, she proposes a new category of rights—the "spiritual rights" of women. By so doing, she names the spiritual harm

---

girls comprise over 80 percent of the estimated 800,000 victims of human trafficking, and suffer from various forms of gender-related violence (Clarke, "Sisters' Keeper" 38). The WHO reports that one in three women world-wide has experienced domestic violence. Domestic violence is more common and entrenched in developing countries. One promising initiative added a series of workshops on gender issues to their microfinancing program. In only two years, women in this project reported half as much domestic violence as a result of women gaining both understanding and leverage to resist their abuse and support one another in their village in South Africa. (Epstein and Kim, "Power of Women" 40)

done to women by theologies that deny the feminine divine in women and the result of physical and spiritual violence that profoundly wounds the feminine soul. She claims that these soul wounds remain beyond speech for most women. These wounds include internalized inferiority, the lack of symbols for the divine feminine (Lanzetta, *Wisdom* 182-195), and as I mentioned earlier in Gebara's analysis, feelings of guilt that are not related to actions but simply to the fact of being women in patriarchal societies. (*Depths* 90-2)

EFFECTS OF VIOLENCE AGAINST WOMEN
Violence against the earth, attitudes related to ownership of the earth, and the indiscriminate exploitation of the earth's resources historically contribute to violence against women and the feminine. This is why theological feminism very rapidly became ecofeminist theology. Intimate violence against women is soul destroying as well as disintegrative of personality. These wounds imperil inner security, precipitate a crisis of faith, and estrange women from their most significant personal and community relationships. (Lanzetta, *Wisdom* 190) Ivone Gebara makes the case that women both experience the effects of social and personal evil pervasively in a gender specific way, but once victimized become abusers or dominators in the specific areas in which they hold power, usually over children in the home. (*Depths* 95-97)

As women religious, we are also not exempt from these dynamics. Some of us have experienced some form of intimate violence in our lives and all of us have exercised some kind of "power over" others in our ministries where we have been in charge, not always non-violently. As highly educated, professionally trained women, we, nevertheless, continue to experience covert and overt forms of gender based discrimination in both church and society. We are both wounded and potentially wounding, spiritually and psychologically.

THE DARK NIGHT OF THE FEMININE
In her contemplative feminism, Lanzetta traces a new trajectory of mystical development in which women pass through stages of the spiritual journey not named by male mystics. Women mystics eventually discover God dwells in them and that we are godly, that we are images of God and do mirror God. This level of spiritual development requires recognizing and resisting all the messages of cultural and religious traditions that deny this possibility of women imaging the divine and becoming divine in their mystical development. To reach the fullness of this transformative healing requires God to heal the unnamed and often unrecognized soul wounds in women that are the result of sexism. Lanzetta calls this healing process the dark night of the feminine divine. This is the impasse/breakthrough I believe many of us may be encountering or approaching. Theologically, we know we are equally in the image of God and that God indwells us in our feminine selves, but our church consistently denies this profound reality in practice. We may live with anger and rage that has no place to go. We live with the sadness of betrayal because our church experience denies our deep feminine wisdom and agency. Apostolic religious life is meant to be prophetic both in church and society. We need to recognize and open ourselves to this deep contemplative healing in ourselves even as we tend the spiritual wounds of other women.

According to Lanzetta, only God can heal this wound of the feminine soul, the spiritual effects of sexism, in our contemplative practice from the inside out. "Contemplation is both source and fruit of spiritual virtues, the former leading to the attainment of humility, compassion, and detachment of soul, while the latter overflows into concern for the happiness and betterment of all beings." (Lanzetta, *Wisdom* 197) Lanzetta uses maternal imagery to describe a mystical ethic of the feminine—bearing the intimacy of the world, bearing the love of the world, and bearing the holiness of the world. To live in intimacy with God and the world, to bring love everywhere, and to manifest the holiness and sacredness of the world, requires internal transformation and not merely a program for social change.

This transformation is characteristically the work of the Spirit, and requires our participation and availability within the contemplative dimension of our religious lives. Our need for the Spirit's nurturance, strengthening, and healing is even more poignant as we, unlike Catherine, are no longer animated by the "kindling" of a rapid influx of vocations. However, we live in different times and can only partner with God's Holy Spirit in mediating God's mercy to our world in our own context. Therefore, we must rely as Catherine did on God's own self so that we can trust that "the Holy Spirit is a burning and shining serenity that will never be depleted and which kindles fiery virtues so that, by the Holy Spirit, all darkness is banished" (*Scivias*, II.4.2) and the fire of God's mercy is kindled even more vibrantly in us.

<h2 style="text-align:center">Works Cited</h2>

Bingen, Hildegard. *Book of Divine Works with Letters and Songs.* ed. Matthew Fox. Santa Fe: Bear and Company, 1987. Cited as *B.D.W.*

_____. *Scivias.* Trans. Bruce Hozeski. Santa Fe: Bear and Company, 1986.

_____. *Symphonia*: *A Critical Edition of the Symphonia armonie celestium revelationum.* With Introduction, Translations, and Commentary by Barbara Newman. Ithaca: Cornell University Press, 1988.

Brackley, Dean. *The Call to Discernment in Troubled Times: New Perspectives on the Transformative Wisdom of Ignatius of Loyola.* New York: Crossroad, 2004.

Clarke, Kevin, "Our Sisters' Keeper," *U.S. Catholic* (January 2006) 38. Proquest Religion accessed on-line September 18, 2007.

Epstein, Helen and Julia Kim. "AIDS and the Power of Women," *New York Review of Books* (February 15, 2007) 39-41.

Gebara, Ivone. *Out of the Depths: Women's Experience of Evil and Salvation.* Trans. Ann Patrick Ware. Minneapolis: Fortress, 2002.

Kristof, Nicholas."Wretched of the Earth," *New York Review of Books* (May 31, 2007) 34-6.

Lanzetta, Beverly. *Radical Wisdom: A Feminist Mystical Theology.* Minneapolis: Fortress, 2005.

Leddy, Mary Jo. *Radical Gratitude.* Maryknoll: Orbis, 2002.

Nolan, Albert. *Jesus Today: A Spirituality of Radical Freedom.* Maryknoll: Orbis, 2006.

Oliver, Mary. "The Summer Day," *New and Selected Poems.* Boston: Beacon, 1992.

Ramdas, Kavita. "Feminists and Fundamentalists," *Current History* (March 2006) 99-104.

Ruffing, Janet K. "Catherine McAuley's Spirituality of the Cross," *The MAST Journal* 2 (Spring 1992) 14-19.

_____ "Proclaiming the New Dawn Centered in God" and "Living in the Mercy of God: Mercy Flowing Outward to the World," Mid-Atlantic Assembly Keynote, July 2006.

_____"Living in the Mercy of God: Our Joy and Our Bliss," Sisters of Mercy of Aotearoa New Zealand, July-August 2007.

Schillebeeckx, Edward. *Christ: The Experience of Jesus as Lord.* New York: Crossroad, 1981.

Sobrino, Jon. *Spirituality of Liberation: Toward Political Holiness.* Trans. Robert Barr. Maryknoll: Orbis, 1990.

Sullivan, Mary C., ed. *The Correspondence of Catherine McAuley, 1818-1841.* Washington: Catholic University of America Press, 2004.

Lessons from the New Ecclesial Movements

Doris Gottemoeller, RSM

The challenge "to be Mercy in the twenty-first century" precisely as *Sisters of Mercy*, from within and in the name of a 175 year old community that bears that name, invites comparison with other contemporary options. Specifically, how is our modality of 'being Mercy' distinct from that of the new ecclesial movements which originated in the twentieth century? What can we learn from these other responses to the Gospel imperative to respond to the needy of our time? What distinctive contribution can we make to the trends addressed in our Summary Paragraph, precisely as Sisters of Mercy? In the pages which follow I will profile the new phenomenon in order to address these questions.

New Ecclesial Movements

To begin with, the movements are difficult to define and classify neatly. An Irish theologian, Tony Hanna, describes them as "groupings, mostly comprising lay persons, but also clerics and religious, who are striving for an intense religious life in the community and a renewal of the faith in the Church."[1] In a letter to the World Congress of Ecclesial Movements in May 1998, Pope John Paul II defined a movement as "a concrete ecclesial entity, in which primarily lay people participate, with an itinerary of faith and Christian testimony that founds its own pedagogical method on a charism given to the person of the founder in determined circumstances and modes."[2] Given the generality of these definitions, it's not surprising that they assume many forms. Some of the better known are Communion and Liberation, the Neo-Catechumenal Way, Regnum Christi, Focolare, the Community of Sant' Egidio, and the Charismatic Renewal. To illustrate the power and reach of some of the movements, I will briefly describe three of them, drawing as much as possible on their own sources.

The Fraternity of Communion and Liberation[3]

The movement took its present name in 1969, growing out of a student movement founded by Fr. Luigi Giussani in Milan, Italy in 1954. It continued to grow until, in 1982, it was recognized by the Pontifical Council for the Laity as a "juridical entity for the universal Church" and declared to be an Association of Pontifical Right.[4] In recognition of its thirtieth anniversary in 1984 John Paul II received 10,000 CL adherents in an audience, giving them this mandate: "Go into all the world to bring the truth, beauty, and peace that are encountered in Christ the Redeemer. This is the task that I leave with you today." In a letter to Giussani in 2002, on the occasion of the twentieth anniversary of its juridical recognition, John Paul II described CL as "[aiming] at helping people rediscover

---

[1] *New Ecclesial Movements* (Staten Island, NY: Alba House, 2006), p. 3.
[2] Pope John Paul II, "Movements in the Church," *Laity Today* (1999), 18. Cited in Hanna, p. 5.
[3] For the data which follows, see the official website of Communion and Liberation, www.CLonline.org.
[4] Canons 321-326 provide for Private Associations of the Christian Faithful, and Canons 312-320 for Public Associations. The former possess autonomy, subject to the vigilance of ecclesiastical authority. The latter are erected by competent ecclesiastical authority, whether the Holy See, a conference of bishops in its own territory, or a diocesan bishop in his own territory.

the Tradition and history of the Church, in order to express this in ways capable of speaking to and engaging the men of our time." CL defines itself as a movement because it does not take the form of an organization or structure with formal membership, nor as a special insistence on some particular aspect or practice of the life of the faith, but as a call to live the Christian faith in the present social, political, cultural, and educational environment. There are no membership cards but only the free association of persons in groups called fraternities. The basic instrument for the formation of adherents is a weekly catechesis, called the "School of Community." Despite this seeming informality, the movement claims more than 44,000 men and women in seventy countries who have committed themselves to a program of personal asceticism, daily prayer, participation in encounters of spiritual formation including an annual retreat, and commitment to the support, financial and otherwise, of the charitable, missionary, and cultural initiatives promoted or sustained by the fraternities. It is supported by extensive publications in more than a dozen languages. There is a General Council (commonly called the "Center") presided over by an international leader and uniting the directors in Italy and abroad for every sphere—school, university, work, culture, etc.—in which the movement operates. Each of these spheres is led by its own group of leaders.

Within individual nations, regions, or cities the movement is guided by 'diakonias,' i.e., groups of leaders available for service to the life of the community.

In addition to the fraternities there are special sub-groups or off-shoots:

- Memores Domini is an association of lay persons in CL who have made a choice to dedicate themselves to a life of virginity, living in houses of women or men and following a rule of group living and personal asceticism.
- The Fraternity of St. Joseph is made up of those who wish to dedicate their lives definitively to Christ in virginity, while remaining in their current life situations.
- The Priestly Fraternity of the Missionaries of St. Charles Borromeo is a clerical missionary group recognized since 1989 as its own Society of Apostolic Life. Members live in communities on five continents.
- The Congregation of the Sisters of Charity of the Assumption is a pontifical institute which separated from the Little Sisters of the Assumption in 1993. Its principal ministry is aimed at the family, through helping in the home, caring for the sick, for children in difficulty and for the elderly. It currently has about one hundred members.

The Neo-Catechumenal Way[5]
This movement was founded in the slums of Madrid, Spain, in 1964 by Kiko Arguello, an artist and musician, and Carmen Hernandez, a graduate in chemistry. Moved by the plight of the poor and dispossessed, they began a program of evangelization of adults which took the form of a post-baptismal catechesis, hence the name. At the invitation of bishops and pastors to establish the program in their parishes, it spread rapidly. By 1990 the movement was established on five continents, and Pope John Paul II, in a letter to the

---

[5] For the information which follows, see www.caminoneocatecumenale.it

Vice President of the Pontifical Council for the Laity, recognized it as "an itinerary of Catholic formation valid for our society and modern times." In 1997, in the course of an audience given to the initiators and the itinerant catechists of the Neo-Catechumenal Way, the pope encouraged them to carry on the work of crafting their statutes. The statutes were subsequently approved by the Pontifical Council for the Laity on June 28, 2002.

Facilitating the spread of the NC Way are special diocesan seminaries, called Redemptoris Mater seminaries, which possess their own statutes and a rule of life approved by the respective bishops who have erected them. In 2000 there were about 1500 seminarians enrolled in forty-six of them: twenty in Europe, fourteen in the Americas, six in Asia, one in the Middle East, three in Africa, and two in Australia. By that time 731 priests trained in the NC Way had been ordained. At the same time it was reported that about 4000 young girls from Neo-Catechumenal Communities had entered religious life, especially in enclosed orders. These priestly and religious vocations were nurtured in the 16,700 local Neo-Catechumenal Communities inserted into 5000 parishes within 880 dioceses.

According to the Decree of Approval, the NC Way "places itself at the service of diocesan bishops and parish priests as a means of rediscovering the sacrament of Baptism and of a permanent education in the faith, offered to those faithful who wish to revive in their life the richness of Christian initiation, by following this itinerary of catechesis and conversation. The Neo-Catechumenal Way is furthermore an instrument for the Christian initiation of adults preparing to receive Baptism." In practice, new members, called 'catechumens,' undergo a seven-year long formation program. Although they continue to live at home, they are organized into communities of fifteen to thirty individuals who meet at least twice a week for catechesis and to celebrate the Eucharist. Day-long meetings are held monthly, as well as occasional social gatherings and regular 'scrutinies' and liturgies to mark the transition to a new stage of formation. Eventually some members become 'itinerants' and move on in order to establish communities elsewhere.[6]

Regnum Christi (and the Legion of Christ)[7]
Like the NC Way, Regnum Christi is also closely associated with a clerical movement. It was founded in Mexico City in 1959 by Marcial Maciel, eighteen years after he began the Legion of Christ in Mexico City as a twenty-year-old seminarian. After his ordination, Maciel had taken his followers to Spain and then to Rome for further studies. By 1948 Pope Pius XII had granted the Legion a Nihil Obstat and the Bishop of Cuernavaca raised it to the status of a diocesan congregation. In 1965 Pope Paul VI recognized the Legion as a clerical congregation of pontifical right. It operates educational institutions and centers for the formation of the laity.

---

[6] Description of the formation program is found in the *New Catholic Encyclopedia* article titled "The Neocatechumenal Way" at www.christusrex.org.

[7] The information in this section is largely drawn from www.regnumchristi.org.

Meanwhile, the movement known as Regnum Christi continued to grow. It describes itself as "an international Catholic movement of apostolate at the service of the Church." Its participants number in the tens of thousands in some two dozen countries. Some fifteen thousand members participated in the 60th anniversary celebration of the foundation of the Legion of Christ in Rome in 2001. It chooses not to be identified with a particular project (education, missions, youth work, works of Christian charity, etc.), but rather it "endeavors to prepare a specific type of person who will be able to respond to the needs of the Church and the world. Its specific contribution is to place at the service of the Church men and women committed to Christ, enthused with his message, and capable of establishing far-reaching apostolic projects." To live this spirituality members rely on a personal commitment to daily prayer, regular spiritual direction, and the frequent reception of the sacraments. They also benefit from working with other members, coming together in teams that meet weekly to reflect on the Gospel, apply it to their concrete circumstances, and review the progress of these apostolic activities. Priests from the Legionnaries of Christ usually provide spiritual and apostolic direction for the members.

The extent to which these movements have penetrated the United States is not clear. The United States Conference of Catholic Bishops publishes the *Directory of Lay Movements, Organizations, and Professional Associations 2007-2009*, but none of the foregoing are listed. However, their websites do reference United States locales. Anecdotally there are stories of bishops who have welcomed them into their dioceses and at least one who has banned the NC Way.

Observations and Reflections on the Movements

Each movement owes its origin to a charismatic founder whose personal spirituality and passion for mission attracted followers. In addition to the founders already identified, we could cite Chiara Lubich, the founder of the Focolare movement, Andrea Riccardi, the founder of the Community of Sant' Egidio, and Dorothy Day, the founder of the Catholic Worker Movement. Furthermore, the more successful movements have grown rapidly, spreading from country to country around the world, attracting the allegiance of hundreds of thousands of participants, whether or not they have specific membership rolls.

This rapid diffusion is not a consequence of minimalist requirements for participation. On the contrary, the movements call for uncommon generosity, the gift of time and talent and even money beyond what is expected of the average Catholic. Their requirements include explicit and demanding formation programs and rigorous ongoing spiritual and apostolic practices. Frequent meetings, spiritual guidance from senior members, and personal accountability to movement leaders are all typical.

At their best the movements represent a flowering of the gifts of the laity, congruent with the insights of Vatican II. At the same time, they also involve clergy and religious. As noted above, CL includes various types of lay fraternities as well as a priestly fraternity and a religious congregation of women. The NC Way runs seminaries around the world, preparing priests who will propagate the Way. Regnum Christi is associated with the Legionnaries of Christ. On September 4, 2007, the NC Way held a youth rally in Loreto,

Italy, attended by about 100,000 young people and presided over by Archbishop Stanislaw Rylko, president of the Pontifical Council for the Laity. When the leaders made a 'vocation call,' some 2,000 men and 1,200 women stood up to show their readiness to become priests or consecrated religious.[8]

At present the movements occupy a kind of legislative vacuum in the church. The Pontifical Council for the Laity has general oversight, as noted above, but the generality of the relevant canons provides opportunity both for creative experimentation and for aberrant or heterodox development. The latter observation leads to some critical reflections which have been leveled at the movements.

The first criticism is that the movements can become divisive and cult-like. The NC Way is particularly open to this criticism, since its practice is to provide a separate celebration of the Eucharist for its members within each parish (including a separate celebration of the Easter Vigil). These celebrations are held on Saturday evening, often at a place other than the normal place of worship, and are frequently not listed in the parish bulletin as available to all parishioners. While the celebration generally follows the *Novus Ordo Missae*, certain parts have been deleted or placed in a different location.[9] This exclusivity and allegations of heterodoxy have prompted some bishops to ban the NC Way in their dioceses. The most extensive inquiry was undertaken by Bishop Mervyn Alexander, in Clifton, England, in 1996. The panel charged with reviewing the NC Way concluded that it had damaged the spiritual unity of the three parishes where it was established, and it was subsequently banned. On December 1, 2005 the Congregation for Divine Worship and the Sacraments sent a letter to the leaders of the NC Way admonishing them to follow the liturgical norms for the celebration of the Eucharist. Pope Benedict XVI reaffirmed the message in an audience with them on January 1, 2007. Archbishop Harry J. Flynn of St. Paul-Minneapolis banned the Legionnaires of Christ from his diocese. He further instructed parish heads that Regnum Christi is to be "kept completely separate from all activities of the parishes and the archdiocese," not using parish or archdiocesan property for any meeting or program. His objection was that "pastors sense that a parallel church is being encouraged, one that separates persons from the local parish and archdiocese and creates competing structures." The diocese of Columbus, Ohio, has a similar policy.[10]

Doctrinal positions of some of the movements have also come under criticism. CL is sometimes described as fundamentalist in its theological focus, idealizing the Middle Ages as a time of unity between faith and life, without appreciation for the contributions of the Enlightenment and modern culture. It aroused considerable controversy in the 1980s with its allegations of a huge conspiracy among Communists, Protestants, secular humanists, progressive political parties, liberal Jesuits, and Catholics committed to ecumenical dialogue for 'selling out' true Christianity.[11] Other issues have arisen with

---

[8] www.zenit.org.

[9] See Hanna, pp. 60-62, for a more detailed description.

[10] Jerry Filteau, Catholic News Service, "Minnesota archbishop bars Legionnaires from his archdiocese," Dec. 22, 2004.

[11] See Hanna, pp. 39-45, for further examples.

both the CL and the NC Way over their relationship to dioceses, including that of priests to their bishops.

Finally, some of the movements have been criticized as lacking social awareness or an appropriate commitment to inculturation of the Gospel message. Because the movements are so numerous and extensive, it would be far beyond the confines of this paper to document all of the relevant testimonies and experiences, both positive and negative. My purpose here is only to sketch out the reality with enough detail to illustrate some challenges for the church today and particularly for religious congregations such as the Sisters of Mercy.

Learnings and Challenges for the Sisters of Mercy
Our Institute itself may be regarded as an expression of a movement. Through the centuries the church has been enriched by the monastic, the mendicant, and the apostolic movements. Each was a distinctive response to the Spirit's gifts to the church; each responded to the needs of the time. The foundation of the Sisters of Mercy was part of the apostolic movement—the birth of hundreds of congregations in Europe from the 16th to the 19th century and their rapid diffusion to the New World, as well as new foundations in North America which, in turn, moved out to Africa and Latin America. These movements yielded distinctive congregations which conformed to the canonical regulations of their time. Except in a few areas of Eastern Europe and Africa, the movement of apostolic religious life is in decline today.

This is not a judgment based on an appraisal of the sincerity of current members, but simply an observation that our numbers have declined precipitously since the 1960s and a reversal does not seem likely in the near term. According to the Center for Applied Research in the Apostolate, the number of women religious in the United States has dropped from 179,954 in 1965 to 63,699 in 2007.[12] The membership in the Institute of the Sisters of Mercy of the Americas has declined by approximately a third since its founding in 1991. It is true that there are 165 "emerging communities of consecrated life and lay movements" in the United States founded since 1965.[13] CARA justifies the grouping together of religious institutes and lay movements on the grounds that many of the groups have not yet determined the type of community they hope to become or the ultimate status they will seek within the Church. However, the editors observe that most of the new groups follow, or plan to follow, traditional models of religious life. While this may seem like a new flowering of religious life, 45% of the groups report having six or fewer members. Only 25% have more than fifteen members. And, perhaps as telling, twenty-four of the communities listed in the 1999 CARA directory had ceased to exist by 2006 and another thirty-seven were determined to be ineligible for the later listing.

I would suggest that there are three learnings from the new movements which address challenges inherent in today's world and which are applicable to the Sisters of Mercy.

[12] *The CARA Report*, Vol 13, no. 1 (Summer 2007), p. 6.
[13] See Mary E. Bendyna, RSM, ed., *Emerging Communities of Consecrated Life in the United States 2006* (Washington, DC, Center for Applied Research in the Apostolate, Georgetown University) for the data cited here.

These are observations based on the evident power of the movements to attract and retain members as well as on the treasure of our Mercy heritage.

The first learning is *the necessity of a clear and distinctive spirituality which unifies a group.* Each of the movements profiled, and many others that could be referenced, has a characteristic approach to Gospel living, bequeathed to it by a charismatic founder and nurtured by subsequent leaders. By spirituality here we don't mean something casual or superficial. Sandra Schneiders, IHM, defines spirituality as "the experience of conscious involvement in the project of life integration through self-transcendence toward the ultimate value one perceives."[14] "Experience" suggests that spirituality is not an abstract idea or theory, but a personal lived reality. "Conscious involvement in a project" means that it is neither an accidental experience such as witnessing a beautiful sunset nor the result of a drug overdose nor a collection of practices such as saying certain prayers or going to church. It is an ongoing and coherent approach to life as a consciously pursued and ongoing enterprise. "A project of life-integration" means that it is an effort to bring all of life together in an integrated synthesis of ongoing growth and development. "Self-transcendence toward ultimate value" implies that spirituality is the choice of a direction toward a value that one perceives as positive not only in relation to oneself but in some objective sense. Now I am not suggesting that every participant in the movements we have briefly profiled achieves this integration and intensity of personal spirituality—only that a vision of the spiritual life is laid before each one with powerful clarity and urgency and that the followers collectively embrace it, thus encouraging and supporting one another.

It's not necessary to persuade Sisters of Mercy that we have had an equally powerful vision laid before us in the life and example of Catherine McAuley and reiterated by countless of her followers. From the day that the doors of the first House of Mercy opened in 1827 Catherine was showing us the way of mercy. Words spoken or written by her echo in our collective consciousness today; practices of sheltering the homeless, caring for the sick and for women in distress, instructing young people still occupy our days. The convents she established followed a prescribed Rule and horarium. Many of our documents since the post-Vatican II renewal began give contemporary voice to our inherited treasure.

At the same time, there are tendencies among us to an individualism in spirituality and a lack of shared practice that threaten to undermine the collective witness. The challenge of renewal has been to deepen our appropriation of our shared charism and to adapt our expression of that charism to contemporary needs—tasks of interior and exterior change that are reciprocally related. Without a doubt the Council (and our leaders) under-estimated the difficulty of the task, particularly of the interior change required. Perhaps forty years is too short a time to accomplish it. But the example of the movements tells us that a deeply appropriated common spirituality has the power to unite members and attract others. Moreover, the spirituality of Sisters of Mercy is an ecclesial one, nourished by the Eucharist and sacraments, a point which connects us to the next learning.

---

[14] "Religion and Spirituality: Strangers, Rivals, or Partners?" *The Santa Clara Lectures*, Vol. 6, no. 2, published by Santa Clara University. Lecture given Feb. 6, 2000. Passages cited here are from pp. 3-5.

A second learning from the new movements is *the importance of our ecclesial identity and relationships*. One of the characteristics of the movements we have profiled is their cultivation of episcopal and papal support (sometimes to the detriment of parish participation). They are also closely aligned with clerical groups (CL's priestly fraternity, the Redemptoris Mater seminaries, the Legionnaries of Christ). And, whether one participates in a CL fraternity, a NC Way community, or in a Regnum Christi team, there seem to be clear requirements and boundaries of belonging.

One of my favorite passages from the Apostolic Constitution on Consecrated Life, *Vita Consecrata*, reads as follows: "The consecrated life is not something isolated and marginal, but a reality which affects the whole Church . . . [it] is at the very heart of the Church as a decisive element for her mission . . . it is a precious and necessary gift for the present and the future of the People of God, since it is an intimate part of her life, her holiness, and her mission." (#3) It is my observation that we have not always embraced this central role nor considered ourselves as being at the very heart of the church. Perhaps we subconsciously generalize from an experience of an unsympathetic bishop or a misguided pastor to the totality of the church and choose to stand apart from it. An aid to a deeper reflection might be the lines from the *Constitutions of the Sisters of Mercy of the Americas*, "We carry out our mission of mercy guided by . . . the pastoral priorities of the universal and local church." (#7) Unlike some of the lay movements, religious congregations have historically interfaced well with local churches. For this reason pastors and bishops have sought them out, knowing that the establishment of a new congregation in a parish or diocese will bring blessings in its wake. Thus religious life became a reality which affects the whole church, a decisive element for her mission. The witness of a distinctive way of life contributes to the holiness of the church.

Another task for our future might be to give clearer identification and focus to our lay associates. How are they distinct from the members, while nourished from the same spirituality?

The challenge of choosing an ecclesial identity and cultivating ecclesial relationships was certainly known by Catherine McAuley. The fact that she only chose to found the Sisters of Mercy when it became evident that it was a necessary step to ensure the continuance of the mission she had begun, and the correspondence she maintained with numerous priests and bishops, attest to the attention that she gave to this responsibility.

The third learning has to do with *the centrality of corporate mission*. Here I am raising up something which is not a particular strength of the movements. This is an area where the gift of the Sisters of Mercy to the church can be most clearly demonstrated and where our visibility can be most evident. The Gospel rootedness of the spiritual and corporal works of mercy is direct and unequivocal. The works of mercy address the widespread phenomena and specific problems with which our Conference is concerned. But the fact that the works of mercy embrace so many human needs can mean that our corporate effort becomes diffused.

Fifteen years ago a study entitled, *The Future of Religious Orders in the United States,* came up with the observation that "Under the guise of 'we are more than what we do,' many individual religious and groups have relinquished the power of corporate witness for a variety of individual commitments in effective but unconnected ministerial positions. The emphasis on individual ministry or at times on simply procuring a position, has eclipsed the symbolism of and statement previously made by corporate commitments."[15] I find that statement perhaps even truer today than when it was first published. More recently, sociologist Patricia Wittberg asserted that the loss of connections with institutions contributes to a diminished sense of congregational purpose and public identity, lessens the sense of communal identity and culture, re-directs the energies of the members into diverse and unrelated services, impacts personal and professional development, including mentoring of new leaders, and, finally, diminishes a group's power in the church and society.[16] While the authors of both studies are generalizing about religious congregations in the United States, I find their observations pertinent to the Sisters of Mercy as well. The situation will not be easily reversed.

There is a need to reaffirm our corporate mission for our times, not necessarily to choose corporate ministries—although these can be powerful expressions of the shared mission. The twofold test of whether a congregational mission is more than rhetoric is how effectively it shapes each member's choices (and the leadership's affirmation of those choices) and how much it contributes to the public perception of the congregation.

After Thought
Any conclusions from this brief review of the phenomenon of the lay movements would have to be tentative and partial. My purpose has been rather to introduce a topic which deserves greater examination and analysis from the perspectives of sociology, theology, and religion. My suggestion is that the movements are a sign of our times, that they address "the fundamental hunger for happiness and for genuine spiritual, even religious understanding and peace," and that the Sisters of Mercy have the resources to examine them further. Our goal should not be to adopt their characteristics, but to embrace more decisively what makes us unique and distinctive, while learning from their genuine gifts. The same Spirit animates both religious congregations and lay movements. The church is richer for this diversity.

---

[15] David J. Nygren, CM, and Miriam D. Ukeritis, CSJ. Chicago, IL: De Paul University Center for Applied Social Research, 1992.
[16] *From Piety to Professionalism—and Back? Transformations of Organized Religious Virtuosity.* Lanham, MD: Lexington Books, 2006.

Forgiveness: A Work of Mercy Newly Relevant in the Twenty-First Century

Margaret A. Farley, RSM

The historical and contextual analyses provided (in this Conference) for our interpretation of worldwide experiences in the 21st century are profound and thought-provoking. The essays that probe these experiences constitute a serious challenge for discernment of what the Sisters of Mercy must do and be in this unfolding new century. The narratives (whether from Canada or Kenya, Oceania or Ireland, Guyana or Australia, Jamaica or the U.S.) offer a kind of book of pain. The particular foci (whether on human trafficking, or gender troubles, or globalization, or economic and environmental injustices) intensify the urgency of our continuing to read this book. Essays that connect what is in the book of pain to biblical and ecclesial guidelines for response, and to the past and present vision and labors of the Sisters of Mercy, offer new chapters, and perhaps a new book, of hope (whether through biblical explorations of embodied forms of mercy and justice, or critical interpretations of traditions of spirituality, or evaluative overviews of new movements in the church, or constructive proposals based on Catherine McAuley's commitments and the extension of these through time).

Out of all of the essays there emerge moral imperatives, some explicit, some implicit. For us, there may be no genuine moral dilemmas as to what love and justice require in the human situation. Pain can be remedied, at least in part, and the inhumanity of humans in relation to humans must stop. The more difficult question is what actions to choose that are possible or feasible, and what strategies to develop in the face of our own and others' deep human limitations. We now know almost too much about the intractability of sheer greed, abuses of power, and systemic evils that lie hidden behind "business as usual," genuine ignorance, or fear. Yet perhaps every situation in which the Sisters of Mercy have found themselves has been like this. There has always been the problem of more pain, more poverty, more oppression than this band of women could by themselves remedy. It seems abundantly clear, however, that this never made them turn back in despair, or yield to paralysis of action. There were always works of mercy to be done— whether in response to pain of body or spirit. "Little by little" is a strategy of its own.[1] Each work of mercy done in a "spirit" of mercy constitutes a work of peace against the works of war, a work of instruction against the forces of deception, a work of healing against the damages of individual or societal poison.

For the Sisters of Mercy there have always also been designated priorities for choices about what and for whom works of mercy are to be done: priorities for the poor, for women, for the sick, for those hungry in body and in mind. Moreover, from Catherine McAuley, the Sisters of Mercy learned the importance both of perceiving genuine needs (of concrete persons in concrete situations), and of taking "any kind of opening" (rather

---

[1] I borrow this phrase and its significance both from St. Paul and from Dorothy Day. Yet much of what Catherine McAuley said and did expresses its meaning just as fully. See *By Little and By Little: The Selected Writings of Dorothy Day*, ed. Robert Ellsberg (New York: Alfred A. Knopf, 1983).

than waiting for the perfect opportunity) to respond to need with the works of mercy.[2] Hence, although the challenge of the Sisters of Mercy to discern what they must do in this century remains a serious and difficult one, we are not without general moral principles or more particular strategic and ethical guidelines.

Given this, my aim in this brief essay is not to specify what we ought to do in every part of the world today. I take extremely seriously, and affirm, the recommendations for concern and action contained in the other essays, and I expect these recommendations to become even more compelling as we enter the process of the Conference itself. Here, however, what I will try to do is to identify a particular work of mercy called for in a new way by the multiple situations in our time, in our world.

The work of mercy I have in mind is the spiritual work of "forgiving all injuries." Given the terrible needs that characterize our world, it seems odd to focus on this particular "work." I do so not to obscure the other urgent works of mercy, both "corporal" and "spiritual," but to shed new light on these works and the "spirit" of mercy that informs them. Given the massive injustices that lie behind many of the terrible needs in our world, it may also seem dangerous to begin with forgiveness as an urgently needed work of mercy. I do so not by ignoring calls to resistance and restitution, but by incorporating them into my proposal regarding forgiveness. My argument will be that an attitude of "anticipatory" as well as "actual" forgiveness constitutes today a necessary challenge to the church as well as to groups, nations, and societies around the world. And those whose particular calling is to bring mercy to the world, both as agents and as signs, have a new and urgent responsibility for this work of mercy.

My effort to unfold this two-part argument involves four steps, each taken in the four brief—and largely, therefore, only suggestive—sections below. (1) I begin with a biblical text that asks of the church something it has little understood through the centuries, perhaps particularly in our own day. (2) Following this, I describe ways to understand forgiveness in experiences both of forgiving and being-forgiven. (3) I turn then to examples and possibilities of the power of forgiveness in societal and ecclesiastical contexts of conflict and stark injustice. (4) Finally, I propose new ways of "seeing" that can be brought to situations of religious and civil conflict when an attitude of forgiveness is introduced.

Forgive Them
The church has long believed that Jesus established it with a special power and responsibility to judge individuals and groups. It bases this belief, in part, on a text in the gospel attributed to John. In this text (John 20:19-23), we find the post-resurrection Jesus meeting with his disciples, greeting them in peace, giving them his Spirit, and sending them forth with this charge: "If you forgive the sins of any, they are forgiven them; if you

---

[2] I take the point about "any kind of opening" from Mary Clare Moore's "Bermondsey Annals 1841," cited in Mary C. Sullivan, *Catherine McAuley and the Tradition of Mercy* (Notre Dame, IN: University of Notre Dame Press, 1995).

retain the sins of any, they are retained."[3] In the Roman Catholic community these lines are traditionally (and certainly popularly) understood to refer to authority. They are frequently put together with Matthew 16:19 ("On this rock I will build my church...give you the keys of the kingdom of heaven, and whatever you bind on earth will be bound in heaven, and whatever you loose on earth will be loosed in heaven"). Together these texts are thought to establish not only authority to judge on the part of the disciples of Jesus, but beyond this a structure and content for authority in the church that followed. Hence, most Christians (especially Roman Catholics) hearing this text, think of judgment, and of the authority of the church to whose judgment they are to submit. As those empowered to judge in and by the church determine, so sins will be either forgiven or not forgiven; the gates of heaven will be either opened to individuals who sin, or closed.

But what if there is another meaning to the text in John? What if its primary meaning is not that the disciples of Jesus, and the church, are to sit in judgment on individuals and groups, but that they are to *free* people, and if they do not do so, the word of God is left silent? "If you forgive them, they are forgiven and freed; but if you do not forgive them, they remain bound. So then, *forgive* them, because if you do not, they will remain bound and unfree. And *if you do not forgive them, who will?*"

John 20:23 is not like Matthew 16, where there is reference, apparently, to technical rabbinic procedures. In the gospel of John, Jesus shows the disciples the marks of his wounds, and then gives them a mission of forgiveness. As some theologians have argued (though not necessarily commenting on this particular text): the message of forgiveness is in a sense the Christian message in its entirety. It is the decisive gift of the Holy Spirit.[4] It is what makes possible a "new heart." We are taught to ask for it every day: "Forgive us our sins, as we forgive those who sin against us." It reaches to communities as well as individuals. It requires repentance, but not total innocence. It is to be offered to all who desire to come to the waters to drink of the Spirit, to all who desire to come to the table of the Lord. Only a power that stretches between heaven and earth can provide such forgiveness, such undeserved but yearned for acceptance. And it is a power given not only to a designated few but to all who share in the gift of the Spirit, all who gather to receive God's mercy and the mission to reveal it to others.

But *is* this the truth that Jesus said the Spirit would teach in his name, reminding us of all he had said? Jesus, after all, did make judgments; he did not offer instant forgiveness to all. Yet who were those he challenged and judged? only the self-righteous—those whose hearts were hardened with their own self-assurance, those who recognized no need to drink of new waters or ask for greater mercy. Others—so many great sinners—Jesus did not examine for the perfection of their repentance; he simply forgave them when they approached him. He rejected no one—not Peter, who had his troubles; not James and John who needed a long time to learn humility; not any of those who betrayed him; not

---

[3] Scripture quotations used in this essay are taken from the New Revised Standard Version Bible: Catholic Edition, copyright 1993 and 1989 by the Division of Christian Education of the National Council of Churches of Christ in the U.S.A.

[4] See, e.g., Walter Kasper, "The Church as a Place of Forgiveness," *Communio* 16 (Summer, 1989): 162.

even Judas, with whom he shared a life and a table (and who today may shine in heaven as a blazing testimony to the power of a forgiven love). No evil is so great that God's forgiveness cannot overwhelm it.

What does all of this mean for the significance of forgiveness as a work of mercy in our time? What is the "new heart" that is made possible by the power of the Spirit and that is characterized by forgiveness? Jesus said he did not come to judge, although Christians (especially Christian nations and churches) have been jumping into the judgment seat ever since. What attitudes, dispositions of the heart, would be possible if this were not the case? And what would this mean in the multiple contexts of conflict and injustice today?

The Meanings of Forgiveness
To forgive is not to be passive in the face of injury, neglect, betrayal, persecution, abuse. Indeed, forgiveness may be one of the most active responses possible in the face of whatever sort of breach occurs in human relationships. It is easy to understand the necessity and the role of forgiving when treasured personal relationships are damaged. We reach out to the one we love, participating in the restoration of the bond between us. Or at the very least, we wait patiently, holding on to the love and the hope that the relationship represents. It is not so easy to comprehend the necessity or possibility of forgiving when we are harmed by institutions or groups, or injured by those in power, violated by those who are in some real sense our enemies.

To forgive is to "let go" of something within us, in order to *accept* someone who has harmed us. But what do we "let go" of? Not our sense of justice, nor a sense of our own dignity as a person. Yet in forgiving another, we let go (at least partially) of something *in* ourselves—perhaps anger, resentment, building blocks of stored up pain. And we let go (at least partially) of something *of* ourselves—perhaps our self-protectedness, our selves as desiring renewed self-statement in the face of misjudgment or exploitation by another.

To fathom our experiences of forgiving—whether by gaining insight into our reasons to forgive or into the elements in the experience itself—it is useful to recall our experiences of being-forgiven. When we recognize our own responsibility for hurting another, marring a relationship, losing what we treasured in the other and in our way of being with the other, we are afraid for the future which we had taken for granted and in which we hoped. To experience being-forgiven, however, is to experience new acceptance, in spite of ourselves, and the restoration of a relationship with now a new future. It generates joy in us, gratitude that our failure has not finally broken the bonds of friendship, colleagueship, or family. The greater our infraction and our realization of its seriousness, the greater the possibility of our gratitude at being-forgiven, and the greater our new love in response. Pointing to the depths of the mystery of a "forgiven love," Jesus himself observes that the one who is forgiven much, loves more than the one who is forgiven only a little (Luke 7:41-41).

Between and among humans the need for forgiveness is commonplace in our experience. Although, as Hannah Arendt notes, "willed evil" may be rare, "trespassing is an everyday occurrence . . . and it needs forgiveness. . . ."[5] Why else are we enjoined to forgive "not seven times but seventy-seven times" (Matthew 18:22)? Even when we know not what we do, we are in need of forgiveness (Luke 23:34). "Only through this constant mutual release from what we do are we freed to live into the future."[6]

Although we no doubt learn what it means to be-forgiven within human relationships, the potentially paradigmatic experience for us is the experience of being-forgiven by God. Our experience with humans helps us to understand our experience with God, but God's forgiveness is unique; and it sheds distinctive light on what being-forgiven means in every context. To experience the forgiveness of God is to experience ourselves accepted by the incomprehensible source of our life and existence, accepted even without becoming wholly innocent, without being completely turned around in our ways, accepted even while we are "still sinners" (Romans 5:8). From the almost-incredible "good news" of this forgiveness, this acceptance, we learn of the love of God that exceeds our understanding and our telling, that invites us into communion with infinite goodness and beauty. And the one response that is asked of us, and made possible within us, is the response of trust. To trust in the Word of God's forgiveness is to let go all of our objections and our fears, and to believe. It is to surrender our hearts in our acceptance of being-forgiven. It is, to use a phrase of Emily Dickinson, to "drop our hearts," to feel them "drop" their barriers and burdens, in freedom, accepting eternal Acceptance. It foreshadows the ultimate experience, of which we have inklings: "By my long bright— and *longer*—trust—I *drop* my Heart—*unshriven!*"[7]

At the center of human *forgiving*, too, is a kind of "dropping of the heart" that is the surrender, the letting go, of whatever would bind us to the past injuries inflicted on us by others. It entails a letting go of our very selves, a kenosis, that alone frees us to become ourselves. At the center of human *being-forgiven* is another "dropping of the heart," another kenotic letting go of whatever would prevent our acceptance of the new life held out to us in the forgiveness of those we have injured. "Dropping our hearts," surrendering our selves, in forgiveness (or trust in being-forgiven) is the beginning choice that makes renewed relationships possible. It comes full circle in the mutuality that restored relationships promise.

But what if the injuries we undergo leave our hearts incapable of the kind of love that makes forgiving possible? And what if those who injure us continue to do so? Whether knowing or not knowing "what they do," what if there is no regret or remorse, no willingness or ability to accept our forgiveness? What if the perpetrators of oppression believe their actions are justified—by whatever twisted stereotyping, judging, stigmatizing? How can forgiveness be a remedy in the new killing fields of the century, this era's tangled webs of enslavement, and new levels of destitution? Must our focus now be not on forgiveness, but on justice? Not on "dropping our hearts," but on a struggle against the evils that cry to heaven for change?

---

[5] Hannah Arendt, *The Human Condition* (Chicago: University of Chicago Press, 1958), 240.
[6] Ibid.
[7] Emily Dickinson, *The Complete Poems of Emily Dickinson*, ed. Thomas H. Johnson (Boston: Little, Brown and Company, 1987), 108.

Forgiveness and Resistance

Forgiving and being-forgiven have nothing to do with tolerating grave wrongs, or—as I indicated earlier—with being passive in the face of massive injustices. Neither the forgiveness offered by God in Jesus Christ, nor the forgiveness that can be a graced and towering human work of mercy, is to be equated with "premature reconciliation" or a covering over of exploitation and ongoing violence. Christian and even human forgiveness can include a radical "No!" to the world as a place of injurious conflict, of gross injustice and needless destruction. It can require that we resist the forces of evil until we can do no more. The attitude of forgiveness, however, the disposition of heart required for this work of mercy, does entail that we must not return lies for lies, violence for violence, domination as a supposed remedy for domination. In relation to these evils, a stance of forgiveness can, nonetheless, mean "Never again."

Three stories come to mind that provide glimpses of the power of forgiveness (or at least its attendant possibilities) in diverse historical situations. The first is a story from the Catholic Worker movement during World War II; the second comes from more recent experiences of the role of "truth commissions" in bridging the gap between claims of justice and needs of broken societies; and the third emerges, perhaps most clearly, in the context of fractures within the church.

1. Dorothy Day and World War II: Who Are Our Enemies, and How Shall We Love Them?

Shortly after the United States declared its official entrance into World War II (which in the eyes of many was a "good" and necessary war), Dorothy Day wrote the following:

> Lord God, merciful God . . . shall we keep silent, or shall we speak? And if we speak, what shall we say? . . . 'Love your enemies, do good to those who hate you, and pray for those who persecute you'. . . . We are still pacifists. . . . Our Works of Mercy may take us into the midst of war. . . . I urge our friends and associates to care for the sick and the wounded, to the growing of food for the hungry . . . . 'But we are at war,' people say. 'This is no time to talk of peace. It is demoralizing to the armed forces to protest, not to cheer them on in their fight for Christianity, for democracy, for civilization.'[8]

Catholic Workers were being attacked in person and in the press for their ongoing refusal to support military action as such. They were accused of being cowardly, timid, too frail to stand up for allies unjustly overrun by hostile armies. Day's response was "Let those who talk of softness, of sentimentality, come to live with us in the cold, unheated homes in the slums."[9] She resisted the counsels even of friends who urged her at least to keep silent about the war. "But we cannot keep silent. We have not kept silence in the face of the class war, or the race war that goes on side by side with this world war . . . ."[10] Day

---

[8] Dorothy Day, *By Little and By Little: The Selected Writings of Dorothy Day*, ed. Robert Ellsberg (New York: Alfred A. Knopf, 1983), 261-63.
[9] Ibid., 263.
[10] Ibid., 264.

took her stand on the words of Jesus: "'Greater love hath no one than this, that he should lay down his life for his friend' . . . . Love is not the starving of whole populations. Love is not the bombardment of open cities. Love is not killing, it is the laying down of one's life for one's friend."[11] Here forgiveness (of perpetrators of violence) is coupled with resistance, kenosis with action, and judgment (if you will) with love.

2. Truth Commissions: Can Truth Serve Forgiveness? Forgiveness Serve Justice?

Since the 1970s, "truth commissions" have been established in nearly twenty countries—in, for example, El Salvador, Chile, Argentina, and perhaps the best known of them all, South Africa. Although their results have varied, many of them offer insights into possibilities of transforming hostilities, equalizing relationships, and starting anew in ways that do not always reach the level of forgiveness but also do not descend into the quagmire of past horrors of conflict and oppression.[12] The commissions aimed precisely to structure new approaches to rebuilding societies in the aftermath of horrendous acts perpetrated against innocent people—acts of abduction, torture, exploitation, widespread murder, and sometimes full-scale genocide. Previously, in similar situations, when the killing stopped there might have only been courts to re-establish justice, to judge and to punish perpetrators, perhaps to require some restitution. But when so many were involved in so much evil, the task of bringing all to justice in court systems appeared impossible. Judicial processes alone could not ferret out all who were guilty, nor determine exact degrees of guilt, nor heal the desire of victims for revenge. Courts by themselves could not bring about in a timely manner the healing of whole societies whose fabric had been torn apart by wide scale violence. Above all, courts could not mend the fissures from years and years of conflict between groups, now marked by so much blood.

If countries or societies were to have a future, something more was needed—that is, the freeing of the voices of the victims, the telling of their stories in order to make visible the truth of their suffering, making it known to the world, and receiving an official, public acknowledgment of what had happened. Not all victims lived to tell their stories; of those who lived, not all could by themselves tell the truth of their experiences; not all by themselves could forgive. But with truth commissions it was possible to develop procedures that might provide healing (and in fact did so in many instances). Here was a shared process aimed at remorse on the part of perpetrators and forgiveness on the part of victims.

---

[11] Ibid., 265.

[12] I rely heavily here on the marvelous analysis of these truth commissions provided in Teresa Godwin Phelps, *Shattered Voices: Language, Violence, and the Work of Truth* (Philadelphia: University of Pennsylvania Press, 2004). For other useful views on the commissions and similar proposals for reconciliation, see Miroslav Volf, "Memory of Reconciliation–Reconciliation of Memory," *The Catholic Theological Society of America: Proceedings of the Fifty-ninth Annual Convention* 59 (June, 2004): 1-13; Denise M. Ackermann, "Reconciliation as Embodied Change: A South African Perspective," ibid., 50-67; Raymond G. Helmick & Rodney L. Peterson, eds., *Forgiveness and Reconciliation: Religion, Public Policy, and Conflict Transformation* (Philadelphia: Templeton Foundation Press, 2001); Robert J. Schreiter, *The Memory of Reconciliation: Spirituality and Strategies* (Maryknoll, NY: Orbis Books, 1998). I note here that while my own rendering of the work of truth commissions emphasizes their positive value, they have had their many critics as well. Some of these are considered in the works cited above.

Words, language, became the way to new life. Previously shattered, silenced voices were able to speak; what they spoke were their own stories, the truth of their experiences. Truth swelled up out of the seemingly dead ashes of broken lives and lost loves. Speaking the truth became a form of resistance to evil: "Never again" was part of its message. For victims, it became a way to recover one's life, once again to gain control of one's own agency and destiny. After testimony was given, witnesses were asked what reparations they desired. The responses were modest: sometimes to go to college, or to have a plaque mounted in memory of lost ones; or just to know the name of the perpetrator who had tried to crush their lives, to silence their voices forever.[13]

Sometimes in this process forgiveness became possible; sometimes it did not. But even when it was not possible, or at least not yet possible, something happened to those who spoke or heard one another. The story is told of a South African woman who, after listening to the testimony of her husband's killer and thereby "learning for the first time how her husband had died . . . was asked if she could forgive the man who did it. Speaking slowly . . . her message came back through the interpreters: 'No government can forgive . . . . No commission can forgive . . . . Only I can forgive. . . . And I am not ready to forgive.'"[14] Yet somehow her dignity was affirmed; she had been given the truth, and an opportunity to choose. Once again her own voice counted; the conditions for forgiveness began to be in place.

What the stories of the truth commissions reveal is that forgiving and being-forgiven have a role deep within large-scale conflicts and injustices as well as small. They offer alternative ways to provide "conditions for the possibility" of both justice and mercy. Thus cycles of external violence and internal violence (the poison of rage and revenge) can sometimes be broken; a new future can sometimes emerge.

3. Anticipatory Forgiveness: The Greatest Challenge of All?

There are situations, however, in which injury is ongoing; abuse, violence, and exploitation do not stop. How, then, is forgiveness possible, and what would be its point? In such situations, is forgiveness simply a naive and futile work of mistaken and ineffective "mercy"? Is it here that struggles for justice must take priority over efforts at forgiveness? How, otherwise, are we not to be seduced into "premature reconciliation," the kind of covering over of evil that allows it to continue unchallenged and unchanged? Is the disposition to forgive even relevant at all to responses of the oppressed to their current oppressors?

The challenge in each of these questions is not to be taken lightly. I want to argue, however, that even in situations where injustice still prevails, where the rights of individuals and groups continue to be violated, the dispositions in the heart of the

---

[13] Phelps, 110 and 158 n. 19.
[14] Timothy Garton Ash, "True Confessions," *New York Review of Books* (July 17, 1997): 36-36; as cited in Phelps, 112.

oppressed and violated ought to include (insofar as this is possible[15]) forgiveness—or more precisely, ought to include the readiness to forgive. To argue this in no way contradicts what I have said about the need for resistance—against exploitation, abuse, domination. If we think that forgiveness all by itself is a sufficient antidote to injustice, this is a mistake. But if we think that struggles for justice are sufficient, no matter what is in our hearts, this, too, is a mistake. The challenge and the call to forgiveness in situations of ongoing humanly inflicted evil and suffering is a call to forgive even those we must continue to resist. Forgiveness in such situations is what I call "anticipatory" forgiveness.

Anticipatory forgiveness shares the characteristics of any human forgiving. That is, it involves a letting go within one's self of whatever prevents a fundamental acceptance of the other, despite the fact that the other is the cause of one's injuries. It is grounded in a basic respect for the other as a person, perhaps even love for the other as held in being by God. It does not mean blinding oneself to the evil that is done to oneself or to others. It does not mean passive acquiescence to subservience, or silence when it comes to naming the injury that is imposed. It does not mean failing to protect victims or to struggle with all one's might to prevent the "breaking of the bruised reed." It does mean being ready to accept the injurer, yearning that he or she turn in sorrow to whoever has been injured; it means waiting until the time that the enemy may yet become the friend. It is "anticipatory" not because there is as yet no disposition for acceptance and love, but because it cannot be fulfilled until the one who is forgiven (the perpetrator) acknowledges the injury, and becomes able to recognize and accept the forgiving embrace.

Nowhere is this challenge and call to anticipatory forgiveness more clearly demanded than in the community of the church. It is here that the moral imperative comes forth to love our enemies. It is here that grace should be passed from one to the other, making possible the melting of our hearts and the acceptance of friend and enemy, neighbor and stranger, alike. It is here that we are to be marked by the encomium, "See how they love one another." It is here we learn of the model of God's anticipatory as well as infinitely actual love and forgiveness—whether as expressed in the story of the "Prodigal Son" where the son is awaited and greeted with open arms, seemingly without judgment, seemingly only with yearning desire for the son's return; or in the story of salvation historically enacted in the forgiveness of Jesus Christ, which holds out for our recognition and acceptance, the forgiveness of God.

Many stories could be told, however, of those who have experienced injury in and from the church itself—from its leaders or co-believers. I know of one that remains vivid in my mind. A woman religious was judged by church leaders to be unworthy of her status as a woman religious. The reason for this judgment was that although she served primarily the poor in her role in state government, the budget of her department also distributed funds for abortion for women with no other recourse. She could therefore, it was determined,[16]

---

[15] "Ought" may be too strong a term here. By using it, I do not want to impose yet another burden on those who suffer under ongoing oppression of whatever kind. I simply mean that it is an appropriate disposition, one that can be freeing and strengthening, even under these circumstances.
[16] The determination was made by church officials, not by the leaders of her own community.

no longer continue as a member of her religious community. The rest of her life's journey was marked, not only by utter service to the poor, but by a form of exile, by swords of sorrow, and by the cross. She responded to what was "done unto" her with integrity and visible humility. She remained faithful to her call no matter what forces tried to pluck it out of her heart. There was in her no bitterness and no loss of who she was. "I shall always be a Sister of Mercy in my heart," she said to reporters in those most painful years. She remained in relationship to the community with which she said she had "cast her lot." She lived simply, even frugally. She prayed her office daily, said her rosary, shared in Eucharist. When, just before her death from cancer, she was asked whether she still needed to be reconciled with those who had harmed her, she said simply, "I forgave them." This is what I mean by anticipatory forgiveness. In one context or another of all of our lives, it is asked of us—whether in the church or in the world. And my argument is that it is of particular need in the multiple conflicts, oppressive contexts, of the 21st century. It may be especially needed but also especially possible in the church, where people die because of unreflective traditional teachings regarding sexuality, where people are starved spiritually because they are denied access to the table of the Lord, where actions for justice are sometimes considered betrayals of the gospel, and where power is exercised in ways that are harmful to the marginalized; but also where grace works in ordinary and extraordinary ways and can be counted on still to abound.

New Ways of Seeing
A primary source of conflict among peoples, as well as of desire to maintain dominance, one people or group over another, is the way in which we "see" those who are different from ourselves. Hence, for example, perceptions of gender, racial, and class differences have long undergirded assumptions about superiority and inferiority among human persons. The same is true of cultural and geographical differences. Longstanding conflicts are sustained by myths of human difference, assumptions regarding "each one's place," and memories of the conquered and the conquerers.

The attitude of heart that I have been describing in terms of forgiveness, trust, and readiness to forgive, makes possible new ways of understanding human difference. It allows us, for example, to step back and to look again at biblical warrants for divine valuation of the importance of difference. A quick but extremely thought-provoking instance of this lies in new interpretations of the Genesis account of the story of the Tower of Babel (Genesis 11:1-9).[17] In most of the traditional articulations of this story in Christian churches, it is said that God punished the descendents of Noah by confusing their language and dividing them, scattering them across the earth. In this rendering, the creation and reinforcement of difference is a punishment for human pride. An alternative reading of the story of Babel, however, is that God did not act out of wrath to punish the people who wanted only to stay together; who wanted only to build a city for themselves, with a tower in the midst high enough ("reaching even to the heavens") *not* to challenge God, but to identify themselves among themselves, to give themselves a name so that they would not lose their unity.

---

[17] These interpretations are not as new to the Jewish tradition as to the Christian.

On this alternative reading, God intervened not to punish the people but to prevent them from frustrating God's *original plan* for diversity among humans. These people were not intentionally rebellious against God. Rather, out of fear of loss of one another, they attempted to absolutize their human community, in order to protect themselves from vulnerability and to enable progress in human invention and shared public discourse. The Christian ethicist John Howard Yoder has argued, for example, that what God may have done in this case was to respond graciously to this defensive effort on the part of a people, and thereby to restore God's original plan for human diversification.[18]

Sometimes, in earlier efforts at interpretation, this text has been coupled with the Pentecost story in Acts 2:1-11. And the question is raised: If diversity was God's intent all along, why should there be—by the power of God's Spirit—a seeming reversal of the importance of human difference, now making irrelevant the different languages, cultures, experiences that had marked the history of humans since God's scattering them across the earth. Perhaps the answer to this question lies in the text of Acts which says, after all, not that everyone now spoke and heard the same language, but that *hearing and speaking different languages, they nonetheless understood one particular message.* Those present at this graced moment said to one another: "How can each of us hear [these Galileans] speaking of the mighty deeds of God in our own native language? speaking in our own tongues?" It seems that differences were not erased; deep human difference, that is characterized by diverse languages, histories, cultures, did not become irrelevant. From this we discern that the word of God is not foreign to any human experience; that difference can not only be accepted but needed (and blessed) because it forms the ears that can hear in every tongue the voice of the Spirit.

Today we can recognize in human relationships two meanings of difference, two attitudes in perceiving the "other." "Othering" can be negative or positive. It can mean our projection onto an "other" all the things we consider (however unconsciously) negative in ourselves; it can mean seeing the "other" as always a stranger, making it easier to see her or him as an enemy, or as less than human. In this first way of perceiving the "other," difference becomes a source of violence.

On the other hand, as my colleague Letty Russell has said many times, difference can be understood primarily as a gift needed for human community. If we were all exactly the same, the possibilities of community would be extremely limited. But if difference is necessary for the richness and vitality of community, then in a sense there is no real "other." As some groups have learned to say, "She is not the other; she is my sister." Or "he is not the other; he is my brother." The response made possible, then, to difference is not enmity, not exploitation, not violence, but hospitality.[19]

---

[18] See John Howard Yoder, *For the Nations* (Grand Rapids, MI: William B. Eerdmans Publishing Company, 1997), 61-65. This same view is articulated from a Jewish perspective in Jonathan Sacks, *The Dignity of Difference: How to Avoid the Clash of Civilizations* (New York: Continuum, 2002).
[19] I am indebted to Letty M. Russell for key insights in this regard. See her forthcoming, posthumously published work, *Just Hospitality*, ed. Shannon Clarkson & Kathryn Ott (Louisville, KY: Westminster John Knox Press, 2008).

There remain, however, tendencies in us to make of difference a kind of eternal barrier between and among us. Religious diversity, for example, has been a tragic source of violence through the centuries. In our era it has returned in multiple forms—the violence of judgment and rejection, exclusion and persecution, and even the ultimate violence of killing. Radically new ways of approaching this phenomenon must be tried, ways that will foster the "conditions of possibility" of acceptance, forgiveness, and friendship. Significant work is being done, especially but not only, by feminist religion scholars.[20] A new initiative has been undertaken, for example, to heal the breaches among Christians, Muslims, and Jews. It involves a "new way of seeing" the heritage of these religions and the potential for peace among them. Instead of focusing, as in the past, on a putative unity among these traditions based on the common fatherhood of Abraham, women scholars of Christianity, Islam, and Judaism choose now to focus on their two mothers, Hagar and Sarah. These scholars believe that the problems and possibilities of the past and present can better be understood by following the history of these two women. They believe also that the responsibility of mutual understanding and shared actions for justice falls now to "the myriad children of Hagar and Sarah, now unto the thousandth generation," including those of us who are their daughters and sons today.[21]

A new "way of seeing" is made possible first by at least the minimal "dropping of our hearts" in *respect* for adherents of religions other than our own. Each tradition must find in itself reasons to respect the others. The new way of seeing is then forged through interacting, learning, attempting to understand the beliefs of other traditions, and to comprehend the histories that have led to the imposition of terrible harm. The farther we travel in this new way, the better we "see" our sisters and brothers, and the more clearly we recognize the imperative for being-forgiven and forgiving.

I began this essay by proposing that a particular work of mercy is called for in a new and urgent way in the 21st century, and that those whose whole vocation is to bring mercy to the world have a special responsibility for this work. I suggested that this work of mercy, the "spiritual" work of forgiving all injuries, would not substitute for or counter the other works of mercy or of justice. As a disposition it is radical enough, and sufficiently "embodied," to shape genuinely compassionate love at the heart of all the deeds of love, all the works of mercy. It is conducive to forming hearts that will comfort the sorrowful, counsel those under the stress and pain of doubt, share insight and wisdom, reveal God's beauty in God's mercy so that the hearts of others are awakened and turned to God and neighbor, endure wrongs not passively but actively, reaching out to forgive and transform. It is conducive, too, to deeds of loving justice, and the further works of mercy: finding food and drink for the hungry and thirsty, clothes for the bereft, shelter for the homeless poor, companionship as well as fairness for the imprisoned; and it can motivate responses to the sick, and reverence for the dead.

If Sisters of Mercy can learn to embody this particular work in new ways, in all the troubled and troubling contexts of human distress and need, we will, I believe, be able to

---

[20] See, for example, the many relevant writings by Rosemary Radford Ruether, Diana Eck, and others.
[21] See *Hagar, Sarah, and Their Children: Jewish, Christian, and Muslim Perspectives*, ed. Phyllis Trible and Letty M. Russell (Louisville, KY: Westminster John Knox Press, 2006), 1.

speak truth to power, stand in solidarity with those powerless and injured, challenge forces of evil whether in systems or ideologies, surrender our hearts in a plea for divine forgiveness for ourselves and for all whom we refuse to judge as our enemies. Insofar as this is today's challenge and call to all the world, and within the church, surely it is our call in a particular way.

Women as the Image of God: *"Fire Cast on the Earth – Kindling"*: Being Mercy in the Twenty-first Century

Patricia A. Fox, RSM

This conference, "Fire Cast on the Earth – Kindling," is one expression of our globalization as Sisters of Mercy. Some of the preparatory papers inform and challenge our reading of the signs of these times, others offer light and direction from our history and tradition. The issue we are pursuing together is about "being Mercy in the twenty-first century." Doris Gottemoeller focuses the question more finely when she asks: "What distinctive contribution can we make to the trends addressed in our Summary Paragraph,[1] *precisely as Sisters of Mercy?*[2] It is this question that I would like to address in this paper. Given the capacities for communication and travel that have existed now for decades, it could be considered surprising that as a world-wide community of religious women, we have not responded to such a question with practical intent and in a sustained manner before. However, with the strong strands of autonomy and localization so firmly entrenched within our tradition, we can rejoice that, at last, in this twenty-first century, largely facilitated by the agency of Mercy International Association, we are finding ways to look at the big picture of our world and our times together. Both the urgency of our times and a more vivid and immediate access to Catherine's vision and charism prompt us to a deeper, responsive reception of our charism of mercy for the church and world.

It was the joyful commitment and energy of a group of attractive women recently arrived from England to join the new Institute of Sisters of Mercy, which evoked Catherine McAuley's animated description to her friend Elizabeth – "the fire Christ cast upon the earth is kindling very fast."(*Correspondence* 270)[3] Her use of this vibrant gospel image indicates that she recognized this event of their arrival to be *God's deed*, an initiative of the provident loving God in whom she had placed her trust and her hopes for the future of the Institute of Mercy. I believe that the invitation to us in these days – to discover our global call as Sisters of Mercy in the twenty-first century – provides an opportunity for us to attend to *God's new deed* in us. The global and local pictures of the current social reality could leave us disempowered by their sheer weight and complexity.[4] However, since it is God's Spirit who creates events of communion, I want to recognize this event of our gathering as God's deed which offers us, a newly emerging international body of Mercy women, some deeper wisdom and insight towards collective decision and action. This time together has the potential to 'open a new way of "being centered in God" in life and in ministry in [the] 21st century.'[5]

---

[1] A one-page collation of the issues that those participating in this conference identified as descriptive of the world in which we minister today. See page 9 of this volume.
[2] Doris Gottemoeller, 'Lessons from the New Ecclesial Movements,' International Mercy Research Conference, November 2007. p.176 of this volume. Emphasis is mine.
[3] See Mary Sullivan, 'Catherine McAuley in the Nineteenth and Twenty-First Centuries,' p. 91; Janet Ruffing, ' Fire Cast on the Earth: Spiritual Implications for Mercy in the 21st Century,' p. 163.
[4] See 'Summary Paragraph of Experience' (26 December 2006). Participants in Mercy International Research Conference, November 9-12, 2007, p. 9.
[5] Ruffing, ' Spiritual Implications,' p. 166.

The Spiritual Works of Mercy

I want to focus on an issue that has been raised in several papers and which I believe is intrinsic to our being Mercy in the 21st century, and therefore to our common corporate mission as Sisters of Mercy. Mary Sullivan, when referring to one of the strands we identified to be within our present global reality, suggests that:

> [t]his present-day hunger and ignorance – whether in the rich or poor – is not unlike the lack of religious understanding Catherine McAuley perceived in women, men, and children of her world, nor unlike the poverty of religious awareness to which she ministered through the spiritual works of mercy which were always her stated goal, in and through the corporal works.... [6]

She goes on to emphasize that: "the ministry of Catherine McAuley was always directed to enhancing people's knowledge of and faith in God"[7] and that "highly educated people were often, in Catherine's day as they may be today, spiritually ignorant of a mature theology of God."[8]

Spiritual ignorance of a mature theology of God is precisely the area I wish to address because of its very practical consequences for our mission of mercy. It is to this end that Elaine Wainwright in her paper on 'Mercy Embodied/Embodied Mercy' chooses to use the nomenclature "G*d," in order to "to interrupt our familiarity with naming the divine." Further, she wants:

> to invite us as women of mercy to be/come deeply aware of the power and pervasiveness of dominant male images in our consciousness, woven into our spirituality and theology and given expression in our language and symbol systems. I believe that unless we shift patterns of thought and language, we will not be able to change structures and systems of power on behalf of all those, especially women and children, whom such language marginalizes and renders invisible and hence of no account.[9]

In a similar vein, Janet Ruffing, following the work of Beverly Lanzetta, draws our attention to "the soul wounds that women suffer as a result of patriarchal religion." She notes that "there are profound spiritual dimensions to gender-based discrimination and violence from which we ourselves are not immune."[10] So that while theologically, we know we are equally in the image of God and that God indwells in us as women, our church consistently denies this profound reality in practice. Consequently, "we may live with anger and rage that has no place to go. We live with the sadness of betrayal because our church experience denies our deep feminine wisdom and agency."[11]

---

[6] Sullivan, 'Catherine McAuley in the Nineteenth and Twenty-First Centuries,' p. 95.
[7] Ibid.
[8] Ibid., p. 97.
[9] Elaine Wainwright, 'Mercy Embodied/Embodied Mercy,' Footnote 6, pp. 141-142 of this volume.
[10] Ruffing, 'Spiritual Implications,' p. 171.
[11] Ibid., p. 172.

Related to this, Elizabeth Davis, having set out a confronting mosaic of realities in contemporary society, identifies a series of "troubling questions". One of these is: "How can women be leaders in this age when gender equity and empowerment of women are still distant dreams?"[12] Any analysis of world poverty almost invariably identifies health, literacy and education of women as intrinsic to its remedy. Over a hundred and seventy-five years ago, our founder, Catherine, recognized with clarity that the agency of women was fundamental for the poor to be freed to live a life of dignity and joy. Since then the full force of the mission of Sisters of Mercy, spread to the corners of the earth, has been directed to that end. Yet it is still true that gender equity and empowerment of women, and therefore the leadership of women, are only distant dreams even while globally, new and urgent determinations are made in our time "to make poverty history."

Women and the Theology of God

I want to argue that a mature theology of the God revealed by Jesus in the Spirit – one that does "shift patterns of thought and language" – is crucial if we are "to be able to change structures and systems of power on behalf of all those [afflicted by poverty], especially women and children."[13] In the past few decades women have had access to a theological and biblical education in ways previously not possible. One consequence is that the women, the "other" half of the human race, are for the first time interpreting sacred texts and contributing in significant ways to current theological and ethical discourse. Women's work in theology, and in a particular way within feminist theologies, has challenged us to receive the 'more' of God, to a deeper, richer knowing of God.[14] Theologian Anne Carr has rightly described this phenomenon as a *transforming grace* as it offers us the capacity for the conversion and transformation that can occur when spiritual ignorance makes way for a more mature theology of God.

My concern is about how the fruits of decades of women's work in biblical and theological research can be made accessible and be "received" by the people of God in ways that enable conversion and transformation. To explore this, I will focus briefly on an area of theology that is familiar to me. As a Sister of Mercy, I have been privileged over years to have been able to study systematic theology with a particular focus on the doctrine of the Trinity. I was prompted to pursue such studies because my pastoral involvements had led me to recognize the practical effects of the beliefs we hold. I recognized in particular that the symbol of God as Trinity, which is at the very heart of our spiritual and theological tradition, has had little if any practical import in people's lives. For so many, it is still largely a dormant symbol, its power to communicate the dynamism of the liberating God Jesus proclaimed by his life and deeds, mostly muted. In recent decades, however, many theologians have contributed to a widespread revival of

---

[12] Elizabeth M. Davis, 'How Can we Dare Wisdom and Mercy in the Mosaic of Our Realities?' p. 13. For two different perspectives on the issue of the leadership of women see also Senolita T. Vakatā, 'Gender Development in Oceania Region' and Sophie McGrath. 'The Political Ministry of Women: An Australian Perspective.'

[13] Wainwright, 'Mercy Embodied', Footnote 6, pp. 141-142.

[14] See, for example, Wainwright, 'Mercy Embodied,' for profound new insights into Jesus as the Wisdom and Compassion of God, and Ruffing, ' Spiritual Implications,' for her enriching work on the Holy Spirit.

this central symbol of our faith. The work of women in this enterprise, as in every arena of theological work, has been and will continue to be crucial.

Many would be familiar, for example, with the work of North American theologian and Sister of St Joseph, Elizabeth Johnson. Johnson addresses the issue of why the doctrine of the Trinity became irrelevant to Christian life. Her focus on the practical impact of the symbol of God uncovers how this central symbol of God as Trinity has functioned for millennia "to support an imaginative and structural world that excludes or subordinates women" and how in turn, this "undermines women's human dignity as equally created in the image of God."[15] She shows how patriarchal religious culture has both confined women to an inferior place and limited speech about God to male images. The seriousness of this situation is emphasized early in her primary publication on the Trinity, *She Who Is: The Mystery of God in Feminist Theological Discourse*, 1992, when she repeats in mantric fashion, "The symbol of God functions."[16] She uses this sentence like a red flashing light to alert the reader that "what is at stake is the truth about God, inseparable from the situations of human beings, and the identity and mission of the faith community itself."[17] In the context of this discussion, we could add to this by owning that the symbol of God can contribute negatively to the phenomenon of world poverty.

Johnson articulates here something that Catherine McAuley knew very well – that there is an intrinsic link between the spiritual and corporal works of mercy. How we speak about God matters because "what is at stake is the truth about God, *inseparable from* the situations of human beings." The symbol of God truly does function. The God or gods worshipped by an individual person or by societies shapes behavior. And it is for this reason that a consideration of the naming of God takes on a particular urgency. Johnson's method evaluates the effects of sexism within society and theological discourse and addresses the debilitating patriarchal effects of the names, imagery and structure of the Trinity, on the Christian community and on women's lives in particular. She draws attention to a fact that has been steadfastly ignored by theologians for centuries: that exclusively male imagery for God has been used in an uncritically literal way, leading to a form of idolatry. This in spite of key theological principles for language about God commonly accepted at the heart of the tradition.[18] Further, she shows that while affirming and promoting the equality of the divine persons and their mutual interrelation, the classic doctrine subverts this by maintaining the rigid hierarchical ordering as Father, Son and Holy Spirit.

Johnson's constructive feminist theology of the Trinity along with those of many others[19] addresses the challenge posed by the limits of the trinitarian theology we have inherited,

---

[15] Elizabeth Johnson, *SHE WHO IS: The Mystery of God in Feminist Theological Discourse* (New York; Crossroad, 1992), p. 5.
[16] Ibid., pp. 4 - 6.
[17] Ibid., p. 6.
[18] Johnson refers to the testimony in scripture and later tradition regarding the incomprehensibility of God, to the centrality of the teaching on analogy within the Roman Catholic tradition, to the need for many names of God, and to the apophatic tradition within Christianity. Ibid., pp. 104-120 .
[19] See for example, Catherine Mowry LaCugna, *God for Us: The Trinity and Christian Life* (New York: HarperSanFrancisco, 1991); Ivone Gebara, *Longing for Running Water: Ecofeminism and Liberation*

and this growing body of work can be accessible to us. While it is not possible within the scope of this paper to draw on the richness of this scholarship, I want to provide one example from British-born Sarah Coakley, presently teaching at Harvard, who elaborates an insight relevant to this present discussion on a mature theology of God. Coakley's trinitarian theology values the apophatic tradition as she examines the capacity of patristic sources to hold the contradictions and ambiguities of language necessary for appreciating both the mystery of God and self. She focuses on the work of Gregory of Nyssa demonstrating that the process of human transformation is the Trinity's very point of intersection with our lives. She suggests that such transformation requires "profound, even alarming shifts in our gender perceptions, shifts which have bearing as much on our thinking about God as about our understanding of ourselves."[20] She refers to Gregory's late work, the *Commentary on the Song of Songs,* where he "charts in highly imagistic and eroticized language, the ascent of the soul into the intimacy of the Trinity." Coakley observes that the message that Gregory wishes to convey is that if the soul is to advance to ultimate intimacy with the trinitarian God, gender stereotypes must be reversed, undermined, and transcended; and that the language of sexuality and gender, far from being an optional aside or mere rhetorical flourish in the process, is somehow necessary and intrinsic to the epistemological deepening that Gregory seeks to describe."[21]

Through such patristic evidence, Coakley attempts to illuminate an "alternative" approach to the Trinity which gives experiential priority to the Spirit and to prayer. In so doing she uncovers what she believes are the false divisions between "theology" and "spirituality."[22]

The careful and creative biblical and theological work involved to redress the major gender imbalance that has been in place for two thousand years is progressing, albeit slowly. It seems to me important that Sisters of Mercy are, and will continue to be, involved in this task, and that this happens through the lens of different cultures and perspectives. This endeavour comes under the rubric of *spiritual works of mercy* and as such has the potential to make a major contribution towards restoring the full humanity of women.

A related dimension of this work is the change that needs to happen at the more primal level of human consciousness. And this is perhaps the most telling and the most difficult arena of transformation because the symbols that reside at the centre of a person's identity and meaning need to be approached with reverence and care. This place is sacred

---

(Minneapolis: Fortress Press, 1999); Sallie McFague, *Models of God: Theology for an Ecological, Nuclear Age* (Philadelphia: Fortress Press, 1987); Patricia A. Fox, *God as Communion: John Zizioulas, Elizabeth Johnson and the Retrieval of the Symbol of the Triune God* (Collegeville, MN: A Michael Glazier Book published by The Liturgical Press, 2001).

[20] Sarah Coakley, "'Persons' in the 'Social' Doctrine of the Trinity: a Critique of Current Analytic Discussion," in Stephen T. Davis, Daniel Kendall SJ, Gerald O'Collins SJ (eds.), *The Trinity: An Interdisciplinary Symposium on the Trinity* (Oxford: O.U.P., 1999), p. 125.

[21] Ibid., p. 142.

[22] Sarah Coakley, 'Why Three? Some Further Reflections on the Origins of the Doctrine of the Trinity,' in Sarah Coakley & David A. Pailin (eds.), *The Making and Remaking of Christian Doctrine: Essays in Honour of Maurice Wiles* (Oxford: O.U.P., 1993), p. 47.

ground. For some, the move to consider the *Holy One* at the centre of their life as *God-She* or even *God-Three* can be so disturbing that it is simply covered over and put aside. For others, even when exposed to excellent theological sources and teaching, and even when intellectual assent is able to be given, the actual move to *receive* a fuller, orthodox, albeit often discordant, understanding of God is finally aborted. When the reception of the incomprehensible God does not have the opportunity to move to the place of the affect, to the place where God is discovered as *Love beyond All Telling,* as *Compassion Poured Out,* theological truth can revert quickly to the previous default position – to the safe place of one's childhood or adolescence. The intellectual entry point closes over. It is all too threatening and *God-He* resumes his throne. This is one of the reasons why the spiritual works of mercy or the ministry of spirituality is so important.

The Ministry of Spirituality

As long ago as 1975 Margaret Farley writing about mutuality in a Trinitarian model and addressing the issue of gender in the naming of God, argued that: "What is important is that there be room… for women to know themselves as images of God, as able to be representatives of God as well as lovers of God."[23] Even longer ago, Catherine McAuley established the first *House of Mercy* in Dublin to provide a space where women could be treated with full human dignity, as persons made in God's image. Today that call from women world-wide is still ours. Moreover, since those first days in Baggot Street, the faces of literally thousands of Sisters of Mercy have been revealing the female face of God to those to whom they minister. As have the faces of multitudes of women everywhere. This fact however has, for the most part, not seemed to contribute to a reception of the truth that woman is made in the image of God and that our naming of the incomprehensible God needs to include female images. Nor has this truth of women as *imago Dei* been translated into practice within the church.

I was profoundly moved recently when I attended a performance of the opera "Dead Man Walking" based on the experience and book of Josephite Sister Helen Prejean. Toward the finale, close to the point of the prisoner going to his place of execution, Helen finally enabled Joseph de Rocher (a fictional name) to own the evil effects of his murderous crime. She tells him he did a terrible thing, and he is despairing of forgiveness. The music from orchestra and voice soars as the climax of this work approaches:

Joseph	But could anyone forgive me?
Sister Helen	God is here, Joe, God is here right now.
Joseph	I did such a bad thing, Sister, maybe my dyin' will give them folks some relief.
Sister Helen	Joseph, when they do this thing to you….
Joseph	Sister Helen, I'm gonna die!
Sister Helen	I want you to look at me, Joe. I want the last thing you see in this world to be the face of love. *Look at me, Joe. I will be the face of Christ for you. I will be the face of love for you.*[24]

---

[23] Margaret Farley, 'New Patterns of Relationship: Beginnings of a Moral Revolution,' *Theological Studies* 36 (1975), p. 643.

[24] Terence McNally, Libretto of the opera *Dead Man Walking,* 2000. Commissioned by the San Francisco Opera. Music Jake Heggie. Emphasis mine.

The crescendo of music and dramatic action draws the viewer into the redemptive power of the moment portrayed and announces powerfully to anyone willing to hear: *a woman's face reveals the face of God!* Besides its being a relief to witness a woman religious portrayed with such authenticity, this opera based on an actual event acknowledges that a woman can indeed reveal Christ's face, God's face. More broadly, it is also a potent example of the ministry of spirituality at work.

Bonnie Brennan traces the evolution of this ministry in Ireland from Catherine and the early foundations until the present and for the purposes of her paper she defines the ministry of spirituality thus: "in an intentional way, [the ministry of spirituality] puts the focus on learning about God; fostering a relationship with God; and finding meaning in our lived experiences in accordance with this relationship."[25] Following this definition, I am proposing that the work of facilitating the recognition that the truth about God is *inseparable from* the truth about women being made in the image of God needs to become one significant dimension of the ministry of a Mercy spirituality. I believe that this recognition is intrinsic to the spiritual works of mercy and an important arena for the ministry of Sisters of Mercy.

Other significant strands of an emerging Mercy spirituality – truly *God's new deed* in us – inevitably arise and are deepened as we listen to each other describe the situations of our corporal works of mercy. Hence the importance to the work within this conference of the papers of our sisters from Kenya, Guyana, Jamaica, Tonga and from the 'places' of ministry like that of Human Trafficking that are now distressingly global. A recent series of postings on *Mercy E-news* from sisters gathered from many countries provide powerful examples of this process at work. I refer to those who participated in the September *Mercy Global Concern* "Bridging the Gap" workshop organized at the United Nations by Deirdre Mullan, RSM. The focus of the workshop was "Promoting Human Solidarity and Care for Earth," and Sisters Claudette Cusack and Mary Daly recorded these entries respectively:

> Deirdre had arranged an amazing program for us that gave us an insight into how the vision of Catherine McAuley was being lived out today in places of dire need around the globe. Day after day we were privileged to hear from our Sisters working to alleviate injustice and to change the systems that perpetuate suffering. Time after time we were made aware of the importance of communication and co-operation between those working on the ground and those working for systemic changes. Both are needed if the poor are to be cared for in the long term. [Paper Number 7]

> The MGC sponsored workshop, "Bridging the Gap," impacted me in several different ways. Hearing from Mercies around the world has deepened my appreciation for and understanding of the Mercy charism. It will affect the work that I do… [in] retreats and spiritual direction…I would like to revisit work I have

---

[25] Bonnie Brennan, 'History of the Sisters of Mercy of Ireland in terms of the Ministry of Spirituality,' p. 100.

done on Mercy spirituality and add or strengthen an emphasis on a contemporary understanding of mysticism and the experience of God; of the role of the experience of chaos and darkness; on the implications for spirituality of seeing God as subject rather than object; of the gift of Mercy emphasis on the relational and on systems for response; on chaos, darkness and the cross and the challenge of hope. [Paper Number 4][26]

This provides a glimpse of the formative effects of our ministries on our theology and spirituality. The fruits of this creative interplay between corporal and spiritual works are also evident more broadly within religious orders and lay ecclesial movements. For example, a recent radio programme in Australia on human trafficking illustrated the creative impact of a nation-wide network of women and men religious. Jennifer Burn, a senior lecturer in law who directs the Anti-Slavery Project at the University of Technology, Sydney, commented:

> There are whole groups of people and networks working across Australia in dealing with anti-trafficking. The religious networks are unique and have made an incredible contribution to the anti-trafficking movement in Australia and they have, in many ways, led the development of law reform and debate in this area.

> Working in anti-trafficking, anti-slavery work is incredibly difficult. It's draining, it's complicated and there have been very few positive outcomes. One of the enormous benefits that I've found from working with religious communities is that they come to the area with a different framework. They have a theology and a commitment that might have a different motivation from the one that I'm working from. One of the things that they do is to think about process... What they will do is to have some period of reflection that's built into discussion...[27]

This observation identifies a distinctive contribution that religious communities as a whole have to offer the "incredibly difficult" work of addressing the raw issues of our time. In pursuing the question of what our distinctive contribution as Sisters of Mercy might be, I have drawn from our tradition of the significance of the dignity of women and linked it to the transformative theological and spiritual implications of women created in God's image. I have connected this to the spiritual works of mercy being intrinsically related to the corporal works of mercy.

Conclusion

In conclusion, I want to draw from the insights that Doris Gottemoeller offers from her analysis of the elements that have contributed to the present flourishing of new ecclesial ministries within the church. Gottemoeller puts forward "three learnings from the new movements which address challenges inherent in today's world and which are applicable to the Sisters of Mercy...The first learning is *the necessity of a clear and distinctive*

---

[26] Mercy Global Concern, Mercy E-News, October 1, 2007.
[27] 'A Light at the Door,' *Encounter,* ABC Radio National, September 23, 2007.

spirituality which unifies a group.[28] She notes that "the example of the movements tells us that a deeply appropriated common spirituality has the power to unite members and attract others."[29]

I am suggesting from all of the above that as Sisters of Mercy in the 21st Century we have the capacity to articulate and draw from a rich and deep spirituality of Mercy that is born of a mature theology of God, of an understanding of the profound importance of knowing women are created in the image of God, and from the cumulated shared wisdom that service of the poor unleashes. I believe that this is *God's new deed* in us – *Fire Cast on the Earth – Kindling.* Our challenge is to find explicit ways to own and appropriate together, as a global entity of Sisters of Mercy, such a theology/spirituality/praxis. If that were to happen, the other two learnings from the new movements – *the importance of our ecclesial identity and relationships* and *the centrality of corporate mission* – would follow.

In 2001, in an article published in the bulletin of the Union of Institutes of Superiors General, Marie Chin quoted from the play, *A Sleep of Prisoners,* by Christopher Fry. Some lines from the play seem equally appropriate for us now:

> *Thank God our time is now when wrong*
> *Comes up to face us everywhere,*
> *Never to leave us until we take*
> *The longest stride of soul [we] ever took.*
> *Affairs are now soul size*
> *The enterprise*
> *Is exploration into God.*[30]

---

[28] Gottemoeller, 'New Ecclesial Movements,' p. 182.
[29] Ibid.
[30] See Marie Chin, RSM, UISG Bulletin, Number 116 (2001), p. 68.

APPENDIX 1

Conference Participants

The Participants in the Mercy International Research Conference in November 2007 were the following Sisters of Mercy:

- M. Francis Añover (Philippines)
- Bonnie Brennan (Ireland)
- Tui Cadigan (Waitaha, Ngati Mamoe, Poutini Ngai Tahu—Aotearoa New Zealand)
- Elizabeth Davis (Newfoundland)
- Mary Kay Dobrovolny (Americas)
- Elizabeth Dowling (Australia)
- Margaret Farley (Americas)
- Patricia Fox (Australia)
- Doris Gottemoeller (Americas)
- Janette Gray (Australia)
- Anne Hannon (Ireland)
- Anne Ciku Itotia (Kenya, Ireland)
- Dolores Liptak (Americas)
- Theresa Lowe Ching (Jamaica, Americas)
- Mary Lyons (Ireland)
- Sophie McGrath (Australia)
- Elizabeth McMillan (Honduras, Americas)
- Mary Noel Menezes (Guyana, Americas)
- Kathleen Murphy (Scotland, Britain)
- Ana Maria Pineda (Americas)
- Meta Reid (Ireland)
- Penny Roker (England, Britain)
- Janet Ruffing (Americas)
- Mary Sullivan (Americas)
- Senolita Vakatā (Tonga, New Zealand)
- Elaine Wainwright (Aotearoa New Zealand; Australia).

Supporting the Conference were the following Sisters:

- Facilitators—Veronica Lawson (Australia) and Frances Repka (Americas)
- Liturgist—Sheila O'Dea (Ireland; Newfoundland)
- Media Specialist—Adele Howard (Australia)
- Managing financial and other details—Ethel Bignell (MIA Administrator; New Zealand)
- Attending the Conference on behalf of the Members of the Mercy International Association was Patricia Bell, Leader, Institute of Our Lady of Mercy, Britain

Biographies of Conference Attendees (November 2007)

M. Francis Añover, was born in Leyte, Philippines on May 3, 1953 and was baptized Nelinda Burgos Añover. She finished a Commerce course major in Accounting, and worked in a bank before entering the convent. Her Master course is in Pastoral Sociology. She is passionate about women's and children's issues, peace and human rights as well as environmental issues. She has been in the congregational leadership team as a council member twice.

Bonnie Brennan's main ministry is Spiritual Direction, Supervision and Retreat Giving. She is also involved in promoting Mercy spirituality through retreats and talks on Catherine McAuley, and the publication of '*It Commenced with Two ....*', and *According to Catherine.* She is presently co-ordinator, for the Northern Province (Ireland), of the *'Circle of Mercy,'* a form of association which involves Sisters of Mercy and lay women and men as equal members.

Tui H. L. Cadigan is from Aotearoa New Zealand. She is one of two Sisters of Mercy of Maori descent and is the delegate for Maori Religious on Te Runanga o Te Hahi Katorika ki Aotearoa (National Catholic Maori Council). She works primarily with Maori in the community and within government organisations. She affiliates to the three South Island Iwi (tribes) of Waitaha, Ngati Mamoe and Poutini Ngai Tahu.

Elizabeth M. Davis is a member of the Congregation of the Sisters of Mercy of Newfoundland (Canada), a doctoral student in Scripture at the University of Toronto, and a part-time faculty member at the Toronto School of Theology. She has taught high school, has served as Chief Executive Officer of St. Clare's Mercy Hospital and the Regional Health Authority in St. John's, Newfoundland, and presently serves on several national health boards in Canada.

Mary Kay Dobrovolny is a member of the Sisters of Mercy of the Americas. Her ministerial background is in housing and education, and she is currently teaching theology and directing the Campus Ministry programs at the College of Saint Mary in Omaha, Nebraska. She is in the final stages of the dissertation process and anticipates receiving a Ph.D. in New Testament and Early Christian Origins from Vanderbilt University in Nashville, Tennessee, in December 2007. Her dissertation is: "A Spirituality of Speaking Out in the Gospel of Mark."

Elizabeth Dowling is a member of the Ballarat East Congregation (Australia). Liz completed her Doctor of Theology in 2005 and published a book entitled *Taking away the Pound: Women, Theology and the Parable of the Pounds in the Gospel of Luke* in 2007. She lectures in Biblical Studies at Australian Catholic University. Her areas of research interest are New Testament (particularly the Gospels of Luke and John), and feminist biblical hermeneutics.

Margaret Farley is Gilbert L. Stark Professor Emerita of Christian Ethics at Yale University Divinity School. Her publications focus on issues in historical Christian ethics, Roman Catholic ethics, medical ethics, sexual ethics, and ethics and spirituality. She is Co-director of the All-Africa Conference: Sister to Sister, which addresses the mutual empowerment of women responding to the HIV and AIDS pandemic in sub-Saharan Africa. She is past president of both the Catholic Theological Society of America and the Society of Christian Ethics.

Patricia Fox is from Adelaide, South Australia and has been involved in secondary, and tertiary education, and in formation, spiritual direction and retreat work. She has held leadership positions within the Mercy Institute and the Archdiocese of Adelaide. More recently Pat has completed doctoral studies in systematic theology with a focus on the Trinity and feminist theologies and is presently directing a ministry formation program within her local archdiocese.

Doris Gottemoeller is currently the Senior VP for Mission Integration at Catholic Healthcare Partners, a multi-state health system. She previously served as the first president of the Sisters of Mercy of the Americas. She earned a Ph.D. in theology from Fordham University, with a focus on ecclesiology.

Janette Gray lectures in systematic theology at the Jesuit College of Theology in the United Faculty of Theology, Melbourne (Australia). Her teaching areas are the theology of the human person, church, church-state relations, feminist theology, and Christian-Muslim relations.

Anne Hannon has been Vice Postulator of the Cause of Canonization of Catherine McAuley since 2003. She is currently responsible for promoting the Cause in Europe and Africa. Anne taught primary school for many years, and earned her M.A. in Pastoral Studies from Seattle University and her M.A.C.C from the University of Wales. She served on her diocesan congregational leadership team, and then for six years on the first Council of the South Central Province of the Congregation of the Sisters of Mercy (Ireland).

Kenyan born, **Anne Itotia** first trained as a teacher and worked both in class and school administration for ten years. Currently, she is on sabbatical after six years of Team Leadership at the Congregational level (2000-2006). She has also worked as the African Justice Desk coordinator in Pretoria, South Africa.

A member of the Northeast/Connecticut community, **Dolores Liptak** has authored five books on European immigration to the United States and three on American Catholic women since receiving her doctorate in American History from the University of Connecticut. Dolores is on the faculty of Holy Apostles Seminary, Cromwell, CT; continues to write and edit; and serves as mentor to those needing guidance with historical or archival projects. Her recent publication is *A Testing Ground of Renewal: The Sisters of Mercy of the Union, Detroit Province: 1966-1973.*

Theresa Lowe Ching is a member of the Sisters of Mercy in Jamaica (Americas). She holds an M.A. in theology from Notre Dame University, Indiana and a Ph.D. in Systemic Theology with a concentration in Latin American Liberation Theology from the University of St. Michael's College, Toronto School of Theology. She is presently Director of St. Michael's Theological College in Kingston, Jamaica.

Resident in Galway, **Mary Lyons** is a member of the Western Province of the Congregation of the Sisters of Mercy (Ireland). A former Secondary School teacher, she is now a practicing Canon Lawyer. She received her JCD degree and Ph.D. (Canon Law) from St. Paul University and the University of Ottawa, and is a member of the Mercy International Research Commission.

 **Sophie McGrath** is a member of the Congregation of the Sisters of Mercy, Parramatta, Australia. She has a special interest in religion, church and women's histories, and, in an effort to contribute to breaking the cycle of the loss of women's history, she co-founded the Golding Centre for Women's History, Theology and Spirituality at the Australian Catholic University where she is currently a Research Fellow.

 **Elizabeth McMillan** teaches theology in San Pedro Sula, Honduras, and is engaged in community organizing with women and in religious vocation and formation ministry. In the past she has taught at the seminary of the Missionary Fraternity of Mary in Guatemala City (1992-1998), at Carlow College, Pittsburgh, and at Loyola University in Chicago. Betsy holds a Ph.D. in philosophy from Catholic University of Louvain in Belgium, and an M.A. from Marquette University.

 **Mary Noel Menezes**, Professor of History, has taught in Universities in the U.S.A., England, Holland, India and the Caribbean. She has authored books, monographs and articles on the Amerindians of Guyana and the Portuguese in Guyana and has been the recipient of national, regional and international honours and awards including Honorary Doctorates from College Misericordia, Dallas, Pa., and the University of the West Indies. For 35 years she also administered St. John Bosco Orphanage and currently works with the older boys at Mercy Boys' Home.

 **Kathleen Murphy** is the author of *The Women of the Passion* and a guest writer for "The Scottish Catholic Observer," Scotland's national Catholic paper. Her new book on *The Women of the Early Church* is due to be published for Pentecost Sunday next year. She is experienced in giving retreats and days of recollection and in lecturing in Women's Biblical Studies; for the last four years she has contributed quarterly prayer services for posting on the mercyworld.org website.

 **Ana Maria Pineda**, born in San Salvador and raised in the Latino sector of San Francisco, holds an S.T.D. in Pastoral Theology from the Universidad Pontificia de Salamanca, Spain. She is an Associate Professor in Religious Studies at Santa Clara University since 1997. Ana Maria has received the Yves Congar Award for Theological Excellence from Barry University, Florida, and an Honorary Doctorate in Theology from Saint Xavier University, Chicago, and is a founding member of the influential Hispanic Theological Initiative which provides scholarships and mentoring for Latino doctoral theological students.

 **Meta Reid**, a member of the Western Province of the Congregation of the Sisters of Mercy (Ireland), holds an Ed.D. and Ed.M. from Harvard University, and an M.A. (English) from the University of Chicago. Meta is currently Director of Postgraduate Diploma in Education in the National University of Ireland, Galway. Her interest in organizational change is informed by a passion for social justice and the challenges of building a multicultural society in the Ireland of today.

 After graduating from Cambridge University, **Penny Roker** spent 22 years as a secondary school History teacher. Entering religious life at the age of 45, she worked as a prison chaplain for six years before making Final Profession last year. Her book on Julian of Norwich called *Homely Love* was recently published by Canterbury Press. She is currently living in London and working as a school counselor.

 **Janet Ruffing** spent her first years in ministry teaching English and Religion in Mercy secondary schools in California. After completing her Ph.D. in Christian Spirituality at the Graduate Theological Union in Berkeley, she has spent the last 22 years chairing a concentration in spirituality and spiritual direction in the Graduate School of Religion and Religious Education at Fordham University in New York City. She has published widely in her field, has relished the opportunities she has had to present internationally, and is looking forward to this international gathering of Mercy scholars.

 **Mary Sullivan** taught Literature and Writing courses at the Rochester Institute of Technology for 35 years. She is now Professor Emerita and Dean Emerita of RIT. She is the author of *Catherine McAuley and the Tradition of Mercy* and editor of *The Correspondence of Catherine McAuley, 1818-1841*. She lectures on Catherine McAuley, directs Mercy retreats, and supports poor families in the neighborhood of her community.

 **Senolita Vakatā** is a member of the Sisters of Mercy, Aotearoa New Zealand. She currently ministers on the islands of Tonga, South West Pacific, working with Caritas Tonga and coordinating the diocesan office for Justice and Development. Among many other endeavors, Senolita organizes workshops on Environmental Justice. She holds a degree in theology from Yarra Theological Union, Melbourne, Australia.

 **Elaine Wainwright** is a member of the Brisbane Congregation of the Australian Institute of the Sisters of Mercy. Her passion lies in enabling communities of faith to engage with their sacred story in the scriptures in ways that are transformative of their lives, and she does this through teaching, research and publication, workshops and preaching. Currently she is Professor of Theology and Head of the School of Theology at the University of Auckland, New Zealand.

 **Veronica Lawson** is a Ballarat East Sister of Mercy who taught biblical studies at Australian Catholic University for twenty-six years before taking up her present position as Congregation Leader. Her main research interest is in feminist interpretation of the Christian Scriptures, especially Luke's gospel and the Acts of the Apostles. She has conducted biblical workshops, especially on mercy, in various parts of Australia, the Pacific Islands, Papua New Guinea, Pakistan, Kenya, and Ireland.

 **Fran A. Repka** is a member of the emerging South Central Community of the Institute of the Sisters of Mercy of the Americas. She serves as Executive Director and Psychologist of Mercy Professional Services, a counseling and consultation Center for the uninsured and underserved as well as for Religious and Clergy. Besides her clinical work of over 30 years, Fran facilitates groups, supervises other professionals, consults for Religious Congregations and Leadership Teams, and has done workshops throughout the U.S. as well as in Latin America, South Africa, Papua New Guinea, Russia, Czechoslovakia, and Guam.

 **Sheila O'Dea**, D.Min., from Newfoundland, is Director of Liturgy at All Hallows College, Dublin. Lecturing internationally, Sheila has researched and focused on the connection between liturgy, catechesis, and mission in the life of the community.

Adele Howard is a member of the Institute of Sisters of Mercy Australia, Melbourne Congregation. She is the Director of Fraynework Multimedia, a Mercy ministry which assists organizations to communicate more effectively through digital storytelling. Adele is committed to supporting Indigenous Australians to communicate their culture through the Fraynework Indigital Centre. As convenor of MIACOM, Adele co-ordinates the on-line communications for Mercy International Association, including the mercyworld.org website, the Mercy E-News and the interactive educational resource *Mercy and Justice Shall Meet*.

Ethel Bignell is a member of Nga Whaea Atawhai o Aotearoa Congregation of Sisters of Mercy New Zealand. For several years she has served as the Administrator of the Mercy International Association, in the MIA's office in Dublin.

Patricia Bell is the Congregational Leader of the Institute of Our Lady of Mercy of Britain. She retains fond memories of and a deep love for the primary school children she once taught. Currently a Member of the Mercy International Association, she serves as MIA's liaison to the MIA Archives Committee and the Mercy International Research Commission.

Appendix 2:

International Mercy Research Conference
Mercy Center, Burlingame, 9 – 12 November 2007
**" 'Fire cast on the earth—kindling':
being Mercy in the Twenty-first Century"**

PROCESS

Focus: In the future, what are the vision, theology and praxis that will flourish within the international Mercy mission and ministry and how will they be nourished?

Preparation:
- ✓ Several participants will have prepared and submitted papers in advance of the Conference.
- ✓ All the participants in the Conference will be asked to bring symbols and images that give a grounding for their context as well as symbols and images from their culture that reflect the Conference theme – "Fire cast on the earth—kindling."
- ✓ Maps will show the geographical location of the participants and their congregations.
- ✓ The environment for each set of presentations will reflect the overall theme for each section. Participants are invited to bring any material that will add to the environment.

ARTICULATION OF EXPERIENCE/STORY

Friday, November 9

7:00 p.m. – 7:15 p.m.	***Gathering and Welcome***
7:15 p.m. – 8:00 p.m.	***Opening Liturgy***: use of spiral image, focus on experience of Mercy internationally including expressions of experience already gathered in the process, elements of our history and tradition, ending with expression of challenge to be Mercy in the 21st century. Also images of fire – from different contexts. **(Listening Team 1 – experiences, images, emphases)**
8:00 p.m. – 8:30 p.m.	***Overview of Conference Process***
8:30 p.m. – 9:30 p.m.	***Social***

CONTEXT: SOCIAL ANALYSIS AND HISTORY

Saturday, November 10

9:00 a.m. – 9:30 a.m.	**Gathering threads** of previous evening. At the beginning of each major section, a *designated listener/listening team* reflects on the previous section in any way she/they deem appropriate –analytically, artistically, musically, etc. Each time there is a **Gathering of Threads**, it will be done in a ritual or liturgical context. **(Listening Team 1 and Liturgist)**
9:30 a.m. – 10:30 a.m.	**Presentations** related to Social Analysis. We need to pay attention to the physical surroundings: possibly multiple presentations of globe not all presented in the traditional way with focus on northern hemisphere and western world; and also images of multiple dimensions of our world. **(Listening Team 2: scribe)**
10:30 a.m. – 10:50 a.m.	**Break**
10:50 a.m. – Noon	**Process:** through personal reflection, small group conversations, large group discussion. Possible questions: In what we heard, what excites me? What causes me anxiety? What calls Mercy with loudest voice? Are there common threads and trends which call 'Mercy'? What areas are more particular to location or context? What questions does our analysis raise that we would want to bring to our dialogue with the tradition? Out of this session, we hope to *begin the focusing process* which will link and take forward *two or three key issues* from one stage of the process into the next. **(Listening Team 2: team members join different groups and collate what they hear)**

1:30 p.m. – 2:00 p.m.	*Gathering threads* from morning session **(Listening Team 2)**
2:00 p.m. – 3:00 p.m.	History *presentations*. Again attention to ambience, possibly images from our past re Catherine, early years in missions. **(Listening Team 3)**
3:00 p.m. – 3:20 p.m.	*Break*
3:20 p.m. – 4:20 p.m.	*Process:* personal/small group/large group with possible questions. What links with and reinforces my personal experience and our congregational experience? What aspects of our history inform our analysis of our experience? **(Listening Team 3: team members join different groups)**
4:20 p.m. – 5:00 p.m.	Continuation of *process* with the question: From what we have heard through the process to date, what aspect/s do we take forward into dialogue with our theological tradition that will help us to shape a vision of Mercy into the 21st century? Again this session seeks to focus and take forward *2 key aspects or issues* that would focus the conversations during Day 2. **(Listening Team 3: team members join different groups)**
Evening	Gathering to *celebrate* our shared tradition

DIALOGUE WITH THE TRADITION

Sunday, November 11

9:00 a.m. – 9:30 a.m.	*Gathering threads* from previous afternoon **(Listening Team 3 and Liturgist)**
9:30 a.m. – 11:15 a.m.	Biblical, theological, spiritual and ecclesial *presentations* **(Listening Team 1: scribe)**
11:15 a.m. – 12:15 p.m.	*Eucharistic Liturgy*
2:00 p.m. – 2:20 p.m.	*Gathering of threads* of morning session **(Listening Team 1 and Liturgist)**

2:20 p.m. – 4:50 p.m.	***Conversations*** between panelists and participants (panelists are divided into two groups each with a mix of disciplines. Participants meet in two small groups. Each group will focus on one of the two aspects identified the previous day for one hour bringing it into dialogue with the theological tradition and insights presented in the morning and then for the second conversation change to the second focus aspect or issue.
2:30 p.m. – 3:30 p.m.	***Conversation #1*** Each of the two groups spends time with half of the panelists in discussion on one of the two designated topics, bringing the theological insights of the morning into dialogue with the focus issue and in light of the analysis and historical reflections of the previous day. This is the developing of our theology. **(Listening Team 2 with Panelists 1 and Listening Team 3 with Panelists 2)**
3:30 p.m. – 3:50 p.m.	Break
3:50 p.m. – 4:50 p.m.	***Conversation #2*** Each group changes its panelist group and its topic and develops theological insights as in Conversation 1. **(Listening Team 2 with Panelists 1 and Listening Team 3 with Panelists 2)**
4:50 p.m. – 5:20 p.m.	***Personal reflection*** on the images that captured my attention this afternoon
5:20 p.m. – 5:30 p.m.	***Large group reflection***. We could have a ritual type listening then to what is emerging in people's hearts and imagination and this could lead us into a special celebration **(Listening Team 1)**
Evening	Gathering to ***celebrate*** our present experience of Mercy

Note: Listening Teams to bring together the material from Sunday to be presented Monday a.m. This will involve all the Listeners and in particular Leaders of Listening Teams to continue the writing up of insights emerging.

VISION/THEOLOGY/PRAXIS

Monday, November 12

9:00 a.m. – 9:30 a.m.

Gathering of threads from previous afternoon
(Listening Teams and Liturgist)

9:30 a.m. – 10:30 a.m.

Conversation in small groups about new learning from previous three days
(Team Leaders of Listening Teams to record.)

10:30 a.m. – 10:50 a.m.

Break

10:50 a.m. – Noon

Process re articulating a **Vision** for Mercy in the 21st century. Note: the separation of **Vision, Theology** and **Praxis** will not be as definite as suggested by the three separate processes. The facilitators will help the participants differentiate yet connect the three.
(Team Leaders of Listening Teams to record.)

1:30 p.m. – 2:30 p.m.

Process re defining the **Theology** that will guide us as Mercy Sisters in the 21st century
(Team Leaders of Listening Teams to record.)

2:30 p.m. – 3:30 p.m.

Process re identifying the elements of **Praxis** for us in the 21st century
(Team Leaders of Listening Teams to record.)

3:30 p.m. – 3:50 p.m.

Break

3:50 p.m. – 4:30 p.m.

Identification of **key elements re dissemination** of our deliberations. Content and dissemination process
(Team Leaders of Listening Teams to record.)

4:30 p.m. – 5:00 p.m.

Closing Liturgy

Acknowledgments

The Mercy International Research Commission sincerely wishes to thank Louise Novros, Rochester, New York, for her enormous contribution to the publication of this book; and Nick Paulus and the Rochester Institute of Technology for their computing expertise in relations with Lulu Press.

The Commission also wishes to thank Ethel Bignell, RSM, Administrator of the Mercy International Association, for her generous and multifaceted assistance to the Commission and to the Conference, and for her initial preparation of this book for publication.

Note

In editing this book for publication, the Commission chose to respect the scholarly conventions used by those who prepared papers for the Conference. Hence, while some limited uniformity of style was introduced, variations in citations and footnote formats remain.

Printed in the United States
154307LV00001B/105/P

9 780557 047598